MEMOIRS OF
A CAMP-FOLLOWER

By the Same Author

THE HISTORY OF PIRACY

With Illustrations and Maps

6s. *net*

"One of the most fascinating books which have been published . . . one exciting life story after another."

Morning Post

MEMOIRS OF
A CAMP-FOLLOWER

BY

PHILIP GOSSE

AUTHOR OF
" THE HISTORY OF PIRACY " AND " THE PIRATES' WHO'S WHO "

The Naval & Military Press Ltd

Published by

The Naval & Military Press Ltd
Unit 10 Ridgewood Industrial Park,
Uckfield, East Sussex,
TN22 5QE England

Tel: +44 (0) 1825 749494
Fax: +44 (0) 1825 765701

www.naval-military-press.com
www.military-genealogy.com
www.militarymaproom.com

In reprinting in facsimile from the original, any imperfections are inevitably reproduced and the quality may fall short of modern type and cartographic standards.

To
JENNIFER SARAH GOSSE

CONTENTS

CHAPTER		PAGE
	Preface	ix
I.	The Great Adventure	1
II.	We Go South	54
III.	The Somme	90
IV.	Rats	123
V.	Remy Siding	169
VI.	India	192
VII.	Khandala	229
VIII.	The Nilgiri Hills	246
IX.	Pukka Poona	261
X.	The Journey Home	287

ILLUSTRATION

Etched by Sylvia Gosse - - - *Frontispiece*

PREFACE

"HIS LORDSHIP'S compliments and he is in his bath and will you please make yourself quite at home." With these words the butler placed a copy of *The Times* beside me on a small table on which lay an open box of Egyptian cigarettes, and left me seated on the edge of a great armchair in Lord Wolseley's study.

Although the affair happened many years ago, when I was a callow youth of some eighteen years, it played an unforeseen but, to me, important part in my future career, and for that reason I will narrate how I came to be seated in the study of the Field-Marshal at an early hour on a summer's day in the 'nineties.

Like many other young men, when the time came for me to determine on a profession, I could think of none. I would have liked to be a keeper at the " Zoo," or to go abroad to some tropical country to collect specimens for a natural history museum, but beyond these I had no ideas nor ambitions. As neither of these callings appealed to my father, the choice of several professions was offered me, but all of them, the law, medicine, or engineering, failed to attract me.

One of my father's closest friends at that time was Viscount Wolseley, Field-Marshal and Commander-in-Chief, and it was at his kind suggestion that the proposition of an army career for me was broached.

PREFACE

Personally I felt no desire whatever to become a soldier, but having nothing better to suggest I thought it best to consent. In any case, the chance did not come to every young man to enter the army under the patronage of the Commander-in-Chief himself. So it was settled that I should call upon Lord Wolseley for an interview at his house in Grosvenor Gardens at the early hour of half-past nine. It was a blazing hot summer day when I arrived at the front door dressed up in a new frock-coat, top hat and an extremely high stiff collar, all essential in those days for a formal call.

One habit which I have inherited from my father is that of punctuality, and like him, the more important the appointment, the earlier I arrive. In fact, my father once held the unique distinction of being the first guest to arrive at a Royal garden party at Buckingham Palace, a signal expression of loyalty which caught the palace staff unprepared.

Thus it was that when I timidly rang the bell of Lord Wolseley's house, his lordship was still in his bath.

Having been deposited in the study, unutterably shy and nervous, I leaned back in the deep armchair and tried to concentrate my mind on the columns of *The Times*, but all in vain. What with the heat, the alarming prospect of the interview, my far too early arrival and my very high collar, I was in a condition of misery and perspiration.

At that time I had only just begun to smoke, but the sight of the open cigarette box on the table beside me reminded me that I had heard tobacco had a soothing effect upon the nerves, so taking a cigarette I lighted it and threw the wax match into the fireplace, in which

PREFACE

a fire had been laid ready for the autumn.

But the power of tobacco to soothe the nerves proved a fallacy, and I became more and more frightened. It seemed to me I had sat there an hour at least, and wild panic began to urge me to fly out of the house, when I heard brisk steps outside, the door was flung open and in strode the Commander-in-Chief. Instantly I leaped to my feet and at the same moment noticed to my horror that the fire was blazing in the grate.

His lordship, smiling, shook hands with me, and glancing towards the now roaring fire said, " I am sorry to have kept you waiting, but am pleased to see that you made yourself comfortable." This was, no doubt, meant to be a pleasantry, but to me it was the final straw. I was too young and too scared to explain how the fire had come to be lighted, but subsided into a state of moist inarticulateness.

Of the interview which followed, I retain no memory beyond being stifled by my high collar and a wild longing to run away. Afterwards he and my father talked the matter over and I was given to understand that the Field-Marshal did not consider me to be cut out for the profession of arms.

All this may appear very far from the point in a book which attempts to record the adventures and impressions of a doctor in the Great War, but often and often when in France I had cause to bless the odd chance which sent my flaming match into the ready-laid fire in Grosvenor Gardens, but for which I might well have become an infantry officer and have had to go through all the abomination which was the lot of the infantry, instead of accompanying them into battle in the less heroic and

PREFACE

certainly less dangerous rôle of a camp-follower, or medical officer, to dress their wounds and tend the health of rank and file.

These memoirs of mine make no claim to be in any measure a War book, but possibly they do give a view of the War from a new angle, being the experiences and impressions of a very unmilitant individual who, like thousands of others, suddenly found himself taking part in the great catastrophe.

Far be it from me to criticise, as so many civilian soldier-writers have done, the conduct of my superior officers and professional soldiers. The impression left at the conclusion of the War was that warfare is a stupid, ugly, retrograde business, all very well perhaps in the Middle Ages, but a sorry slur on what we consider our enlightened twentieth-century civilization, and a grave indictment of the abilities of all the diplomats and statesmen who in 1914 could find no better or less crude means of settling an international dispute. One cannot but agree with Voltaire that if there must be wars, they should be conducted by professional soldiers only. There have always been people ready and willing to wear a uniform and go forth to kill strangers, so if wars must be, by all means let professionals fight their battles amongst themselves.

In the good old days this was the rule, and a citizen of a state at war with another was even able to travel from place to place, without harm, in the very country with which his own was at war.

In the Great War, members of my profession of medicine were in a unique position, and on quite a different footing from all other civilians who had donned

PREFACE

a uniform for the duration of hostilities. The R.A.M.C. was the only corps or unit the officers of which were carrying on their own peace-time calling. Not only this, but in a great many cases the temporary commissioned officers were better qualified and more experienced in the technical side of medicine, surgery, or public health than the regular officers under whom they served. This fact made the position of a temporary medical officer a very enviable one, for he was able, in an emergency, to disobey an order which he felt convinced was not one compatible with up-to-date medical standards or not the best for his patients or charges. Probably it was the fact that the vast majority of the R.A.M.C. officers were civilian doctors, who were only soldiers for the War and were doing their own job, that made the medical branch of the army almost the only one which during the whole campaign in France never broke down, whatever conditions unexpectedly evolved. Although the R.A.M.C. had the great advantage over other units and regiments in the army of having ready-trained new-army officers to serve under the old regular ones, its military traditions must often have been rudely shocked by the independent and unorthodox behaviour of its juniors. The part played by the doctors in these memoirs was that of the medical officers attached to divisions, that is as M.O.'s to infantry battalions, field artillery brigades and the other units which went to make up a division. It is these doctors whom I have dubbed camp-followers, and they have nothing to do with the hundreds of doctors doing useful and purely professional work further back at casualty clearing stations and base hospitals. The camp-followers, as

PREFACE

doctors to one particular division, were solely occupied in tending the wounded in the field and dispatching them back to the hospitals as quickly as possible and in looking after the health of the fighting troops.

The relationship between the R.A.M.C. and the fighting troops became very much changed soon after the division got out to France, and we heard no more jokes of " Rob All My Comrades " or the " Linseed Lancers." Before going out to France we had to put up with a good deal of chaff, but after a battle or two were never reminded about our robbing our comrades, and the corps became on a very friendly footing with the rest of the division. A good M.O. to a battalion was a privileged and important officer. He was usually on intimate terms with his colonel, a friend to all his brother officers, and friend and confidant as well as doctor to the rank and file. Often and often I noticed that a battalion with a first-class M.O. was always a first-class battalion, had the smallest sick parade, fewer men falling out on a long march and the lowest quota of casualties from trench foot. A doctor's life in the line with a battalion, or to a lesser degree with a field ambulance, was not without danger and hardship, as will be appreciated when it is remembered that almost eight hundred doctors were killed in the British Army.

Some of my readers may find fault with me for having comparatively so little to say about the " horrors " of war and so much about beasts and birds. The title might well have been, " A Solace of Birds," for without the birds I dare not think how I should have got through the War at all. One friend, after reading my MS. asked if I could not include " more horrors," even at the

PREFACE

expense of some of the birds, but I told him that in any case I could remember no more "horrors," though of birds I remembered so much. The mangled corpse is forgotten, but the warbler with its nest and eggs is remembered. I think the reason for this is largely that at the time the "horrors" were so beastly, so ugly, that one got into the habit of putting them aside by concentrating on the birds, so that now, after many years, the memory retains the birds and to a large extent has got rid of the rest.

I sometimes wonder, when I recall those lovely quiet, peaceful farms and villages in the back areas where my division used to go into "rest," whether I should like to revisit them. But on further consideration I have always decided not to do so. As to the trench area, I believe it is now completely changed and unrecognisable, and to visit it again would be to lose what memory of it I have, while as to the charming, quiet places which seemed so ideal nearly twenty years ago, I suspect that much of their charm lay in the contrast between their peacefulness and the noise and filth which we had so suddenly come out of. There again I fear disillusionment awaits.

The memoirs which follow are not set down from memory only. After the death of my parents a box was found which contained all the letters written to them by me from the time I joined up in 1914 until the end of the War. Opening a few of these at random and reading their contents, scenes, people and places which I had entirely forgotten were vividly brought back to me. I then began to read the whole batch, and with the help of an old note-book I attempted to write a consecutive narrative. This note-book was in no sense a war diary or journal, for it was all about birds and beasts, and no military event or happening appears in it unless it has especial bearing on some bird or animal.

CHAPTER I

THE GREAT ADVENTURE

IT was my first visit to the trenches.

A more perfect September day for the expedition could not have been wished for; the sun shone; there were no clouds—no wind. Scarcely a sound of shot or shell broke the profound, almost eerie silence.

This was not an official tour of duty, but purely and simply an outing; a piece of common sightseeing. A brother officer in my field-ambulance was going up the line to pay a visit to a friend of his, the medical officer of a battalion of the Northumberland Fusiliers, and invited me to go with him. Everything was new to us and exciting as we tramped along through Grispot up to the shattered village of Bois Grenier, where our advanced dressing-station was concealed in the cellar of a brewery. Here we were lent a guide who led us along a road hidden from the Boche by canvas screens, to the entrance to the communication trench. This was followed until we reached the trenches we were in search of. There was still none of that roar of cannon and rattle of machine-guns which we in our innocence had imagined went on more or less continually in trench warfare. In fact—again our blessed innocence—we had been just a trifle disappointed when, as we were stepping down into the communication trench and were feeling a trifle frightened and rather brave, a noisy little French newspaper-boy came running along the road bawling out "Dailimal paper," and took away a good deal of the glamour of our adventure.

Here was evidently another disillusion. The first had been three weeks before, when our division, the 23rd, had landed at Havre. Some of us—I know I was one—had an idea that our landing on the shores of France would be an occasion of public rejoicing. We had pictured ourselves being received by a grateful population with Gallic acclamations of delight and possibly with garlands of flowers. The least we looked for was an official welcome on the quay by the mayor of Havre, followed perhaps by the presentation of a bouquet to our general, by a little French girl in a tricolour sash.

But nothing of the kind had taken place, and the only incident of note, an unrehearsed one, was when a horse, evidently labouring under an overpowering impulse to get to grips with the enemy, leaped overboard and swam ashore. The truth is that our arrival in France passed so unheeded as to suggest that by September, 1915, the sight of British troops landing on their shores had long ceased to be a novelty to our allies. The only portion of the civilian population which welcomed us was the children, who followed us wherever we went, with outstretched hands, crying "Chocolat—bullibef—souvenir" with an occasional sinister and mysterious invitation to go and "jig-a-jig," in a direction indicated by a jerk of the thumb.

Having got out of earshot of the tiresome little newspaper-boy, our guide led us to the medical officer's dug-out, where we found McKerrow, the man we were looking for, seated upon an upturned box bent intently over some occupation. When we drew near and I saw what that occupation was, I knew at once that here was a man after my own heart, for he was attentively engaged in skinning a field vole. From this I wrongly jumped to the conclusion that, like myself, he was an amateur taxidermist and collector, but he repudiated any such claims and confessed that all he was doing was skinning a field vole to make into a muff for his little daughter's doll to wear when it took perambulator exercise.

From that morning McKerrow and I became fast friends, and whenever we could we would meet and talk of all sorts of matters not connected with war or medicine, such as birds and flowers.

This meeting, and the sight of him skinning a vole, was to have a profound effect on my career in the army which I little foresaw at the time.

The 69th Field Ambulance, to which I belonged, had its headquarters and main dressing-station at a big brewery called Fort Rompu, which stood on the banks of the sluggish river Lys, near to the bridge at Sailly, a few miles from Armentières. Our business was to clear the sick and wounded of the whole area occupied by the 23rd Division and bring them down the communication trenches from the regimental aid-posts to the advanced dressing-stations, and eventually to the main dressing-station, whence the more serious cases were sent back to the Casualty Clearing Stations.

We had two of these advanced dressing-stations, the principal and largest one at Bois Grenier and the other at Grispot, a smaller village behind Bois Grenier. Both these villages being under direct observation of the Germans opposite, the casualties could not be sent back to the main dressing-station until it was dark, when motor and horse ambulances came up for them. A few miles behind Fort Rompu, towards Steenwerck, we had our transport lines at a farm, where men and officers went for a rest and a quiet time after doing their spell in the front line.

With another officer I was put in charge of the smaller advanced dressing-station at Grispot, pronounced by all soldiers " Greasepot." This was an ugly hamlet of one straight street of new red-brick, slate-roofed cottages. We two officers were billeted in a cottage still inhabited and there we slept and had our mess.

Our host was anything but agreeable. Sulky and morose, he was popularly believed to be a German spy. Certainly if he had wanted to signal messages to the enemy it would have been easy for him to do so, for from the back rooms which he occupied there was a clear, unobstructed view of the Boche lines and the rising ground behind. It was a curious fact that hitherto his house was the only one in the street which had never been shelled, which no doubt caused the suspicion that the owner was in league with the enemy. One day after we had been there a little while, a major in the R.F.A. called to make enquiries about our host and wanted to arrest him as a spy. This we most earnestly begged him not to do, because we looked upon him as our mascot, and as long as he remained in the house we felt safe. After some argument and a good deal of whisky we persuaded the major to go away and leave us and our mascot in peace.

During the daytime ours was a deserted village and scarcely a man was to be seen walking in the road between it and Bois Grenier. Several of the cottages which were not wrecked were still inhabited by French families, who sold chocolate, weak beer, cigarettes, patriotic postcards and candles to the soldiers.

It seemed uncanny to be so close to the German front line, less than one mile, and see—still more, hear—so few signs of active warfare. But at sunset the whole scene would change. During the day not a vehicle was to be seen on the roads, but with darkness the roads suddenly became crowded with marching troops, columns of ammunition waggons and ration carts. Above the noise of wheels rattling on the cobble-stones would be heard the occasional sharp crack of a sniper's rifle, or the tap-tap-tap of a machine gun; while an occasional stray bullet would go wailing overhead. One of our duties, and at first rather an exciting one, was to go at night with a motor ambulance to visit various ruined farm buildings close behind the trenches, to collect any wounded who had been brought in during the day. Of course, no light could be used on the car and the driver had to make the most of the occasional flashes of our own guns or the faint, quivering light of the star-shells from the trenches. Sometimes we used an electric hand-torch, but care had to be taken to flash the light only on the road.

The officers of the field ambulance never remained long in one place or doing the same job. We took our turns at the advanced dressing-stations, at the main dressing-station at Fort Rompu, or at the rest camp on the other side of the river. In addition, we had to be ready to go as temporary medical officer to any battalion or artillery brigade in the division, or do any special work that required an officer of the R.A.M.C.

One of the assortment of odd duties that fell to the field ambulances was the washing of soldiers and their clothes. This took place in a laundry or wash-house, which had several huge tanks, in each of which some fifty naked, shouting, laughing soldiers could bathe at the same time. As each battalion came out of the trenches it marched to the Divisional bath-house, where fifteen hundred men a day had a hot bath. While the men were in the tanks, their tunics and trousers were put into an oven to be baked, in order to kill the lice, and then well brushed, and mended by a staff of Flemish women and girls who were engaged to do this. When the men had finished their bath their uniforms were returned to them, and they were issued with clean socks and underclothes, while their old ones were washed and mended for future use.

One of our officers who spoke French well was put in charge of the wash-house, and his post was by no means a sinecure. He was responsible for the smooth running of the baths, laundry, and furnaces for heating the water, and he had to see that the women did not steal too much soap nor too many towels. He had to be firm as well as tactful in settling the disputes amongst his women employees, and to be ready to translate into French the love-letters the girls received from their English soldier sweethearts. The post of O/C Laundry was considered a " cushy " one; it was not.

After every spell at either of the advanced dressing-stations we spent a week or ten days at the rest camp, which stood beside a farmhouse across the river between Erquingham and Steenwerck. I never read Mr. Mottram's masterpiece without recalling that farm, which might have been the original of his Spanish farm.

It was a single-storied, red-brick building, had the same old thatch, the same midden of steaming dung in the courtyard, the odour of which filled every room. Mr. Vanderlynden owned the farm, though under another Flemish name, and Mrs. Vanderlynden was still alive and very active, and as efficient as was Madeleine to cope with British quartermasters and billeting officers.

Here one was one's own master; got up in the morning when one felt inclined, and did just what one liked. After breakfast, an English breakfast of fried eggs and bacon, I would go out to parade my small army of sixty men. Then the men's billets were inspected, as well as the horse-lines with its thirty-odd horses, and the A.S.C. grooms and drivers. After the short duties of the day were over I could settle down to what, I fear, interested me a good deal more than inspecting soldiers' kits or going on route marches.

It was the sight of McKerrow skinning a vole that prompted me to write a letter to my old friend, Oldfield Thomas, the keeper of Mammals in the Natural History Museum in Cromwell Road, to ask him if the Museum was well provided with specimens of the small mammals of Flanders, and if not, whether he would like me to procure some. Thomas, who was always ready to encourage amateurs to collect, wrote back to say that they were in great need of specimens from Western Europe, and he sent also some of the museum labels and some arsenical soap for preserving the skins. I then asked my mother to send me a dozen " break-back " mousetraps, and as soon as they arrived I set about collecting and skinning mice and shrews.

The lack of skinning instruments was easily solved by my purloining the ambulance chiropody outfit, a magnificent set of instruments, scalpels, forceps, etc., fitted into a brass-bound box, which was never used for its legitimate purpose, and which is still in my care.

The daily life of an M.O. to a battalion or a field ambulance consisted of quiet periods varied by occasional bursts of work, when fighting was on, which might keep you hard at work for a few hours, or for one or two whole days and nights in a big " strafe," without sleep or rest. When out of the trenches in reserve or in the back areas, where the division went from time to time, it was different, if your interests lay in wild life or country pursuits. Of course, this did not apply to combatant regimental officers; for them there was always plenty to be done, fortunately, perhaps, for their stability of mind. When in the trenches, after the short sick parade and the inspection of a latrine or two, the regimental M.O. had a long day before him with but little to do except smoke, read, or play patience.

My collecting always kept me busy.

In the evening I would go out with my haversack full of traps and a piece of ration cheese for bait. Creeping about in the wet ditches and hedgerows I would look out for the tiny beaten tracks of my small jungle game; woodmice, voles, or shrews. Setting traps for even such small game as this calls for a certain amount of skill, or at least, hedge-cunning, for a dozen traps placed anyhow and anywhere will catch nothing. As each trap was set a small piece of cotton wool was fixed to some bramble or twig close by to help locate it the following day, otherwise many would be lost. Then first thing next morning I would be off again on my rounds, visiting my traps and taking them up.

Of course, there were blank days of disappointment as in every other branch of field or blood sport. But then again there were red-letter days, when in one of your cunningly set and baited traps, you discovered some small animal the like of which you had never seen before.

On returning to the dug-out, each specimen was carefully examined and measured. These measurements had to be written on the labels and recorded in millimetres, the length from point of nose to stump of tail, the length of tail, which must not include any hairs at the tip, and the length of the ears and paws. Then the place where the specimen was caught, the date, and its sex, had to be noted down. On the back of the label I would put down anything I thought worth while, such as the position of the trap when set, in a hollow willow tree, for instance—a favourite site for pigmy shrews—or the edge of a dyke, a hole in a wall, or under a hay-cock. Perhaps the bait would be noted down in the case of a rare creature which had fallen to the temptation of some other lure than ration cheese, such as bread, almonds, or raw apple. The label being completed, out came the chiropody set and the actual skinning began. To make a good skin of a small mammal, such as a mouse, is not such a simple and easy matter as it may sound. The most difficult part and the one which requires greatest patience and practice is to remove the bone out of a mouse's tail, and insert in its place a long thin wire, on which cotton wool has been spun, gradually tapering in thickness to the tip, to correspond exactly with the bone which has been withdrawn.

When this has been done, and the mouse stuffed with army cotton wool and the skin sewn up with needle and thread, it has to be pinned out on a board to dry, and the label attached to the off hind leg. It all sounds very easy, but taxidermy, even the skinning of mice, is quite an art, or certainly a craft of no mean order.

This hunting of small mammals was all very well in the back areas, miles away from the line, but in or just behind the trenches the risks were not only on the side of the small mammals. Sometimes the hunter became the hunted. Well-intentioned sentries and other armed patriots, seeing a suspicious person, dressed—more or less—in the uniform of a British officer, skulking in waste places, or creeping about in water-logged ditches, were apt to jump to the conclusion that he was an enemy spy. When challenged I found that the simple truth that I was only setting traps for field mice, failed, in most cases, to allay suspicion, and on one occasion I was hurried, under an armed guard, to explain my suspicious actions to higher authorities.

When the division went into " rest " somewhere well away behind the line it was the business of my batman, Bob Church, to make enquiries in the neighbourhood if any corn stacks were being threshed. On discovering one he and I would go off, and after explaining to the astonished but always polite farmer what we were after, would join in the threshing, and as the last of the stooks were being lifted and there was a general stampede of small game in all directions, we would dash into the arena, coatless, and armed with sticks; many a fine specimen now enjoying embalmed immortality in the British Museum was procured at one of these battues.

But it must not be thought that, like the adult collector of British birds' eggs, I was merely after numbers. A few good specimens of each species was enough, for during many years of collecting birds and beasts for the museums in Newfoundland, South America, the Balearic Islands and other countries, I had always made it a strict rule never to kill anything needlessly. Indeed, when collecting birds I very seldom shot one until I had stalked it and had an opportunity to examine it closely and carefully through my binoculars, for I know only too well the bitterness of finding that a life has been sacrificed unnecessarily. I always enjoyed the week or ten days at the farm. After the morning inspection and the route march, there were generally animals to skin and the men's letters to censor, then the day's work was done. The one great occasion of the day was the arrival of the mail-cart. If Church entered my room with a beaming face, I knew there were some letters for me and perhaps a parcel as well, but if he looked crest-fallen I was prepared to learn there was nothing. A ride perhaps in the afternoon, and a book to read after tea. It was a lazy, pleasant life.

In the winter there was little to see during the rides, the country being flat and treeless and much built over. The most interesting objects were the estaminets, which played so large, if unrecognised, a part in the War. There were many which possessed delightful names. There was "le Retour des Hirondelles," "le Chant du Rossignol," and another popular one "le Chant des Oiseaux"; each one illustrated by a descriptive painting. A favourite of mine was "le Lit Tranquille," and I can imagine no inn sign more alluring to the tired traveller than that. There was one signboard over the entrance to a small estaminet on the road which runs from Sailly to Estaires which by no means suggested peace nor tranquillity. On it was written, in bold characters, these words :

"To the Terrible Years, 1914
1915"

after which a large, ominous space had been left for the terrible years to come. Almost every cottage offered cheap articles for sale to the soldiers; and almost every other one had such notices as these in the window: "Beer Heer" or "Beer, Chips, Vin, Café," while another frequent sign was "Beer Washing for Soldiers."

Wherever I am I always keep a friendly eye open for cats. Up here in Flanders I was sorry to find cats were all too few, and those I did see were poor skulking specimens of a noble race. But there was one exception at our farm, Félicité. She was a small and rather scrubby white and tortoise-shell cat, but very intelligent and affectionate. She was the most confidential cat I ever knew, and was for ever whispering something in my ear which I never could quite catch. While I was writing she would come and sit very close beside me and read what I wrote and purr loudly. As the door of my bedroom could not be shut she had the *entrée*, and every night after I had gone to bed she would stroll in and leap up on to my bed and sleep curled up beside me. This adoration was, I fear, largely cupboard-love, for each day after I had finished skinning a mouse or a vole I would give her the carcass, for I only wanted the skin and Félicité would oblige me by disposing of the corpse, and nobody at the farm was more concerned than she over the success of each night's trapping.

After ten pleasant days at the rest camp it was my turn to go to our headquarters at Fort Rompu and luxury. It had central heating, on one day a week, which was useful for drying wet clothes, and also electric light which was cut off at 7 p.m. It had fireplaces in all the bedrooms, but as these had their chimneys blocked up they were ornamental rather than useful. In fact Fort Rompu had all the appearance and appurtenances of great comfort, but was in reality a gross sham. News reached me here from the British Museum that quite a stir had been caused by the arrival of one of my specimens, an exceedingly rare shrew called *Crocidura leucodon*, which piece of news encouraged me to even greater efforts of trapping. My mother was now sending me wonderful parcels each week, foods of all sorts, especially fresh fish, which if fried at home kept quite well, and was a popular addition to our mess. Also she supplied me with mouth-organs for the men of my section, who were always glad of them. Secretly I carried a mouth-organ myself, and when alone in the trenches or on the roads behind at night, I used to play simple airs for my own pleasure, and—what a confession—to keep up my courage! The mouth-organ is almost the only musical instrument out of which melody can be coaxed by the quite unmusical.

After the spell at Fort Rompu, with its pretended grandeur, my turn came again for the advanced dressing-station, this time at Bois Grenier. This was a disagreeable village, in full view of the Boche and already shelled to pieces. As so often happened, the R.A.M.C. occupied the capacious if dark cellar of the local brewery. This cellar was divided into three parts, one for the detachment of R.A.M.C. stretcher-bearers, another to be used as a dressing-room for the wounded, while the third I shared with an army chaplain, a most unusual roommate at an advanced dressing-station, and an exception to the run of Anglican chaplains, for he preferred being near the trenches to stopping at the main dressing-station farther back. He was in and out of the trenches all day long, and so became liked and respected by the men of his battalion. For his pains and pluck he was wounded and was on his way to England in the hospital ship *Anglia* when she struck a mine, and he had to swim for twenty minutes before being rescued by a destroyer. I missed him very much and missed as well the fresh roses which he used to pick each day in the ruined gardens to decorate our cellar.

A little light and air came into the cellar through some small windows on the level of the street outside, but as these opened on the German side of the building, they had to be blocked up by sandbags. There was a stove to warm the place, but as it only radiated smoke, little comfort could be got from it. Bob Church cooked our meals and his skill improved each day. Though a boilermaker by trade, he showed a natural aptitude for cooking, and was a genius at making Welsh rarebits out of a lump of ration cheese and a couple of rounds of toasted ration bread.

Our first experience of real shelling took place in the middle of November, when my friend, J. B. Woodrow, and I were together at Grispot. We were sitting in the cottage having lunch when an appalling crash was heard just behind the house on the German side. A few moments afterwards there was a second explosion in the street. The shell must have just missed the roof, for it fell on the cobbled road and sent up a cloud of stones, earth and dust, as well as bringing down an avalanche of slates. Though still novices to this sort of thing we had been warned that the third shell was likely to drop between the two previous ones, so we darted out of the house and got into a shelter a little way up the street. A moment later we heard the third shell coming, and up went our billet. The bombardment lasted about twenty minutes and when the air was cleared of dust we saw that our two-storied residence had become one-storied. Several men had been hit and Woodrow was himself struck by a piece of shell casing while going back to rescue one of our wounded ambulance drivers. Among the things we lost as a result of the bombardment was our faith in our mascot, the surly landlord, most of my clothes, and worse than all of these, a bottle of home-made sloe-gin. This was, for sloe-gin, of great age, seven years in bottle, the last of its vintage, and had been specially sent out to me. It had arrived while I was at the main dressing-station at Fort Rompu, but I knew better than to open it in the mess there.

Until he was wounded Woodrow and I always worked together, and whenever either of us had any particular luxury to eat or drink we used to hide it until we were alone at one of the advanced dressing-stations. We did this not only for reasons of greed, but from sad experience. The headquarters mess might consist of any number of medical officers from six upwards, and the usual assortment of army chaplains. The latter were mighty trenchermen and anything we produced for the general mess would disappear in the twinkling of an eye. So this precious bottle of vintage sloe-gin—1908 Chateau Curtlemead—we kept until we went to Grispot, where one day it was uncorked and with due ceremony placed on the dinner-table. We were just about to sample it, the wine-glasses were set out all ready, when the first shell exploded. In our panic to escape I forgot to seize the bottle and never learned what happened to it.

When Woodrow had been safely got away I went back to the billet to find it had received a direct hit from a very heavy shell, and I was just in time to make some men of the R.F.A. and R.E. who were busy plundering disgorge various belongings of ours or our landlord's. All my books were missing, amongst them *Erewhon* and *Erewhon Revisited*, *Crime and Punishment*, and one of Fabre's. But worse than all, the bottle of sloe-gin had gone, though whether stolen or smashed I do not know.

The bombardment did me one good turn, for a shell had struck and destroyed our dressing-station across the road, and when I came to indent for replacements I played the " old soldier " and included the loss of "instruments, chiropody, set of, one." The original set is still in my safe keeping, should the War Office wish to have it back.

The next day the village was shelled again and a message was brought asking for stretcher-bearers to go to a battery half a mile away, where they had sustained some casualties during the recent bombardment. We went to the gun pits where we dressed the wounded and sent them down in a motor ambulance to Fort Rompu. The battery commander, a major, then invited me into his dug-out where he produced a bottle of whisky and two tin mugs. We talked of various things, trying to find some subject or interest in common. As I began to think about leaving, a little mouse came out of a hole in the wall and began to dart nimbly about the floor. The red-faced major swore, kicked a boot towards it, and the little mouse vanished as suddenly as it had appeared. The major cursed the mouse, declaring it was always running about like that, and wished he could get rid of it. I offered to rid him of it, if it really bothered him, and so the next day I brought one of my mousetraps, baited it with a piece of cheese, and set it near the hole in the wall. The whisky bottle was again brought out, and the major and I sat drinking and smoking, when all at once the major whispered, "There it is!" I looked and there was the little mouse. It was exciting to sit very still and watch it. More than once it seemed to be making straight for the trap, but each time as it drew near it turned in some other direction.

The excitement became intense. The major and I dared not move or whisper, and our pipes went out.

Then once again the mouse approached the trap, and seemingly getting wind of the cheese, drew closer still and remained motionless, listening. Then suddenly it seized the bait in its two tiny paws and began to gnaw hungrily at the cheese. Click went the trap, which sprang high into the air as the spring was released, and fell clattering down on to the floor, with the little mouse beneath it.

I went and picked up the trap and showed the major the little soft body, quite warm, the cheese still between its minute, sharp teeth. I felt a curious feeling of pride that by my own ingenuity I had outwitted it. But this sensation did not last for long, and began to ebb away while I held the little limp thing in my hand. After all, I reasoned with myself, it's only a mouse, and it annoyed the major. But all the same I wished I had not killed it. Bother the major, why on earth had I told him I had a mousetrap; why had I not told him to catch the mouse himself if he wanted to? But it would never do to let him see how I was feeling about it; he would despise me for a sentimental fool. I finished off my whisky and turned to say good-bye. The major was holding the little mouse in his hand, and surprised me by saying, " I wish now we hadn't killed the little chap. I believe I had grown quite fond of him."

Colonel Walker who commanded our field ambulance came up next day and seeing I was rather shaken by the two bombardments, sent me back to the peaceful farm for a few days' rest where, in spite of the incident of the gunner major's mouse, I continued my trapping and sent off to the British Museum my sixtieth specimen, a pigmy shrew which I had caught in a hollow willow tree. A few days' quiet rest at the farm and the tranquil companionship of Félicité soon put me right, and I was sent up to Bois Grenier to spend Christmas in the underground cellars of our advanced dressing-station. I was now in charge of some forty stretcher-bearers and two A.S.C. motor-drivers, who were kept at Bois Grenier to drive a Ford ambulance, in case of emergency, during the daytime.

It was decided to hold a Christmas dinner which was to be followed by a concert in the big cellar. By way of a treat I had bought at the field canteen several dozen bottles of English ale, the favourite drink of English soldiers. Also my mother had sent me for the occasion quantities of Woodbine cigarettes, and a dozen mouth-organs, my sister Tessa a large home-made cake from Bideford, while my sister Sylvia contributed a big tin of peppermint bulls-eyes. What more could any host or guest wish for?

The Christmas feast was a great success and so was the concert which followed, to which came many gate-crashers, uninvited but welcome guests, gunners from the field artillery battery next door and various odds and ends of the R.E. and signallers who inhabited other cellars in the village.

A stage was improvised by partitioning off one end of the large cellar with stretchers placed on their sides. Behind these were the footlights, made of tin boxes which held candles whose feeble light dimly illuminated the abdomens of the performers but left their faces in shadow, a fact of no little satisfaction to the more shy and retiring artistes.

At one side of the stage a small table had been placed

for myself, the chairman. On this stood a real bedroom candlestick, "won," no doubt, from some ruined and deserted house near by, and two bouquets of fresh flowers, one late roses, the other chrysanthemums, gathered for the great occasion in the wild gardens of the wrecked village.

The programme was opened by the chairman in the conventional manner by reading out telegrams of regret from various distinguished persons. One, I remember, sent from Berlin, was from the mayor of Bois Grenier, who was believed to be in a German prison. He deeply regretted he was unable to be present that evening but was sending some bulls-eyes for the ladies—loud applause. Another telegram, bearing the Potsdam postmark, ran as follows: "We had fully intended being present at Bois Grenier this evening, but have been prevented from doing so by the verfluchten Schweinhunde of the 23rd Division, Gott strafe them. Wilhelm R.I." These and other innocent jokes put the audience in the best of high spirits and the concert began.

Most of the songs were of the lugubrious sort so beloved by the British soldier, all about young soldiers dying slowly but vocally on battlefields, with visions of their mothers, to whom the expiring heroes sent maudlin messages of love and remembrance, seated at home by cottage fires. There were, of course, the usual comic songs about mothers-in-law and fat ladies bathing at the seaside, and some of the popular soldier songs with such choruses as:

"Far, far away would I be,
 Where the Alleyman cannot catch me,"

or the equally unheroic one:

> " Oh my! I don't want to die,
> *I* want to go 'ome."

But the star turn of the evening was one of our A.S.C. ambulance drivers who gave " impersonations " of different members of the Ambulance, both officers and N.C.O.'s. The take-off of our adjutant was quite lifelike and was received with deafening applause. So was that of the quartermaster, which made us all laugh like anything. After several turns he suddenly announced " a certain officer very angry on parade " and proceeded to stump up and down the stage, impatiently plucking at a small moustache. Something about it seemed familiar to me but I could not at first decide who it was he was imitating. Unlike his former take-offs, this one was received in dead silence, and when, wondering why this was, I glanced round at the audience, I was surprised to see that every man was watching me. Then looking again at the performer, I suddenly recognised myself and burst out laughing. Instantly the whole audience which hitherto had refrained out of politeness from laughing shouted aloud with delight. I had never before seen a living caricature of myself; it was a curious revelation and gave me much food for thought and reflection.

Now and again during the concert a wounded man would be brought in from the trenches near by. There was a small tunnel in the wall of the cellar, which led up to the street outside. Probably in the old days it had been used to transport barrels of beer. A curtain of sacking hung over the opening so as to hide any light in the cellar from enemy eyes. When a " case " arrived, a voice would call down the tunnel and the orderlies on duty would slip away from their places at the concert and get ready to receive the stretcher. The first objects to arrive would be the handles of the stretcher and a pair of muddy boots. Gently and slowly the stretcher would be lowered until two legs and then a tunic appeared, but not until the face of the wounded man came into the candle-light would it be known if he was a smiling soldier happy to be on the first stage to " blighty " or a dying one. Sometimes the stretcher held a dead soldier who had expired on the short " carry " from the trenches to our cellar. One boy arrived with a bullet wound in his arm. This was dressed and bandaged and shortly afterwards he was seated among the audience, with a mug of tea in one hand, the other arm in a sling, singing the choruses as lustily as any. It was strange to think that this lad had been shot by a German sniper only half an hour previously and now was happily and safely enjoying himself. Between the songs we could distinctly hear the ominous steady tap-tap-tap of the German or the more irregular spasmodic sound of the English machine guns, and from time to time a bullet would crack against the wall outside.

At 8.30 the concert ended with " God Save the King," which somehow appeared to be sung more heartily and to have more significance in it than when sung at a soldiers' sing-song at home.

Two days after the concert the " impersonator " was hit by a piece of shrapnel which penetrated one lung, and we sent him to the nearest Casualty Clearing Station. When I called to see him the following day he was dying, but he recognised me, and I was able to tell him before I left him how much I had enjoyed his "take-off" of myself.

The Christmas dinner and concert did not complete our round of Yuletide festivities. On New Year's night I was present, again as a spectator, at a quite different performance. It had occurred to the great and the wise that a good way to usher in the New Christian Year would be to make a raid on the opposite German trenches. Certainly it would help to check the growing tendency on both sides to fraternize, a manifestation of goodwill and war-weariness which had appeared in that part of the line, and which alarmed and horrified the powers which directed battles from the base. Raids were a new feature of trench warfare and were soon hated and feared by the bravest of regimental officers and men.

This raid was carried out by five officers and one hundred other ranks of the 9th Yorkshires, under the command of Major Prior. To render the raiders inconspicuous their faces were blacked with burnt cork, and the pass-word chosen was "Charlie Chaplin." At midnight the party filed out of the trenches and began to crawl towards the German lines. An hour afterwards they came hurrying back under heavy fire from rifles and machine-guns. The principal object of the raid, the taking of prisoners, had not been attained, but in the words of the official historian of the 23rd Division, "The casualties suffered by the actual party were very light, amounting to a total of seven men slightly wounded, but some twenty-four casualties, including an officer and three other ranks killed, were sustained from hostile

artillery fire brought on to our trenches in retaliation....
This was the first of many successful raids carried out by
the 23rd Division during the War."

At the conclusion of this " successful " raid, when the
enemy shelling had ceased, the wounded began to arrive
at our cellar at Bois Grenier. The first to appear were
the members of the raiding party, and I shall always
remember the singular spectacle of those seven black-
faced soldiers as they sat in a row on seven small
children's chairs " borrowed " from a ruined school
near by. They looked for all the world like a troupe of
nigger minstrels on the sands at Margate. The contrast
between their coal-black faces and the white and blood-
stained bandages was striking. The men themselves
were in the highest spirits, the anti-climax had not yet
begun, and they laughed and joked while having their
wounds dressed. They enjoyed the cups of hot tea we
gave them and my mother's Woodbine cigarettes. One
excited boy described how as they were stealthily
creeping towards the enemy trench, a huge Boche—they
were all giants—suddenly seeing the black-faced soldiers,
shouted out—apparently in colloquial English—" Gawd,
look at them black-faced beggars ! "

The other casualties which were brought in later that
morning were much more seriously wounded than the
black-faced members of the raiding party. Amongst
them was a man whose face had been blown off. It
was the first time I had seen such a thing and it was
very dreadful. His face was not merely skinned, but
entirely gone, slashed off by a splinter of a steel shell.
He died in the cellar.

It is generally supposed that a surgeon or a doctor is

so hardened to seeing ghastly sights that nothing can disturb him; but actually a surgeon is no more callous than other men, but has learned to hide or suppress his feelings.

Although never an operating surgeon, naturally I have been present at, or assisted at, hundreds of operations, great or small, and was never upset by them. But all the same, when the surgeon made the first incision with his scalpel into healthy, human skin, I always had to glance away from that one moment. Once the first cut had been made I lost all feeling that the subject being operated on was a human being and it became simply a " case," a piece of living anatomy.

How those raids came to be abominated by those who had to make them! To judge from what appeared in some of the newspapers, as well as in the official communiqués, known as " comic-cuts," the British soldier longed, above all things, to be allowed to take part in a raid. If this was indeed the case he certainly concealed his desire very successfully from his friends. No doubt the Staff knew best and these persistent raids did " keep up the fighting spirit of the troops," and who was I, a non-combatant of humble rank, to question that what they did was for the best? But all the same the thought often did occur to me, what would have happened if that precious " fighting-spirit " had not been continually whipped up? The French, until egged on by us, did not go in for raids. Their comfortable policy between battles was to " live and let live," and the French are no mean warriors. I still wonder what would have happened if the friendly meetings between German and English soldiers in No-Man's-Land where they exchanged cigars for cigarettes and chattered together, had not been nipped in the bud.

If two men fall out and fight, the time for friends to step in and persuade them to make up the quarrel and reconcile them is when their first anger passes off. But if the friends and backers shout insults and urge their respective champions to go on with it, then the fight continues. Would the Great War have lasted for more than six months without the stimulus of eloquent politicians and press propaganda? Who knows?

After a longish spell of subterranean existence in the dark cellars of Bois Grenier I was "lent" to the 103rd Brigade R.F.A. to look after them while their own M.O. was on leave. This was one of the advantages, or as some thought, disadvantages, of belonging to a Field Ambulance, that at any moment you were liable to be sent off to do a temporary job elsewhere in the division. It did me good to leave the safe darkness of the brewery and live a normal, healthy life above ground. The moral effect of living always below ground was beginning to show itself, for the longer you remained safely underground the more scared you became of going out into the open. However, I found my troubles soon vanished when living in the open and above ground, with a cheerful mess and a charming colonel. I thoroughly liked making my daily round of visits to the different batteries and the horse-lines.

As there was no room for me to sleep in the farmhouse called Rolanderie, where the brigade had its headquarters, I had a small room under the roof of a filthy estaminet near by. This hovel—it was nothing better—looked straight across the trenches, and with my field-glasses I could sometimes see from my bedroom window small grey objects creeping about like lice, which were German soldiers. As a billet this estaminet was the worst I was ever in. The woman who owned it was a bedraggled wench, for ever scolding her litter of small, ragged children. The building seemed on the point of collapsing, and at night when lorries passed the door the whole house shook as if it would fall down in a heap, and even if a door was slammed it trembled. Another drawback was that every sound could be heard all over the house, and when I was in bed I could hear all that went on in the estaminet below as if I was in the same room. The customers were all Tommies going into or coming out of the trenches. One morning I heard a soldier's voice demand " doos oofs," and then the landlady called out to one of her children to go to the farm near by and fetch some eggs. Then the voice of the soldier shouted out, " Toot sweet . . . 'urry, I'm waitin' for 'em."

All day long soldiers kept coming in to buy eggs. It was a surprise to me to learn what a lot of eggs were asked for. If the customer spoke French he asked for " doos oofs." If madam did not " compree " French, he then asked again in Belgian, " eegs," which never failed.

One day while I was with the 103rd Brigade, one of the batteries telegraphed up to say they had been shelled. The colonel and I walked down to the battery which was in an orchard behind Bois Grenier to see what damage had been done. One very old and hollow apple tree had received a direct hit from a shell and lay scattered in fragments on the ground. Amongst these we found a small, grey, fluffy animal, a fat or garden dormouse, curled up fast asleep. The colonel gently picked the little creature up in his hand, when suddenly the dormouse woke up, gave his thumb a severe bite, then curled up and went to sleep again.

The healthy life above ground with the R.F.A. quite cured me of my agoraphobia, and when my time was up and I was about to leave, Colonel Henning asked me if I would like to be his permanent M.O. if permission could be obtained. I was in rather a fix as to what to answer. I liked the brigade, its colonel and its officers and felt altogether a different person after living the life of a sewer rat at the advanced dressing station, but at the same time I did not want to be disloyal to Colonel Walker or my field-ambulance. Anyhow, it was settled for me by the application being refused on the grounds that Nimmo Walker did not wish to lose any of his section commanders, and so I returned to my old friends.

After a short spell at Fort Rompu I went for eight days as "locum" to the 9th Yorks, doing four days in the trenches and four at a ruined farm building in reserve. The dug-out was dry, a fact worth recording, and measured six feet long by five wide and six in height. It had a glass window, an unusual luxury for a dug-out, and an elegant and tall cheval glass. I did not have the dug-out to myself, for I shared it with a house-mouse, but he lived beneath the floor-boards. He suffered from a nasty cold in his head and was continually sneezing. After my experience with the gunner-major of Grispot and his mouse I made no attempt to catch him.

At the end of the four days we went back a little way into reserve, and the second-in-command, Major Prior, and I were billeted in a dug-out beneath a ruined cottage. Everybody was tired and very dirty. In the afternoon as Prior and I were standing together outside our dug-out, we were astounded to see a motor-car coming slowly towards us down the straight road which was close behind the trenches and in full view of the Boche. We wondered whoever the two dare-devil officers could be who were reclining on the front seat. To our surprise and relief the car reached the shelter of our ruined cottage without being shelled, and out jumped two immaculately dressed young A.S.C. officers, a captain and a first-lieutenant, who told us they came from St. Omer, and that having nothing else to do they decided to have a look at the War, but had missed their way, and asked if we knew where the road led to.

"Germany," replied Prior, the blunt Yorkshireman.

We took them into our dug-out, and with a map showed them exactly where they were, and how to get back to St. Omer, and told them we should be glad if they would return with their car as quickly as they could, for our sakes as well as their own. What really annoyed us was their care-free spirit of the holiday maker, and their spotless raiment. We felt ourselves to be, as indeed we were, both verminous and filthy, while these two were dressed in spotless tunics of Savile Row cut, light cavalry riding breeches and spurs, and in place of the regulation khaki ties they both were adorned with folded hunting stocks. They took our advice not to dally on the way back and the car dashed up the road at sixty miles an hour.

As the car disappeared round a corner, Prior turned to me and murmured, " Thou shalt not covet the A.S.C."

Nothing else of interest occurred while with the 9th Yorks, and when my eight days were up I returned to Fort Rompu.

I now began in earnest to collect and skin specimens for the British Museum. In the fields round Fort Rompu there were many mole hills, which filled me with a desire to procure a mole or two to add to my collection of Flemish mammals. So I wrote to one of my sisters who had a cottage at Withypool on Exmoor, asking her to get me a couple of traps. Within a week an odd-shaped parcel arrived which contained two steel mole-traps. These I set in what I thought to be likely places, but I met with no luck whatever. Mole catching seemed to be like many other ancient crafts, a business for experts.

I had already learned in the army that whenever at a loss the regimental sergeant-major was the right man to appeal to for help. So I sent for him and explained that I wanted some moles, that I had some traps, and asked if he thought he could find a man in the ambulance who knew how to use them. Off went the regimental sergeant-major, and half an hour later, while I was still sitting at the desk in the orderly room, I heard sounds of approaching steps and the regimental sergeant-major marched in, followed by a depressed and rather scared-looking Army Service Corps driver.

"Driver Pugh, sir," bawled the R.S.M., "admits to being a mole-catcher in civil life."

Then stepped forward Driver Pugh, who in reply to my questions said that before the War he had worked on a farm in Wales near a village with an unpronounceable name, and that his principal duty at this farm had been to catch moles. The very man I wanted. So it was arranged that Driver Pugh should be excused all duties that afternoon, and he was sent off with my traps. This piece of news, coupled with the sight of the traps, brought about an instant and miraculous change in the Welshman's demeanour, for in place of a sad, browbeaten man, he instantly became alert, smiling, and self-confident.

How he did it I do not know, but next morning, chaperoned by the R.S.M., Driver Pugh entered the presence bearing in his hands two handsome Flemish moles. These when skinned proved to be a male and a female, so that strictly speaking I had enough for the collection. But the mole-catcher had so obviously enjoyed his outing and being allowed for once to do his own job, that from time to time, while we remained at Fort Rompu, I told the R.S.M. that I needed some more moles, so Driver Pugh had another happy half-holiday and never failed to produce one or two moles the following day.

It was sometimes quite pathetic to see how much the men liked following again their old peace-time callings. Once while I was acting as temporary medical officer to a battalion, an order arrived from Divisional Headquarters instructing the commanding-officer to make enquiries whether there were in his battalion any men with first-hand knowledge of the care of carrier pigeons, because several experts were required to take charge of some mobile pigeon lofts which were being sent out. This news soon spread and caused much excitement. The battalion had been recruited in a Yorkshire town where pigeon fancying and pigeon racing were popular hobbies and sports. Here, it seemed, was a chance to get a " cushy " job well away from the line, near some comfortable estaminet, with no officer, still more no R.S.M. and no parades. Indeed, it seemed to hold out the realization of the golden dreams of almost every infantry soldier. At noon the battalion paraded, the order was read out and any man who knew about the care of carrier pigeons and how to fly them, was instructed at the word " Advance " to take two steps forward. When the order rang out . . . Advance " . . . the whole battalion moved two paces forward and halted.

The adjutant had a difficult task before him, to select the two or three required, when confronted by some four hundred carrier-pigeon experts from which to choose.

Sometimes the field ambulance would remain at one place for quite a long while and become more of a hospital for light cases than a clearing house for sick and wounded.

Amongst our men were two tin-smiths and the things these two contrived to make, with old biscuit tins, a pair of cutters and a blow-pipe, were quite extraordinary. Once at a derelict brewery, they made from old tins and some odd pieces of lead piping a complete hot water supply with a boiler and a dozen wash-basins.

which could be filled with hot or cold water day or night.

At Ypres, in the deserted prison, one of our officers invented an ingenious contrivance to dry trench boots. One of the bugbears of trench warfare in the undrained, waterlogged salient was trench-foot. This was caused by the men's feet remaining cold and damp for days together when they were in the line. In every battalion there was a daily foot inspection, at which the men's feet were dried and then well rubbed with whale oil; and every man was issued with a dry pair of socks. Often half the benefit of all this was lost, because the feet went back into sopping wet long rubber boots. The difficulty was to dry the inside of the boots; hot bran was tried and hot crumpled newspapers, but these failed to dry the boots in time. Then this ingenious officer got the tin-smiths to make a machine which blew hot air along a pipe off which at intervals of about a foot upshot smaller pipes. The boots were placed upside down over these smaller pipes, much like snuffers on a candle, and the hot dry air was turned on, and in theory the difficult problem solved.

We never learned if this apparatus proved satisfactory, because just as it was got going the division was sent off, post haste, to take over a section of the line further south and another field ambulance inherited our invention.

There were some men whose civilian work always led to them being giving similar employment in the army in whatever branch they might be. Thus, all club or hotel waiters became mess-servants, and some fortunate officers had peace-time valets for batmen. My own batman was a boiler maker by trade, and although he made a clumsy and seemingly hopeless valet at first, he ended by becoming a veritable Admirable Crichton.

Quite by chance it was found out that a somewhat lady-like nursing orderly was a barber in private life. At the time of this discovery my hair needed cutting more than that of anybody else, and so it was agreed to try the orderly on me. The result was excellent. Before submitting my head to him I asked him if it was true that he had been a barber before the War. " Oh no, sir," was his shocked reply, " I was a Court hairdresser at Slough." Having proved his worth on my head, the orderly was promoted to lance-corporal and installed in the place of a carpenter who had hitherto shorn the heads of the ambulance.

Lance-corporal Hill soon made quite a reputation for himself as a hairdresser, for besides his official duties as haircutter to the ambulance, he practised his tonsorial art with success, both financially and in other ways, amongst the fair ladies of the villages in which we were billeted from time to time.

Colonel Nimmo Walker held very strongly the opinion that no man should remain always at the safe and comparatively comfortable headquarters, and made it a rule that every N.C.O. and man, whatever his special duties might be, should from time to time take his turn as a stretcher-bearer at one of the advanced dressing-stations.

Once when I was on duty at one of these advanced dressing-stations in some trenches near Fosse 10, and Lance-corporal Hill was one of the detachment, I suddenly came round a corner to find him engaged in a most unwarlike pursuit. Seated on the ground at the mouth of a dug-out was Hill in the act of combing with great earnestness a human scalp.

"What on earth are you doing, Corporal?" I asked.

"Just keeping my hand in, Sir," was his answer.

What had appeared to me to be a human scalp was really a wig, with curling locks, known to the profession as a switch. I learned, what I did not know before, that without constant practice, the Court hairdresser, like the pianist or conjurer, loses his cunning.

One of the most useful men we had in the ambulance was a thatcher. I had never before met or heard of a thatcher under the age of seventy, but this man could not have been more than thirty. Wherever we went, in the winter time he would make thatched roofs for our horse lines, and this protection kept our horses in very good condition.

All too often we camp-followers, as well as the fighting men, were the victims of the profound ignorance of some Great Thinker at the War Office. One of these, probably a relic of the South African War, would conceive some measure or "stunt" by which the allied cause would benefit—at least in theory, but which when put into practice by those on the spot more often than not fell far short of the high hopes of the originator. Ask any infantry officer; he will tell you, for he suffered worst of all from these muddle-headed projects.

One such scheme led to a deed of barefaced mutiny which must, I believe and hope, have been unique in the annals of the British Army. It happened some time during the wet early spring of 1916, while we were in the Armentières sector, in front of Fort Rompu.

An order came to us from headquarters with several

large crates. When these were opened and unpacked they were discovered to contain those garments, euphemistically described by men's outfitters as " gents' slumber-wear," but by ordinary persons as pyjamas. The accompanying War Office letter had to do with these useful, if unwarlike, garments, but before disclosing its contents certain facts connected with the treatment and evacuation of wounded soldiers must be touched upon.

One of the most troublesome and difficult wounds to treat on the battlefield was that described in the army reports as " G.S.W. femur." These were cases where a bullet or piece of shell had struck and penetrated a soldier's thigh and in doing so fractured his thigh-bone. They were always serious and the percentage of deaths amongst them very high. This was due in part to loss of blood, but still more to shock, which was brought about by damp and cold. A man might be shot in the thigh during a trench-raid or while mending barbed wire, and as likely as not he would crawl into some water-filled shell-hole to wait for several hours or until the following night, when he could be attended to and carried back by his regimental stretcher-bearers. They were very difficult cases to deal with, as they were always very badly shocked, and there was the difficulty of the broken leg requiring a long splint which had to reach from the man's armpit to beyond his foot. It was the custom to dress the wound at once with the first-field dressing, which every soldier carried sewn into the lining of his tunic, apply a splint and after wrapping the man up in blankets, carry him down the communication trench to the nearest ambulance advanced dressing-station. Here the wound was re-dressed if necessary, a long splint applied, and he would be given an injection of anti-tetanus serum, and if in great pain, another of morphia. To guard against an overdose of either of these, the surgeon would write on the man's forehead with a blue skin pencil A.T. to show the next doctor who saw the man that he already had been inoculated, and put an M. on his wrist to give warning that he already had been given morphia.

Then with fresh dry blankets round him the wounded man would be sent off by motor ambulance to the main dressing-station a few miles further back, where he would be examined again by a doctor, and if it was found that he was cold or shocked, he would be wrapped in more blankets and kept warm by two, three or even four hot water bottles. The great thing was to disturb the wounded man as little as possible and above all things not to remove his clothes, however wet they might be, until he was at the C.C.S. hospital, where he would be operated on by expert surgeons, his wounds properly and thoroughly explored and cleaned, and his fractured bone securely set.

As long as a man in wet clothes is well covered up he comes to no harm, and retains his natural heat; but if his clothes are allowed to evaporate he soon becomes cold, and a man wounded severely may easily die of cold.

Now the orders which we got with the crates of pyjamas were that in future all " G.S.W. femur " were to be completely undressed at the advanced dressing-stations, and that the wretched man was then to be got into a suit of pyjamas before being sent back to the main dressing-station and so to the C.C.S. It was evident that the instigator of this fantastic order knew little of the practical side of treating wounds in the field.

Colonel Walker called us all together and read out the order, and then asked each of us in order of seniority what we thought about it. H——, our senior captain at that time, was a regular and he, very rightly, asked to be excused from giving his opinion of an order from the War Office. But the rest of us held temporary commissions, and had nothing to lose or fear in our future careers by saying exactly what we thought. One and all declared the new order to be preposterous, and surgically mischievous, and that anyhow the soldiers in the trenches had quite enough to put up with already, without our adding to their troubles, and we ended up by telling the colonel that orders or no orders, we flatly refused to carry this one out. Much as Colonel Walker disapproved of the order, he was not in the same happy position of irresponsibility as we junior officers were, so we retired to the mess-room, where, after a lively discussion, we sat down and wrote a round-robin to the A.D.M.S. of the division, in which we stated that as medical men we felt bound to refuse to carry out the recent order, and gave our reasons.

This precious document we all signed except H——, and sent it directly to the A.D.M.S. so as not to involve the Colonel who, although in agreement with our views, could scarcely be expected to join in such a gross act of insubordination.

The first result of our round-robin was an infernal row; the second the rescinding of the stupid order.

It was in such cases as this that we temporary officers who were engaged in our ordinary calling had the advantage over combatant temporary officers, who often had to carry out with blind obedience orders which they knew to be wrong.

On looking back at it all now, I see that in many ways I made a very unsatisfactory soldier. For one thing, there was my kit, the despair of my commanding-officers and of all transport officers. I think we were limited to one hundred and forty-five pounds weight of personal luggage; it may have been forty-five or one thousand one hundred and forty-five; I forget now which; I was never good at figures, but forty-five came into it. Whatever it was, I found it impossible to get mine down to the regulation degree of lightness or bulk.

There was the bulging valise, the collapsible washing-stand and canvas bath, the folding armchair, the kit-bag, the portable gramophone, the books, the skinning outfit and traps, and last, but far from least, my fishing-rod. This fishing-rod was a treasured possession, a constant companion, and not to be taken from me by colonels, quartermasters or transport officers.

What a lot of fun I got out of it and so for that matter did the rank and file of the 23rd Division. It was quite by accident that I learned at Fort Rompu, on the banks of the slowly flowing river Lys, that my nickname in the ambulance was Harry Tate. The original Mr. Tate used to give a clever and amusing music-hall sketch entitled " Harry Tate goes fishing." After I recovered from the first shock I could not but admit to myself that the nickname was apt. Whenever we were out of the line and there was a river, canal, or pond near—and there was generally one or another—off I would go in uniform of sorts, and high rubber boots, with my rod and a bag containing bait for the quarry and lunch for myself, and spend long, peaceful, quiet hours with rod and float, seated among the rushes or beneath a willow tree.

On setting out one day on such an expedition I happened to see my reflection in a tall mirror which stood in the hall of the big house we were billeted in, and it gave me quite a shock to see how like I was to Mr. Tate, even to the newly grown moustache which nature had planted slightly awry, and my way of wearing my soft cap at rather a jaunty angle. In my bird diary I find many brief entries of happy days spent in the gentle sport of angling.

At Vieux Berquin, by the forest of Nieppe, the days passed pleasantly enough fishing for tench in an old clay pit, with Monsieur Berthoud, the schoolmaster, with whom I was billeted. He pointed out to me the footmarks of an otter on the banks of the pond, though I was never fortunate enough to see the animal which made them. I never fished in the lake at Duckebusch, though enterprising young bombing officers used to go out in a crazy old boat, and after dropping a bomb into the water, row quickly away. Then after the bomb had exploded, stunned fish would float to the surface and be caught and taken back to make an addition to the ordinary mess menu—a doubtful one, but at least a change.

There were many singular rôles a soldier might play in France.

There was one elderly soldier at Zillebeke whose

business was this. Now and again an enemy shell would fall into the lake there which supplied drinking water to thousands of men and hundreds of horses in and about Ypres. It occurred to one of the Great that the Boche, to whom no frightfulness was too frightful, might take it into their heads to drop shells into the lake filled with poison or with the microbe of some deadly water-borne disease.

To guard against this danger the all-wise installed this elderly soldier at Zillebeke lake, and whenever a shell plunged into the lake his orders were to row as rapidly as he could to the exact spot where the shell had fallen; quickly to procure a sample of the water in a special sterilized container, and return. Although nothing was down in his orders about returning speedily, the inspector, having got his specimen, used to row back at a pace which would have placed him among the favourites for the Diamond Sculls, for often as not one shell would be quickly followed by a second in the same place. This scare of poisoned water was on a par with many similar and no more grotesque.

In the summer of 1917 there was a persistent rumour in the back areas behind Poperinghe that German aeroplanes were dropping sweets and toys, the former being poisoned, the latter highly infected with all sorts of deadly microbes, which would spread disease and death amongst the French children who found them.

We may smile at the credulity of persons who could believe such a preposterous idea as an enemy scattering poison to kill innocent children, and yet to-day it is no secret that every Christian power has stowed safely away vast quantities of poison gas in great bombs, ready to drop them on to towns and cities to kill innocent civilians; men, women and children.

I never realised before going to France what vast numbers of Scotch doctors there were. Although the Board of Trade in its annual returns makes no mention of them, yet without any shadow of doubt doctors hold the honour of second place amongst the native industries of Scotland. I have heard it claimed by some that marine engineers come before doctors in the list of national manufactures and exports, but closer enquiry would convince these doubters that the production of marine engineers, although an important industry, is purely a local one, confined to the banks of the river Clyde. Indeed I go so far as to maintain that more doctors qualify each year at Glasgow University to practise their art and mystery on English patients than marine engineers are turned out to tend and oil English and Scotch ships.

All our field-ambulances were richly provided with Scottish graduates of medicine; all the four medical schools, Edinburgh, Glasgow, Aberdeen and St. Andrews were well represented, but Glasgow could claim more alumni than the other three put together. They were most formidable disputants, those Glasgow doctors. No fact could be stated, no opinion aired, but it would be seized upon by the Glasgow contingent to become a bone of contention. No flippant remark nor mild English joke but it would be argued and wrangled over until the joker bitterly regretted his humorous venture.

They were practised masters at the game, and woe betide one of us Sassenachs who attempted to dispute a point with them, for short work would they make of an Englishman, or even an Irishman in any discussion.

But a dispute amongst themselves was a battle of giants, of experts, and many a controversy, carried on in the high, querulous Glaswegian dialect, would drag on far into the night.

A good, honest, straightforward joke they tolerated; and indeed told many a good story themselves, generally at the expense of Scotchmen, but what they could not allow or overlook was a flippant English aside or light remark, which collapsed at once under cross examination.

It was one of these Glasgow doctors who told me a story about Lord Kelvin at one of his lectures to the students at the Glasgow University. The subject was electricity, and Lord Kelvin opened his lecture by asking if any gentleman present knew what electricity was. Immediately a student in the middle of the crowded hall stood up.

"Well, Mr. McGregor, will you kindly tell us what is electricity?"

But Mr. McGregor remained silent, shuffled his feet in an embarrassed way, and then subsided into his seat.

"Now come along, Mr. McGregor, we are all waiting for you to tell us what is electricity."

At last poor Mr. McGregor who had now become more uncomfortable and very pink in the face, blurted out that he had forgotten.

"Dear me," replied the lecturer, "what a misfortune. Only two persons know what electricity is; one is God, who won't say, and the other is Mr. McGregor, and he has forgotten!"

It was not a Scotsman who told me about a society

of which I had never even heard, one inspired by the most altruistic motives. This was the Society for the Repatriation of Scotchmen.

I learned that when the last Scotchman was safely back in his own country, this public spirited Society intended to spend any funds it might have left over on repairing the great wall of Hadrian, to keep them from getting out again. How all these repatriated Scotchmen were to find room or make a living was not very obvious, but it seemed to me to be a society deserving of every support.

Although Scotch doctors predominated, we had officers from other lands as well. A field ambulance was in some ways like a servants' registry office. It continually had R.A.M.C. officers coming to it from the base as reinforcements, who remained with us until a post was found for them as M.O. to one or other of the units in the division. Some of these were Canadians, others Australians, who had immediately joined the Imperial (as they called it) Army on the outbreak of war. The Australians had a permanent grievance because had they not been in such a hurry to come over to England to join up as first lieutenants in the R.A.M.C. but had waited to join their own Australian Army Medical Service, they would have started, whatever their age or however short a while they had been qualified, as full-blown majors and would have been paid on a much more generous scale than were we, either temporary or territorial R.A.M.C. officers.

One of the Australian doctors, a very young one and very popular, was known throughout the division as " Squeaker " Martin. How he came by this nick-name

I never learned. He was afterwards posted to an infantry battalion which was commanded by a gallant but extremely jumpy colonel. Like so many nervous commanders, he liked always to be accompanied by his M.O. when in the trenches. Whenever the colonel went up the communication trench at night " Squeaker " Martin would follow close behind him, and now and again by some dexterous twist of his fingers, spin a wooden match past the colonel's head in such a way that the match made a whining noise just like a rifle bullet. Each time Martin did this the colonel would quickly duck down and call back " that was a near one, Squeaker ! "

One of our principal occupations at headquarters, and quite the most irksome and dreary, was the censoring of the men's letters. This was a task I never cared for, but as I came to recognise the different handwritings I got into the habit of passing many letters without so much as glancing at their contents, knowing all too well what sort of letter it would be, and that it would contain not one syllable which could possibly assist the enemy. I do not think a man's letters home ought to be read by anybody to whom the writer is known. No doubt it was quite necessary that supervision should be kept over letters written from the front, and very occasionally I found facts or places mentioned which the writer had no business to give away, although it was only done in thoughtlessness.

I remember reading one letter written by a private to his girl at Huddersfield. After the usual opening sentence of every soldier's letter home, about being in the pink and hoping the recipient was equally in the pink, the writer hazarded the conjecture that his fiancée went to many evening parties, and asked, wistfully, if ever at these gay festivities, her thoughts turned to her " missing link " out in France.

There was one sort of letter I always put my censorial blue pencil through, filled with the imaginative outpourings of the embryo news-reporter, or descriptive journalist. Many of these gave glowing and truly terrifying accounts of the writer's experiences and sensations under heavy shell and rifle fire, and were, almost without exception, written by nursing orderlies who had never heard the sound of a rifle bullet, but who might occasionally have heard or even seen a shell burst in the distance.

Such passages I blotted out, not to prevent them reaching the bewildered enemy, but to save the feelings of an anxious parent, wife, or sweetheart from being harrowed. In very extreme cases I would speak privately to the " literary " soldier, give him back his letter and at the same time a short, but kindly word on the subject of writing home letters.

The general conversation in our mess differed from that of most other messes, in that being all members of one profession we talked " shop." Otherwise it was much like the conversation to be heard in any other mess in the old or new armies. We exchanged local divisional gossip, and discussed the latest rumours, the wilder and more improbable the better, which the padres had picked up during the day. When these topics failed there were certain stock subjects which could be drawn upon for argument and debate ; one which never failed to draw the Colonel concerned a member of the Royal

Family. The Colonel stoutly maintained that if he or any other officer of or above the rank of captain should meet the Prince of Wales, who held the rank of captain, and was often in and about the trenches, he should salute him as being the Heir to the Throne. As the self-elected mouthpiece of the opposition, it always fell to my lot to champion the opposite school of thought.

I held the view, or pretended to, that His Royal Highness should be treated exactly as any other officer of his rank on active service, and no distinction made.

This harmless and aimless bone of contention never miscarried, but led to long and amusing and, sometimes, quite heated discussions.

Then one day as I was walking alone to visit an advanced dressing station near Ypres, I saw coming away from the trenches, a young officer, also alone. As we drew near it seemed to me that I recognised him; and a second later it flashed upon me that this was the Prince of Wales. For the moment I forgot all about my championing of the cause of equality of rank and snatched my pipe from my mouth ready to salute him. Then suddenly my conscience pricked me. Was I, now that they were to be put to the test, to go back on all my theories, oratory and arguments, and betray my party? No! such treachery was unthinkable. I would greet the Prince in the way I had so often assured the mess he would prefer to be greeted, as one captain by another. So as we passed on the duckboard, with my pipe in my mouth, I nodded and said cheerily " Good morning." I had expected to be able, when I got back to the mess, triumphantly to tell my story, of how our democratic Prince returned my democratic greeting, but not a bit of it; he cut me dead, and I loved him all the better for it.

Other subjects were discussed in the mess than what an officer should or should not do if he met the Prince of Wales. One of the most popular of these was " early memories." Whenever conversation flagged, it was only necessary for someone to recount his earliest recollection for everybody present to remember something yet more precocious that had happened in his childhood or even babyhood.

One evening there had been an extra long bout of this topic and we were getting wearied of incidents of infantile memory, some bordering on the incredible. For instance, one of the nonconformist chaplains declared he could still remember his feeding bottle which had a long rubber tube attached to it, and recalled the gurgling sounds it made as the last drops of milk passed down the tube from the empty bottle into his mouth. This feat of memory he claimed, could not be surpassed by any of us. Then, when it all seemed over and done with, the nonconformist parson met his match, from an unexpected quarter.

A new claimant entered the lists, an unknown and dark horse. This was a medical officer named Bell, a quiet, shy man who had only just come from the base, and was stopping with us until appointed to a battalion. Hesitatingly and modestly he said that he had been very much interested in all he had heard, but with all due deference to the chaplain, he believed he could justly claim his own memory went back even further. Though a little dim now after so many years, he still remembered lying on his back in a crib or cradle, when a tall man with a kind, grave, clean-shaven face bent over him, lifted him up and carried him into the light of an oil lamp. Then the grave-faced man raised the shawl or whatever it was that covered the small, naked Bell, looked earnestly at him, and then went to the open door of the room and called down to somebody below, who he thought must have been waiting for some such message, " It's a boy ! "

The next day Bell left us and I never saw him again, but was ever grateful to him for ending, once and for all, one of the most interminable topics of conversation of our mess.

One of the compensations for being in France during the war was the opportunity it gave for reading. Whatever I should have done without my collecting and books I dare not guess. I had no desire to read exciting stories, and least of all, those about war. Above everything, I enjoyed reading natural history books, those of W. H. Hudson in particular, which carried you away from the noise and beastliness of war to wander with the writer in search of birds and flowers in the New Forest, or on the high Wiltshire downs, or else to stalk the wary wild geese which settle every autumn in the marshes on the Norfolk coast. It was after reading *Birds and Man*, which made me homesick for the New Forest, that I did a thing I had never dared to do before. I wrote to an author whom I did not know.

In my letter to Hudson, after saying how much I had enjoyed *Birds and Man*, I told him how well I knew many of the places in the New Forest he described, and told him also a little about the birds I had seen in Flanders, hoping it might interest him. Having written and posted my letter addressed to his publisher, I became uneasy at my boldness. Several days went past, and I began to think that perhaps I had offended Hudson; that my letter would be ignored, as indeed it deserved to be. But one day a letter arrived for me in an unknown handwriting, with a Cornish postmark. On opening the envelope, I discovered a long letter from Hudson, and was relieved to find that he had not taken offence at my writing to him.

His letter was dated 26th October, 1915, and written from Woodside, Lelant, Cornwall.

It ran as follows :

DEAR MR. GOSSE,

I was very pleased to receive your interesting letter this morning from the front and glad to know the book has given you some pleasure. It is not strange that one of your name should be a bird lover, if, as I suppose, you are a grandson of Philip Gosse the naturalist. I used to read his books long years ago. I know all that beautiful country about Beaulieu and down to the sea and rather wish I was there just now to see all that oak forest in its yellow foliage. But I wish too that I could be on the East coast at Wells where I have been accustomed to go in October just to see the wild geese congregate in thousands on the marsh between Wells and Holkham. Unfortunately my health has been bad for some time past and I am here for a couple of months for the sake of the milder climate. Here I have the estuary of the Hayle before the window and can hear all day and night the piping and thrilling conversation of the curlews going on. A few nights ago we had a flock of wild geese to visit us too; their cries woke me up some time after midnight.

Your bird watching must be a rather difficult and

dangerous business out there; I suppose the hawks you saw were hen harriers.

I sincerely trust you will come back to Beaulieu some day unhurt when this horrible business is over. Most of my young literary friends, who until a little while ago never dreamed of doing anything but write books, are now in it, and my unhappiness is because I can't knock 30 years off my age to be with them.

Yours sincerely,
W. H. Hudson.

My mother kept me well supplied with books, most of them cheap reprints of standard works, such as the "Everyman" edition. When I had read these they were passed on to others, often to men in the ranks who liked reading something other than occasional newspapers or cheap magazines, which was all that ever came their way.

Those "Everyman" volumes of my mother's probably circulated up and down the line, from Ypres to Arras, until they were worn to shreds.

I heard, after the War, that some philanthropic people in England formed a committee to collect books and send them out to the men in the trenches, but certainly none of their books ever got up to our division.

For good, but interrupted reading, there is nothing better than Hakluyt's Voyages. I read practically all the eight volumes of the "Everyman" edition. Another book I remember enjoying was the life of Frank Buckland, the naturalist. I liked particularly the extract from his diary, which he kept while a schoolboy at Winchester. It runs:

Tuesday: Lost hedgehog.
Wednesday: Found hedgehog.
Thursday: Lost hedgehog.
Friday: Found hedgehog.
Saturday: Ate hedgehog.

Occasionally I found myself without anything at all to read, and at places where there were no birds to watch, or no small mammals to trap and skin, was in a sad way.

One such place was the cellar of a ruined estaminet at Fleurbaix. It was in the winter, the rain was falling in torrents and so were other and worse things as well. There was no inducement to go out, and it was just the time and place for a good book. In despair I began to search the cellar to see if I could find something—anything—in print, for anything would have been better than nothing, to pass away the time. The search was without result except for a torn sheet of an old newspaper. With this poor treasure I retired to my bunk to squeeze what entertainment I could from it. This was little enough, to be sure, except for the concluding sentence of one paragraph which seemed to be pregnant with unconscious humour.

It was an account of some revolting murder, and described how, in a street in Bermondsey, the neighbours had reported to the police that an old man, a recluse who lived alone in the street and was suspected of being a miser, had not been seen for several days. The article went on to describe how the police had broken into the old man's room, where they had discovered his body lying on the floor in a welter of blood. It then went on to give revolting details of how the poor old man's head and face had been bashed to a pulp, his throat cut from ear to ear, and his body stabbed in several places. Around the body lay the overturned furniture, the cupboard and drawers had been ransacked and any money or valuables the old man might have possessed were missing.

This gruesome account ended with these cryptic words, " The police suspect foul play."

CHAPTER II

WE GO SOUTH

IT was a bitterly cold February day when the Division left the Armentières sector, but nobody was sorry to leave. Our time there had been a fairly quiet one; in fact, by far the quietest the Division was ever to experience; but the country was low-lying, ugly and uninteresting.

Where we were going we did not know, nor very much care. All we wanted was a change.

After marching for a few days we eventually stopped in the neighbourhood of the ancient town of Aire.

The Division was "in rest" and scattered about the countryside. My friend Pye-Smith and I, with our section, found ourselves quartered miles away from the rest of the Ambulance, at a village called Blaringhem. Of my billet there I have none but the happiest memories. The cottage belonged to a couple of dear old French peasants, Monsieur and Madame Pouvillion, who lived there with their two grown-up daughters, Cécile and Jeanne and a son Paul, a lad below military age. My bedroom was a sort of cupboard which opened out of the kitchen and living room. It was spotlessly clean and had one minute window formed by a single pane of glass which did not open. Pye-Smith had a billet at the other end of the village, but used to join the

Pouvillions and me for meals, which were taken at the kitchen table; and we were soon on the very best of terms.

I made an arrangement with Madame Pouvillion by which she agreed to do the cooking in return for our army rations. These consisted of fresh meat or bully beef, with potatoes or tinned dried vegetables, bread, cheese, and jam and tinned milk; but it was the fresh meat the family most hankered after. She would cook these, adding her own fresh vegetables and supply us with salads, and when procurable, fresh milk. Madame Pouvillion proved a first-rate cook and we all enjoyed the Anglo-French meals she provided, particularly after our usual fare with the ambulance. It was wonderful what tempting dishes she could turn out with a tin of bully beef or a scrap of bone and a few of her own home-grown vegetables. And what fun it was. My halting French was no bar to general conversation at the happy board, and all sorts of rural subjects were discussed and jokes bandied.

After dinner every evening Bob Church would help the young ladies to clear the table and then bring in my portable gramophone, while the family settled themselves in chairs round the stove to listen to the concert while they roasted chestnuts. I had no French records, but the fact that my hosts knew no English did not spoil their enjoyment; who knows but that many a song on a gramophone record would sound far better if one did not understand the words?

The one great and universal favourite which was always called for and always encored was a song by Harry Lauder called " Stop your tickling, Jock,"

The song had a catchy, hilarious chorus, which represented the sounds made by a highland lassie while being tickled in the heather by a highland laddie. The louder Lauder laughed, the more uproarious did the Pouvillion family become, though none more so than Madame Pouvillion. This lady was short and plump and when seated in a chair her feet did not reach the floor. The more the singer laughed, the more the lassie chokingly implored her true love to desist, the louder did Madame Pouvillion laugh and rock from side to side with delight until she was in danger of falling off her chair. In spite of the cold and bitter weather those were happy days at Blaringhem. Being alone with our section, and having no other troops near, Pye-Smith and I had little to do. It was a real rest, for except for the daily route march every man was free to do as he pleased.

Blaringhem, like almost every other village or small town we stopped at, had no doctor, for most of the French doctors had been called up for military service, and it often fell to the R.A.M.C. officers unofficially to take their places. Thus it happened here, and I soon had quite a practice. Madame Pouvillion would act as go-between and tell me who was ill and needed visiting, and direct me to the patient's house. Of course we never charged a fee for our professional attendances, though many of the patients, even the very poorest, would try to press some small gift on us. This generous feeling was the cause of my becoming quite ill at one village in which we were quartered. There was a good deal of sickness about, particularly among the children, and I would visit and prescribe for perhaps eight or ten patients in a morning. After each of these visits a friendly wrangle took place between the mother and myself over the question of a fee. The only way, I found, to satisfy them was to accept a cup of alleged coffee or a glass of very fiery cognac. The coffee tasted of pure chicory or something even worse, and as for the cognac, it certainly was no credit to the grape. The result of drinking several cups of this noxious black mixture, and several stirrup cups of fiery cognac was disastrous to my digestion. More than once I returned home after my round of visits a wreck, a victim to acute chicory poisoning and chronic French hospitality.

One of my patients at Blaringhem was the village curé. His white house stood opposite the red-brick church, which had a tall square tower on which was a tablet with the date, 1679. Not only was the curé the most important patient, socially, in my practice, but the most seriously ill, and I used to visit him every day. I found his French almost as difficult to understand as he did mine, but Madame Pouvillion explained to me that he spoke bad French with a strong Flemish accent, being indeed a Fleming.

In appearance he was a very tall man, about sixty-five years of age, with black eyes and snow white hair. His room was filled with musty tomes, and I imagine his windows were seldom opened. He was very interested when he heard my name, and explained at great length—for fear I did not know it—that gosse in French signified a small boy—about *so* high—but not a *very* small boy, and that gosse was not a good French word, but patois. He then went to one of his bookshelves and drew out a dictionary and showed me the word gosse; and also pointed out the name of a French painter called Gosse who flourished, I think, between 1750 and 1822.

Often R.A.M.C. doctors who were stationed for long periods in small towns near the base had quite big practices amongst the French civilian population. One, a Scotch doctor, had an exceptional experience at a small town not far from Boulogne. When he joined the army he left a flourishing lower-middle-class practice in one of the suburbs of Edinburgh, made up largely of earnest but rather narrow-minded kirk-goers. His military duty in France was to look after the health and sanitation of a large camp which stood just outside the town. During this while Captain McDonald got to know a large number of French families, attended them in their illnesses, and gradually built up quite an extensive practice. When the Armistice came, and he was getting ready to return to Scotland, a subscription was raised among his French friends and patients to buy him a farewell gift as evidence of their affection for him and as a token of their gratitude for all he had done for them, in his unofficial capacity as family physician.

On the day of the presentation the hall of the Hôtel de Ville was packed with French men, women, and children, dressed in their best. The Mayor presided and before making the presentation, delivered an eloquent address. In the name of France, of Humanity, of his fellow townsmen and townswomen and in his own name, he thanked their good friend Monsieur le docteur Capitaine McDonald from the bottom of his heart for all he had done for them. Had he not left a lucrative practice in his native land, Caledonia, the ancient ally of France, to come and succour the sick of their town? Before he left them they wished Monsieur le médecin to accept a slight souvenir, something which he could place in his consulting room at home, and which, whenever he glanced at it, would bring back to him the many friends who would, as long as life was spared them, remember and pray for the good doctor McDonald. The speech concluded and the applause having died down, the doctor was invited to ascend the platform, where a large object, shrouded by a cloth, lay upon the table in front of the Mayor.

With a sweeping gesture the Mayor whipped away the covering cloth to disclose an elaborate piece of statuary in white porcelain.

McDonald in accepting the gift replied in a few well chosen words of thanks, and assured them all that the beautiful present they had honoured him with would never leave his consulting room and never fail—even if that were necessary—to bring back to his memory his dear friends in France and the happy years he had spent among them.

McDonald being somewhat shortsighted, had at first taken the statue to represent St. George killing the dragon; he could just discern a figure bending over another which lay grovelling on the ground. When he got back to camp he put on his spectacles in order to examine and admire the statue more closely, and found his sight had played him false. The stooping figure was not St. George, nor was the figure prone on the ground the dragon. The legendary scene the statue represented was Leda, about to take into her open arms the swan.

Poor McDonald did not know what to do.

He tried to picture in his mind's eye the statue placed on the table or mantelpiece in his consulting room, and knew only too well what his patients would think about it. If only the kind people had given him a watch, or a clock suitably engraved.

But his imagination boggled at the prospect of exposing it to his grim and disapproving patients. The effect on his practice would be calamitous.

A deep estuary ran from the sea up into the town. The night before he was to sail for England, a gale of wind blew, accompanied by torrents of rain. The streets were dark and deserted when the doctor left the camp, wearing a water-proof, his collar turned up, his hat drawn well down, and a large parcel under one arm.

But to return to Blaringhem.

I did not do much trapping during our stay there. The weather was intensely cold, the ground frozen hard as were the little streams and water ditches, so beloved by all sorts of shrews. When the daily march was done, the round of professional calls made, it was pleasant to sit in the warm kitchen and read a book, or talk to Cécile and Jeanne. We were all sorry, hosts and guests, when the time came for us to pack up and leave peaceful Blaringhem.

Cécile was an ardent collector of picture postcards of views of places abroad, so I wrote to my mother to send some photographs of London to her.

A month later I received a letter from Cécile showing my mother had not forgotten. Her letter, dated 18-3-16, ran:

WE GO SOUTH

Monsieur le Capitaine,

Permettez-moi de vous remercier au nom de toute la famille des jolies vues de Londres que vous nous avez envoyées.

Nous conserverons toujours, soyez en certain, un bon souvenir de votre séjour chez nous. Maman se rappelle avec plaisir les morceaux americains que vous lui jouiez pour elle, ainsi que Mme Chevalier qui nous visite chaque jour veuillez je vous prie nous rappeler au bon souvenir de Monsieur le Capitaine Smith et avec nos meilleurs vœux, recevez, de papa, maman, Jeanne et Paul ainsi que de moi même nos sentiments respectueux.

Cécile Pouvillion.

Although none of us knew what our destination was to be it was soon clear that it was not to be the Salient or Armentières again. By long marches the division moved southwards into country quite different from that we had been accustomed to. On the last day of our march, as we drew towards the town of Bruay, we passed a French regiment marching away from the line. These were the first fighting French soldiers we had seen, and were a magnificent body of men.

At last we arrived at our destination, which proved to be one of the most delightful châteaux we ever occupied. It was perched up on the summit of a steep hill at Bois Mont, not far away from the village of Ourton. This château, just evacuated by French troops, stood in a lovely garden, and although the chimneys of the mining town of Bruay could be seen not many miles away, the country in the immediate neighbourhood was charming and unspoiled. At six o'clock in the morning after we arrived I woke up to hear the strange, deep, sonorous notes of a hoopoe. The garden proved a very aviary of birds; white-throats, black-caps and other warblers had arrived and seemed to be in every bush and hedge. A pair of song-thrushes had five eggs in their nest, and several pairs of swallows were building their clay houses in the farm buildings. It was here at Bois Mont I heard the first turtle dove, always an enchanting sound, and particularly so during the War.

After wandering about the garden I went out into the fields and watched two kestrels fighting high up in the air and while they battled feathers floated away in the gentle breeze. Later on in the same day I noticed something brown moving in the grass. Through my field-glasses I discovered this to be another kestrel in the act of killing its prey. On closer inspection the prey proved to be nothing more formidable than a garden worm, which the hawk was gripping in its talons while with its beak it tore the writhing worm into pieces.

While at Bois Mont I continued my trapping and skinning but the only new addition to the collection of mammals was a hedgehog, which proved a difficult and painful subject for taxidermy. A day or two after our arrival at Bois Mont we were surprised to see the Divisional General's empty car drive up, with its small pennant flying on the radiator cap. It brought a note from General Babington inviting me to lunch then and there at his headquarters, an unexpected and rather an alarming honour for a bashful R.A.M.C. captain. During the meal the talk was all of birds, their songs and their ways. Somehow or other the General had heard of me and my fondness for birds and beasts, and as for once he had a few hours to spare from more important things, he proposed we should go for a walk in some neighbouring woods to watch birds. The walk was pleasant enough but not very fruitful in results, for naturally any birds that were in the woods flew away and hid themselves at the unparalleled spectacle of a British General, in uniform, accompanied by his aide-de-camp and another but less resplendent officer, creeping and dodging amongst the trees and undergrowth.

As so often happened whenever we seemed to have found the ideal spot at which to spend many weeks, orders came after a few days for us to leave Bois Mont and move up towards the line. After a march of only a few hours our ambulance entered the gates of another, but very different château from the last one, at Coupigney-Hersin, a small town or village, just on the edge of the coal-mining district, and having as all too near neighbours the ill-favoured towns of Sains-en-Gohell and Noeux-les-Mines. This château, an ugly, ostentatious building, was a modern architectural monstrosity of red, blue and white bricks, and was partly Gothic, partly Norman, with more than a suggestion of the Moorish. It was said to belong to a coal millionaire, which seemed more than likely. The garden, surrounded by a high wall, although suffering from two years of neglect and run to waste, was full of fine trees and shrubs, and had a large vegetable garden and orchard, grown wild and full of weeds; though from my point of view none the worse for that.

Here we were ordered to organise a " special hospital," for the reception of serious cases of gun-shot wounds of the head and abdomen from the near-by trenches, for immediate operation. This news led us to think that at last we were to stop in one place for a while, and taking all things into consideration, we felt ourselves fortunate. As soon as ever the château had been got ready for the wounded I began to explore the garden and soon realised that in spite of the coal mines and slag heaps near by and the unsightly château, the place was a paradise of birds.

Besides several black-cap warblers in full song, and a pair of spotted flycatchers, there was a little serin finch which hunted insects all day long amongst the branches of a big tulip tree, and kept up a constant high-pitched prattle, which brought back to me vivid memories of hot days and scented pines in the Balearic Isles.

This tall spreading tree seemed to be a favourite haunt of birds, so I had my camp bed made up and bivouacked beneath it and only slept in the house when the weather was wet. While lying in my bed the first night I heard a pretty bell-like note which I did not recognise. The sound came from the direction of a pond and suggested frogs, so the next morning I went to look at the pond and found and caught several frogs, some bright green, others brown, but both sorts having a yellow line running down the middle of their backs. These I packed securely in a box with damp moss and posted them to the " Zoo " and heard later on that they had arrived there safely and were edible frogs, and therefore were not the ringers of the little bells I had heard. In fact it was not until two months afterwards that I discovered what made the tinkling sound. One hot day when we were billeted in a farm house high up in the Somme country, after a heavy thunder storm with torrents of rain, I started out for a walk. As I left the farm yard I heard the same tinkling-bell sound, quite close by. After a considerable search I found, beneath a loose brick close to a wall, a pair of little toads, very small, with brilliant orange bellies. When alarmed they made no attempt to escape, but lifted up their four legs and thus disclosed the edges of their bright orange waistcoats, in order, I suppose, to warn an enemy that they were not good eating.

The pond at Coupigney was an endless source of interest. Apart from its frogs, toads, tadpoles and newts, it was the dump to which the swallows came to draw their building material. It was interesting to watch how they arrived, each one carrying a short piece of straw or dry grass held horizontally in its beak, and then after alighting at the very edge of the water where the mud was soft, scooped up a beakful of mud, without losing hold of the straw, and flew off with it to the nest.

On the third of May we arrived at Coupigney-Hersin but not until three days later did I meet with my greatest ornithological surprise. It was at about seven o'clock on a glorious morning as I lay on my open-air bed beneath the big tree that I heard an odd medley of bird notes which were utterly unknown to me.

This was indeed bird-watching de luxe, for I lay there in my sleeping-bag and could gaze up into the green branches above, and wait comfortably until the unknown singer chose to disclose himself.

By and by I perceived a movement high up among the branches, and presently, through my field glasses—which were kept under my pillow when sleeping out of doors—I caught sight of a small, active bird of the warbler family. It had the appearance of a woodwarbler, but its belly was of a yellow tint and its eye streaks very marked.

Then, while I was watching it, the bird began to sing, if the astonishing medley of sounds it poured forth can be described as a song. Perhaps an accomplished ventriloquist rehearsal better describes the performance. The entertainment opened with a run of very sweet notes interspersed with a few rough guttural sounds. Soon tiring of this, it gave a perfect imitation of the chattering song of a swallow; so perfect that I peered about to find the singing swallow, and it was only when, with my powerful glasses, I saw the bird's throat swelling and its beak opening and shutting that I began to suspect my new friend of being a ventriloquist.

No doubt the little green bird was flattered by my admiration and was determined to show himself off and do his utmost, for concluding the swallow song with the alarm note of the same bird, he proceeded to entertain me by a series of imitations—in miniature—of the song of a skylark, the alarm note of a blackbird, a few unmistakable notes of a nightingale, and then closed a perfectly brilliant performance by the long drawn-out whistle of a starling.

When I realised that the "turn" was over, it was all I could do not to applaud and cry out "encore," but my batman appeared with my morning cup of tea and my artist friend in the green roof above disappeared.

This day, which began with such an ornithological feast turned out to be a red-letter day. Amongst the gooseberry bushes in the overgrown vegetable garden I found a pair of common white-throats building their nest, which was completed except for the lining. Amongst the same bushes I discovered the nest of a cirl bunting containing three lovely blotched eggs.

From now onwards, until fate ordered us to leave this enchanted garden and go up the line, each day produced some new delight, and each was heralded by the little green ventriloquist whom I had identified as an icterine warbler.

Every day new nests were built, or eggs were laid in nests which I had watched being built.

On the 14th the white-throats laid their first egg, and a black-cap warbler was sitting closely on her four treasures in a nest well hidden in a holly bush.

Then one day General Babington arrived to inspect our hospital. When the inspection was finished he called me up and asked if I had any birds' nests to show him. I told him I had and off we went, the General and his aide-de-camp Lord Wodehouse, led by myself. What the General had thought about his inspection of the hospital I do not know, but he was certainly pleased with his second inspection. I took him to see in turn all the nests I knew of, black-caps', hedge sparrows', blackbirds', song thrushes', cirl buntings' and many others, and he himself found a goldfinches' nest with five eggs in it, in a stunted Austrian pine, which I had missed. While we were standing a little way off, the cock goldfinch came to the nest and fed the sitting hen. We also saw and heard a gold crest and a serin finch, and our one and only nightingale woke up in the shrubbery and obliged with a few sweet notes. I kept the icterine warbler to the last as being the show turn, and he, no doubt in honour of our popular General and of the great occasion, broke into ecstatic song at the right moment, and followed it by a ventriloquist selection by way of an encore. Altogether it was a most successful garden party and I felt grateful to all my small friends for behaving so handsomely at the General's visit.

These happy, peaceful days at Coupigney were drawing to a close, and ended with an act of frightfulness and vandalism.

One morning towards the end of May I was awakened in my bed beneath the tulip tree by the terrifying shriek of a huge approaching shell. Hitherto we had been left entirely alone by the enemy, but Satan was now about to ravish our Garden of Eden. The first shell, fired from nobody knows how many miles away, crashed into the fair lawn and hurled up masses of earth, leaving an ugly black crater. Ten minutes passed, when another came crashing and splintering amidst a shrubbery a little farther off. During the next hour six or more of these monstrous horrors came, each missing the ugly château but playing havoc with the lovely garden.

Thus it was that when the order came for us to leave and go up towards the line to the coal-mining town of Fosse 10, I, for one, left Coupigney with less regret but with a natural feeling of anxiety for the safety of its birds and fledglings.

As to Fosse 10, it proved to be a new mining-town, drab and dreary beyond belief. The building occupied by the ambulance was a deserted schoolhouse, but even here there were recompenses, for a pair of house martins had a nest under one of the eaves and a pair of black redstarts spent their time on our roof; though the only birds common in the coal towns were swifts, which raced screaming round the school in the evenings.

We had a good deal of work to do at Fosse 10, with the sick and wounded, but I managed to get away sometimes to walk in the neighbouring fields, where I found corn-buntings in a meadow close to Bouvigny as well as a pair of stone-chats. One warm sunny day I watched for a long while a handsome cock cirl bunting, perched on an upper twig of a small tree in a hedge. He sat perfectly still on the same twig for more than an hour, chanting his monotonous ringing one-note song. While doing this he would point his open beak heavenwards and move his head from side to side while the measure lasted, and when it was over, once again subside into his typically sluggish bunting attitude. Although I have an " ear " as they say, for a bird's note, I can rarely distinguish on first hearing it the song of the cirl bunting from that of the lesser white-throat. They both make a similar succession of high, ringing notes. But until the singer can be recognised by sight, the locality from which the sounds come will almost certainly identify it, for whereas the lesser white-throat prefers to sing from the bottom of the hedge, the cirl bunting almost always chooses a topmost branch or twig for his concert platform.

One day I explored a pleasant little coppice standing between Bouvigny and Servins, and added a new bird to my list. This was a grass-hopper warbler, the most shy and retiring of all bush-haunting birds. I would have missed him if he had not been " reeling " in some thick brambles. It was some time before I saw him, but when I did I got a splendid view of him and could watch him turning his head rapidly from side to side as he poured out his singular love-song, which resembles more than anything else the noise made by a quickly revolving fishing reel. In a gorse bush by the edge of this coppice I found a linnet's nest with two eggs in it and not far away in a patch of swampy ground, thick with rushes, I saw a sedge-warbler. On my way back through a field of rye, I heard a song which I had never heard before, and after much stalking and peering about with the field glasses, I had the joy, not only of hearing, but of seeing a marsh warbler.

Even when one could not get away to the woods and meadows, but had to remain in the mining towns, there were birds for those with eyes to see or ears to hear them, though why any wild bird with wings to fly with should have chosen to remain in this squalid, treeless area, made more vile by heaps of slag, and where at any moment great shells might come crashing down, is beyond my understanding. Behind an empty house in Fosse 10 there was a small backyard, in which there contrived to live one green lilac bush. In a fork of this bush I was astonished to find a compact nest made of dry grass, and ornamented on the outside by pieces of lichen. In its cup were five eggs of a delicate purple or lilac colour, freckled over with small dark brown spots. What bird had built this nest and laid these eggs I had not the faintest notion, nor could I imagine what bird it was that had chosen so unbecoming a site for so frail a nursery. But I had not very long to wait in hiding, for soon I heard the familiar friendly chuckle of an icterine warbler, and an instant after there appeared the Puck of the warbler tribe, looking all the more fairy-like in such squalid surroundings. The little bird, after obliging with a parody on the chirp of the vulgar house-sparrow, settled down on its nest. Whenever I could I used to go alone to visit, in their backyard, these icterines who soon seemed to recognise me as a friend. Like my first icterine at Coupigney the cockbird was a clever mimic, and among other accomplishments would give a really good imitation of the laugh of a yaffle and the cheerful cry of the greater spotted woodpecker. During our stay at Fosse 10 I had much to be grateful for to those icterine warblers in the backyard.

Of matters medical or military I will say little, for these have been fully set out in histories written by experts. In spite of strong protests by the British military authorities large numbers of civilians were still living in this much shelled town, and one day the Germans heavily bombarded the place for two hours and many civilians were killed or wounded. One of the latter was a woman who was brought to the ambulance dressing station in labour. The colonel was greatly alarmed at the prospect of having to conduct an accouchement in the 69th Field Ambulance, so, in spite of the shelling which still went on, he ordered the woman to be placed in a motor ambulance and rushed off to the civil hospital at Bethune. With that feeling of nicety which he always shewed on all occasions, our bachelor colonel insisted that the orderly who was to ride in the ambulance with the wounded mother-to-be should not only be a married man, but a father as well.

I have been careful, as far as possible, to keep these memoirs free from medical topics, and the incident which I am about to relate is not included from any clinical interest it may have, but simply as an example of the extraordinary fortitude, under great adversity, of the English private soldier.

It took place at an advanced operating hospital in the mining area, only a short distance behind the reserve trenches. It had been proved that men badly wounded in the chest or abdomen often died before getting all the way back to the casualty clearing stations, or else arrived there in such a condition of shock and exhaustion that they died on the operating table. To this new advanced hospital, run by our ambulance, all cases such as these were brought from any part of the sector. It was one morning after a night of blustering wind and rain, when I happened to be orderly officer, that the arrival of a bad " G.S.W. belly " was reported. One of the wounded man's friends had come with him, carrying his belongings, and from him I heard what had happened.

During the storm the preceding night the Boche had suddenly blown up a mine beneath his company in the front line, and followed this up by an intensive bombardment with trench mortars, rifle-grenades and high explosive. The Germans had then attacked with bombs and bayonets. After a fierce hand-to-hand engagement the enemy had at last been driven back to his own trenches and our wounded got away.

The stretcher-bearers had a very tiring carry, not only because of the shrapnel barrage but because of the deep mud and shell holes. When I went to see the wounded man I found a pale-faced, spectacled boy, covered with mud, soaked with rain and blood, and obviously in a desperate plight. He belonged to the London Irish Rifles; why, I never fathomed, for he was not Irish, but English, and lived at Guildford.

While I was gently examining his wound I asked him, more for the sake of something to say than anything else, if it hurt him very much. His answer, which I shall never forget, was "No Sir, only when I laugh."

I am glad to say little John Bishop surprised us all by surviving a long and dangerous operation and eventually recovered. One day, several years afterwards, he called to see me in London, to prove he was alive and well, and to say certain kind things about the much abused R.A.M.C.

During our stay in the mining area we officers of the field ambulance were often sent away on various jobs, most often to act as temporary M.O. to one of our infantry battalions. Being an old friend of the 9th Yorks, I was always allowed to go to them on such occasions. One day in June, I was ordered to join them just as they were about to do a turn in the line.

When the battalion reached the communication trench which leads to Givenchy it began to rain in real earnest. Owing to the darkness and the slippery deep mud the going was bad, but there was the consolation that there is nothing like steady rain to damp the ardour of the fighting man. A clear, moonlight night may be all very well for lovers' walks, but for a battalion going into or coming out of front-line trenches a good downpour has its points, for it keeps the keenest-eyed sniper or the boldest patrol harmlessly under cover.

After much stumbling and whispering, for the two front lines were less than fifty yards apart, I found the dug-out which was to be my house and home for the next ten days.

We were late getting in, and the medical officer of the outgoing battalion was impatiently awaiting my arrival. Five minutes was enough for him to give me the lie of the land, the position of the aid posts where the stretcher-bearers had their quarters, and any other necessary information.

As he was about to climb up the steep steps leading out of the dug-out he stopped to acquaint me with one other, but very important matter he had forgotten, relating to the Landlady.

This was something quite unexpected and I was eager to learn more. Of course I had heard many of the rumours about the Germans keeping women in their officers' dug-outs, but never before had I heard of a woman in the British trenches.

It seemed that ever since the British took over this line of trenches from the French, the medical officer of each battalion had instructed the medical officer of the next to be careful to look after the Landlady, who proved to be a cat, and was the one and only remaining civilian of Givenchy.

The regimental doctor produced a tin of preserved milk and gave me precise instructions as to its proper dilution and the hours of the daily feeds, just as in peace time he must have done to many a mother over her first baby's bottle.

He explained that the Landlady was out, that she went out at dusk every evening, but would return at dawn and expect to find her saucer of milk ready prepared, and in its usual place.

As to her other rations, it seemed she supplied herself with these by catching rats and field mice every night. These duties I gladly promised to perform and we said good-bye.

Tired and wet after the long march I was glad to get out of my damp clothes and curl up in the less damp blankets on the low bunk which had been made by cutting away the chalk on one side of the dug-out.

I soon fell asleep and must have been so for some hours, when something heavy fell on me which woke me up with a start. At first I thought a shell had struck the roof and that I was buried in débris. Then I became aware that the weight on my legs was moving as though alive and I lay quite still, afraid to stir.

Whatever could it be? I dared not put down my hand to feel for fear it was a rat, but if it was it must have been one of those huge monsters an Irish soldier had told me of " as big as a dog."

In the meanwhile the movements of the heavy object had become rhythmical, a sort of prodding was going on, accompanied by an odd, deep, throbbing sound. Then all of a sudden, as sleep cleared away, it dawned on me that my waker could be no other than my Landlady; and gingerly I reached in the direction of the object and felt the soft fur of a cat, busy at that exercise all cats enjoy, of kneading with alternate paws. She soon settled down in the middle of the bunk, and I made myself as comfortable as I could at one edge. After an hour of fitful slumber Church brought in my breakfast; the Landlady, having had hers earlier, continued to sleep on my blankets the remainder of the day. It was not until now that I got my first sight of my Landlady, and a beauty she proved to be.

But surely no cat of France?

At the risk of being branded narrow-minded or insular, I must register a word of disparagement of all foreign cats. I do this in no amateurish spirit, but as a professed lover of cats. In many parts of the world I have made it a point to talk to all children and to make endearing sounds to all cats. The English cat is, as a rule, a noble beast. Proud and independent, it has preserved its dignity and not bartered its soul to become the fawning slave of man, as has the dog.

But your foreign cat is apt to be an ignoble skulker, a fugitive before strangers, the very dregs of cat society.

Whatever land gave birth to the Landlady, she was certainly as fine a figure of cat-hood as you could wish to see, even in England itself, that home of fair and gallant cats.

Her coat, like that of Joseph, was of many colours, in fact she was a tortoiseshell. She made no claim to Persian pedigree, her hair being short, but it was thick, soft, and scrupulously clean.

During the whole day she slept curled up on my bunk and did not wake up until the evening. Then, a little while before sunset she arose, tripped up the steps of the dug-out and inspected the skies. From where she sat she had a good view of Notre Dame de Lorette, behind our lines, and of the broken spire of the Church of Ablain St. Nazaire, beyond the crumpled village of Souchez.

After a while she sauntered up the trench which led towards the front line, and at a respectful distance I followed her. Presently she reached the fire trench and without warning leaped upon the parapet, where she sat gazing across No-man's-land, with all the tranquillity of a peacetime cat seated on the wall of its own backyard. No doubt from her point of vantage she could see the ruined mine shafts of Lens and even German soldiers moving about in their trenches.

But I trembled for her. Only some fifty yards separated our front line from that of the enemy. At that very moment more than one German sniper must have been watching her; perhaps was then drawing a bead on her with his rifle. Down many a periscope her image was being thrown by artfully adjusted mirrors into the retina of bloodthirsty Boches. Each second I expected to hear the crack of a rifle and to see my Landlady leap into the air and then fall dead or mortally wounded into the bottom of the trench.

But nothing of the sort happened, and I was led to suppose that all Germans were not as black as they were painted.

Then to add to her foolhardiness, the Landlady commenced her evening toilet; in full view of two vast contending armies, each armed to the teeth with every device invented by civilised man to destroy life and limb.

She began by washing her face, licking each paw in turn and rubbing her cheeks, neck and ears. Then the sides of her body were dealt with, and then her tail, held down by one paw, was licked from tip to stump.

Nothing was left undone, not even the final scrupulous ritual in which one hind leg is thrust stiffly heavenward while the particular region is dealt with.

When all this was completed to her satisfaction, the Landlady sat for five minutes to enjoy the view, a view which not one in all the thousands of brave fighting men within a square mile of her dared to look at.

It was strange, I thought, that the Landlady could sit up there for twenty minutes in perfect safety while if I, a non-combatant, whose profession was to succour the sick and wounded, whether friend or foe, showed my head for but one moment above the same trench, I would receive a bullet through my brain. How incalculable are the ways of man.

The Landlady, unperplexed by such reflections, having rested after her ablutions, rose, stretched herself, and then disappeared over the parapet into No-man's-land—and not a sound, not a shot.

What she did there until she came back to bed with me some eight hours later no one knows.

Probably she hunted rats and mice in the long grass that grew so rankly amongst the coils of barbed wire out there. Those small mammals were her sport and her supper.

But who can say if she had not friends in the German lines? Who knows but what she was a spy in German pay? But no, it would be treachery even to think such a thing.

Did she, I used to wonder, leap up on the German parapet and make herself as at home in the enemies' line as in ours? That I can well believe, but what happened beyond our front line she kept to herself, a profound secret.

However, in whatever way she may have spent her nights, to me, or to her dug-out, the Landlady never failed to return at dawn. Each morning it was the same; after drinking the milk I provided for her, she would leap on to the couch, drive me to one side, and then settle down where I had been, and fall into peaceful, happy slumber. When the time came for us to leave those trenches I said good-bye to the Landlady with real regret, and was punctilious to inform the relieving medical officer of her requirements and habits.

Memory is a mysterious thing. After seventeen years I find myself with certain recollections which remain as bright and clear as when they happened, while other matters, often of far greater importance at the time, have faded away, to be forgotten. This is the case with my sojourn in the Souchez trenches, of which but two facts stand out clearly; the Landlady and the officers' latrine.

To enter this temple of Hygeia, the worshipper had to leave the protecting trench altogether, through a gap which seemed to open straight into No-Man's-Land, and expose him to the full gaze of the enemy. A sinister message on a board warned him it was "Dangerous to loiter." Acting on this kindly hint, the suppliant darted across the few open yards which separated the gap in the trench from the temple, which proved to be a low, roofless contraption made of thin boards nailed together.

Inside the holy place were two objects. One was a board on which were written these ominous words, "Keep your head down." On obeying this intimation, the other object came under notice. This was a narrow board, in which two holes had been cut, one at either end. It was supported horizontally by two enormous live shells, whose fuse-caps penetrated the two holes in the board, and thus formed a seat for the votaries at the shrine of the Goddess of Health. I used to speculate as to the weight required to ignite these fuses and explode the shells, and was glad I did not weigh sixteen stone, as did the company commander.

When we were not at the main dressing station at Bully Grenay or with a battalion, we would be at either of our advanced dressing stations. One of these was at the wicked little village of Ablain St. Nazaire.

Poor St. Nazaire, it is wrong to call her wicked; rather was she an innocent victim of man's vileness. Before the war came that way, Ablain St. Nazaire must have been a charming little village, nestling at the foot of the spur of Notre Dame de Lorette, but now little better than the bull's-eye on a target for German guns.

On fine days I used to climb up the steep slope of the famous hill and sit and gaze over the great battlefield spread out below or roam in search of birds. On bright sunny days it was wonderful to be up there alone, but yet it just missed perfection. Although alone, one had all the time a sense of not being quite alone. This feeling may have been due to the knowledge that wherever you wandered, a score of pairs of German eyes were watching you. Unaccompanied one was safe enough, but if half a dozen or more men were seen there together they would soon have been shelled.

Perhaps the sensation of being shadowed was due to the ghosts, the wandering spirits of the hundreds of French soldiers who had fallen there the previous year when they drove the Germans off the hill, and whose white bones and shreds of blue tunic still lay amongst the grass and wild flowers.

And yet Notre Dame de Lorette held an irresistible attraction for me. There were not many birds to be seen, perhaps they too felt ill at ease. Kestrels, though, there were in plenty, who no doubt found abundance of voles and mice to hunt for. In some bushes half-way up the slope a pair of butcher birds—well named at such a shambles—was generally to be seen, but if they had a nest there I failed to find it.

One day, while a small battle raged below, I sat with my back to it, and watched a tree-pipit. It would rise up from a bush and fly at a steep angle until it was some thirty or forty feet above the ground when it would turn, head downwards, and glide swiftly towards the earth, with its wings held behind its back, singing the whole while and conclude this joyous proceeding by perching always on the same bush it had started from.

On one of these outings to Notre Dame de Lorette, Lord Wodehouse, a keen naturalist, came with me to shew me a pair of golden orioles which he had seen on a previous visit.

We were not fortunate enough to find them, but to make up for this disappointment we heard a quail, and after some stalking flushed a pair.

None of us were really sorry when the time came for us to leave the Carency sector. The Germans had become more and more truculent and every village and town in the neighbourhood was shelled regularly and thoroughly.

Where we were to go to next we did not know, or very much care, so long as it was not to the Salient. We moved by easy stages and short marches, for the Division had suffered severely in the Carency sector, and needed rest, reinforcements and training before going again into the line.

After the drab squalidness of the mining area of Fosse 10 and Bully Grenay the fresh green fields and June flowers of Liéttres, a few kilometres south of Aire, were paradise.

I knew directly we arrived at the village that I should be happy there, for the very first thing I saw was a yellow wagtail, running about and flirting its long tail by a stream, hunting invisible winged insects.

The sight of this engaging bird I took to be a good omen, for where wagtails are, will also be peace and quiet. Also, if any other welcome was needed to Liéttres, a black red-start had possession of the roof of the cottage where I was billeted. As soon as possible I set forth to explore the country round about, and before long chanced upon an old disused quarry, always a favourite spot for birds. And I was not disappointed, for there I spied a splendid cock butcher-bird, looking superb in the afternoon sunshine, and fierce with his black eye streaks. I was first attracted to him, not by his conspicuous plumage, but by his unmistakable alarm call. On sighting him I subsided behind some cover to wait and watch.

Persuaded that the danger was past, my red-backed shrike flew up and perched upon a twig at the top of a hawthorn bush, where I got a splendid view of him from my hiding place.

For a long while he remained there singing his pretty little trilling song, which sounded so trivial issuing from that cruel notched beak, made to dismember young living birds and insects.

Occasionally during my walks I would disturb a heron fishing in the little stream, which would rise and flop lazily and heavily away to drop amongst the reeds higher up, or a brilliant blue kingfisher would flash by.

In a meadow of long grass quite close to the village lived a corncrake, which kept up its monotonous rasping cry—creck-creck—creck-creck—from sunrise until dusk.

One day—how well one remembers these trivial events and forgets the important ones—I was strolling through a field where the hay had just been cut and heaped up into haycocks. It was a hot, sunny day and on the top of one of the haycocks I spied a little owl fast asleep. I approached slowly and quietly, until I stood within a few yards of it, and still the owl slept with eyes tightly closed, oblivious of its mortal enemy.

For a good ten minutes I stood there watching the slumbering owl, when at last he woke up, frowned angrily at me for disturbing him, and flew away. Within an hour he was back again on the same haycock.

It might be wondered how a grown-up man could sit down in a hayfield and do nothing for a whole hour, but the truth is that after being in or about the line for several months, one was content to sit in the sunshine, and do nothing at all, beyond admire the flowers and listen to the song of the birds and enjoy the quiet. It was medicine for the mind and solace for the soul.

On such rare occasions and at such a place, it was blessèd, after the noise and the alarms, to sit in the sunshine, forget the past and the future, and revel in the present.

Surely it was Liéttres that Mr. Blunden had in mind when he sang :

> " Now to attune my dull soul if I can
> To the enchantment of this country side
> Where man is not for ever killing man
> But quiet days and quiet waters glide."

During the hour in that hayfield a solitary quail flew low, just over my head, and a lesser—not the common—white-throat sang its rich, trilling song at the foot of a briar hedge near by.

Those quiet days at Liéttres, the peaceful village, were made up of small events, so trivial as to be hardly worth recording. Why do I remember one evening while standing at the gate of the cottage in which I was billeted, seeing a Crocidura Leucodon rush, terror-stricken, with piercing cries, across the road? And yet that sight remains more deeply impressed on my memory than many an important event which occurred during the War. What danger he was fleeing from I do not know, for no enemy followed on his track and the mystery, like many another, remains unsolved. Although the arch-enemy and destroyer of all living things as small or smaller than himself, no beast or bird is known to kill and devour a shrew.

After leaving tranquil Liéttres the Division moved steadily south until we reached the chalky downlands of the Somme, where we camped in an orchard above the winding river and within sight of the spires of Amiens Cathedral. It was now high summer, and I had my bivouac placed beneath a pear tree in a far corner of the orchard. But I was not lonely there, for a fat black dog appeared from nowhere, and would sit close beside me, panting heavily and gazing rapturously up into my face. A flock of geese, not so friendly, but not seriously hostile, cropped the short grass round my bed, and two motherly cows completed my family.

While we were here I managed to get a day's fishing in the river Somme. I caught not a fish, but what did that matter? How better could a long summer's day be spent than sitting alone among tall reeds, watching a red-tipped float, even if it never bobbed?

There were birds in the reed-beds; noisy, suspicious reed-warblers and chuckling sedge-warblers. Dabchicks dived close by, kingfishers hurried up and down the river on urgent business. One, evidently thinking my rod a convenient resting place, perched on it for a while until, unable to keep still any longer, I moved, and the gorgeous bird went off like a flash of blue.

This was one of those rare days of ecstasy whose memory remains but whose charm and mystery are difficult to convey to others.

Whoever planned the postal service to the B. E. F. must have been a genius at organization, and well deserved any or all the rewards or decorations that may have been bestowed on him.

Although we wandered about France, here to-day, gone to-morrow, yet our daily budget of letters reached us almost without fail. My mother, and my father and sisters as well, kept up a regular and steady stream of letters and parcels.

It was not until the other day that quite by chance I learned who that genius was, and what a truly remarkable organisation the Army Postal Service was. After lunching with my sister at her cottage in Normandy this summer, one of the guests, General Price, offered to drive my wife and me back to Dieppe. It was almost inevitable that he and I should talk about the War, and in all innocence I remarked on the astounding way in which our letters and parcels used to reach us, no matter where we went. This proved a happy observation on my part for it turned out that General Price was the very man who commanded and organised the vast Army Postal Service from August, 1914 until after the Armistice. With a little persuasion I got him to talk about his work and most interesting he was, though it is impossible to refer more than briefly to the subject here.

At the beginning of the War the Postal Section of the Royal Engineers took the field in the B.E.F. some 250 strong. The concern grew rapidly and threw off branches for all the subsidiary expeditions, so that by the end of the War the total personnel overseas numbered close on four thousand. Early in 1915 the Base Standing Office was transferred from France to London and employed a staff of 2,540; largely women and disabled soldiers. One branch, for the distribution of parcels alone, was housed at Regent's Park in what was claimed to be the largest wooden building in the world. It covered an area of over five acres of ground. It gives some idea of the magnitude of the postal service to learn that during the four weeks to Christmas, 1916, the parcels dispatched to the B.E.F. alone reached the stupendous number of four million six hundred thousand. All this while some twelve and a half million letters were sent to the various fronts every week. General Price observed that the British soldier was a good correspondent, for the statistics shewed that for practically every letter sent out to the front a letter came back! The work of the Army Postal Service did not end with the delivery of letters and parcels. The average weekly sales of postal orders in the B.E.F. alone numbered eighty-one thousand, representing a value of £56,000.

By April, 1917, the number of parcels received from England by the armies in France was over eight hundred thousand a week, but by the middle of that year the parcel traffic began to some extent to decline, owing partly to food restrictions at home, but principally to the establishment of canteens in the field. Up to that time "T. Atkins" was almost wholly dependent upon the post for luxuries and comforts, but after this the people at home found that the postal order served the same purpose. Not only did the Army Postal Service deliver letters and parcels, but they delivered ballot papers to voters for parliamentary elections from Australia, Canada and the United Kingdom. The Service had much to be proud of, and not least that during the retreat before the great German advance in the spring of 1918, they lost only three bags of mails.

My mother somehow found time to keep up a correspondence with several young soldier friends on active service. One of these was Siegfried Sassoon, to whom she wrote letters and sent books.

Among her papers when she died were found several letters from him, and by his kind permission I am able to print one here.

1st Battn. R.W.F.
Jan. 6th (1916).

MY DEAR MRS. GOSSE,

But how nice to get letters from *both*.

We are having a rest at a quiet village miles from the trenches. We look across the Somme valley; Airaines is 4 miles distant. (They don't mind you receiving this dangerous information, as we are here for several weeks—till the battles begin again, I believe.) Have you ever visited these parts of France? I love the rolling hills, open ploughlands, with gray Dobbins at work, and ridges crowned with woods, and the roads winding and dipping away into the distant country.

But I mustn't lapse into fine writing!

I do hope you will run down to Weirleigh soon and cheer mother with your anecdotes. I am reading a new novel by Conrad at present. I have a nice kitchen to sit in, with tiled floor and open hearth, and a jolly fire-back representing a domestic scene with most elaborate details.

A cock crows discordantly at 6.30 a.m. within a few feet of my slumbering head. He crows with a French accent, I think. Old men ply the flail in dim barns, wild-boars gruntle in the Bois de Riencourt a mile away, and altogether we live in Arcadian surroundings.

I ride a pony over hill and dale sometimes, but the shepherds do not pipe under the hawthorn; perhaps piping is forbidden in war time, or else they are preoccupied with blowing on their fingers. The only music I hear is in the triumphant squeaks and shrillings of our fife and drum band marching up the village street of an afternoon. But I am hoping to get into Amiens some day to hear a solemn strain. How nice of you to want to send me books. I can't think of any book at the moment; just pick out a couple of " Everymans " which you like; if I have read them I shall enjoy doing so again. Anything old-fashioned, quaintly written amuses me.

There is a young poet in this Battn., 19 years old and a

temporary Captain—Robert Graves, son of Alfred Perceval (rather a bad poet, isn't he?). R. G. writes moderately well, and is a great admirer of Samuel Butler (Erewhon), and shocks his venerable sire with violent Trench lyrics about lice and corruption. (Father retaliates with impassioned hymns in the *Observer*.)

Well, I must go to roost; the log has burned itself out.

Best wishes (and a New Year poem) to Mr. Gosse and love to yourself.

From,

SIEGFRIED.

CHAPTER III

THE SOMME

THE village of Fricourt which lies in the valley between Albert and Contalmaison is a place of evil memories. After the first attack the Germans, driven from their old trenches, were holding a line further back, running behind Peake Wood, on the road to Contalmaison. As for the village, it no longer existed when we went there on the morning of July 9th, having been pounded to a mass of rubble and brick dust. The general bombardment was in full roar when the ambulance marched to the spot chosen for us to pitch our tents which were to act as an advanced dressing-station for the coming battle.

The choice seemed to us unpropitious, being in the open and quite unprotected except for a low bank; while a battery of heavy howitzers had their emplacement just behind us. Nor was it reassuring when a soldier who was standing exactly where our tents were to be, had his buttocks blown away by a premature from one of the howitzers.

The rest of the day we spent working hard pitching tents and rigging up tarpaulins in preparation for the rush of wounded expected when the battle began next morning. I shall never forget that night, and it is still a nightmare in my dreams. Without a break or pause the guns far and near thundered and boomed until the deafening uproar threatened to drive one distracted.

All night long those howitzers behind us sent their great missiles shrieking just over our heads, while the ground shook and trembled. However much I tried, I could not get out of my mind the sight of the man whom we had seen killed and wondering what the odds were against another such " premature."

We officers were crowded into one tent, for there had been no time to do more than was absolutely necessary for next morning's work. Hour after hour the din went on without a lull. Fortunately for us no enemy shells came our way, although so great was the din that I doubt whether we should have heard them, unless they fell close to us.

One thought of the poor fellows being shelled up on the crest of the hill above, in deep mud, with no trenches worthy of the name, waiting to attack at dawn, and wondered at their courage; and marvelled how men, however brave, could stand such an ordeal.

Every one of us was dead tired, after the long march, starting at dawn from the other side of Albert, and the hours of hard work till dark. But with all that noise sleep to me was impossible, and the sight of my friends lying asleep on the floor filled me with envy. Many things occurred to my mind, while I tramped up and down; one being that people who do not like loud noises or crowds should keep away from modern battlefields.

At last dawn broke, and the guns moved up, including, to our great relief, the battery of howitzers, and we were thankful to have work to do to occupy ourselves.

As usual, Pye-Smith took charge of the dangerous work of leading the stretcher bearers and he and Nimmo Walker were away all day up the line. Presently the wounded began to pour in, some on stretchers, others more lightly wounded, walking. Each officer at the dressing-station had a bell-tent where he examined and treated each case in turn. Hundreds of wounded men were soon gathered in the open space, some sitting, others lying on the ground. While they waited the orderlies supplied them with cups of hot tea or cocoa, and pieces of bread or biscuit and bully beef. The " walkers " were then sent off in cheerful parties of fifty or more to follow the sign boards which pointed the way to the next dressing-station further back, while the stretcher cases were put on to motor ambulances, or empty ammunition lorries, which hurried as quickly as possible out of the danger zone. So great was the rush of wounded that kept pouring down from Peake Wood and Bailiff Wood that we soon had to give up our tents and attend to them on the open ground outside. Before long the whole place looked like a shambles, with wounded and bandaged men lying everywhere, and it was a most fortunate thing for us all that the enemy was too much engaged elsewhere to have time to shell the areas further back.

After working for several hours, I happened to glance up and saw a very muddy, unshaven and disreputable-looking officer seated on a heap of bricks, grinning at me. I felt cross and tired and rather resented his presence, when he called out, " Hullo, Philip, enjoying yourself? " Directly I heard his voice I recognised my Australian cousin, William Gosse, a captain in the

British R.F.A. On the declaration of war he had left his sheep station in New South Wales and come to England to join the Royal Field Artillery. In the South African war he had enlisted as a trooper in the South Australian Horse and eventually been granted a commission in the gunners. When that war was over he went with his battery to India, but meeting with a serious accident playing polo, was invalided out of the service and returned to Australia, and so probably was unique in having been a gunner officer who had never been to Woolwich.

When he arrived in England at the end of 1914, he supposed he would be taken back to the R.F.A. but was informed that no more gunner officers were required! On hearing this surprising but reassuring news, William enlisted in a regiment of irregular horse which was being formed and trained in Hertfordshire. Being unambitious and not caring in what capacity he served, he was perfectly content where he was, and had it not been for my father, who spoke to Lord Haldane about this waste of a skilled gunner, he probably would have remained a trooper. Owing to the influence of Lord Haldane, he was gazetted a first lieutenant in the R.F.A. and in 1915 found his way to France with a brigade.

My cousin was one of those fortunate and to be envied people who really liked the War; to whom it was one jolly round of excitement.

Having recognised and acknowledged my unshaven and filthy relative, I apologized to him for not being able to offer him anything to drink stronger than tea or cocoa. He at once offered to present our mess with a bottle of whisky if we could send to his battery for it. As the rush of wounded had slackened off, I got leave to go with him to fetch the precious and then much needed whisky.

Near his battery, which was on a ridge about half a mile away, there was a wonderful view right across the German line. He asked if I would like to see what his guns could do, and told me to watch a small green lozenge-shaped wood. Then he spoke into a telephone and in a few moments the little green wood became a leaping cloud of smoke, dust, and flashes. After a few minutes of this he ordered the firing to stop, and we entered his dug-out. We talked and laughed over some articles which were then appearing in a popular daily paper, written by a famous journalist, which claimed to be first-hand accounts of the Somme fighting from the lips of wounded heroes. No doubt they were written for purposes of propaganda at home, for they described how every wounded soldier the writer had spoken with was longing to return to the front to get at the Boches. These preposterous stories were read and laughed at by every soldier in the line and were considered an immense joke. While we were sitting talking, an austere-looking colonel of artillery, the commander of the brigade, entered the dug-out, to whom my outrageous cousin promptly and without a blush introduced me as " Sir——you know, Sir, who writes those ripping articles in the paper about the Tommies."

The colonel at once unbent and greeted me warmly by name, the famous journalist's name, and congratulated me on my articles, which he said would help to bring

THE SOMME

home to the people in England the magnificent fighting spirit of the troops.

Feeling the situation might at any moment become difficult, I made my apologies for leaving so soon, and with a bottle of whisky in my pocket hurried back to Fricourt.

This was the last time my cousin and I met. After the Somme he was promoted Major and given the D.S.O. and command of a battery, but not long afterwards he was killed.

Those days in the Somme were not in favour of bird watching. For one thing there were practically no birds in the battle area, and for the other there were more urgent matters to occupy one's time and attention.

But even at shattered Fricourt there was something pleasing. In the vault of what had once been a house a pair of swallows had their nest, and all day long kept flying in and out through a dark opening in the ground. They must have built their nest, laid their eggs, and hatched their young during an almost continual hail of shot and shell.

I wondered if in happier pre-War summers this same pair of swallows nested under the eaves of the house which once stood there and if, when it was destroyed, the homing instinct had been so strong that in spite of every inducement to go elsewhere they had nested in the cellar of their old dwelling.

While we were still at Fricourt and during a lull between battles, my friends of the 9th Yorks invited me to dine with them. On the evening of the party, I arrived at their dug-out looking forward to a convivial gathering.

It was evidently to be a gala banquet, for there were menu cards which we gloated over: they promised us a four course dinner, with various good wines, and I was shown a box of the best Havana cigars; all the result of a parcel just arrived from Fortnum & Mason.

We were scarcely seated round the table, ready to fall to, when the sound of a gong was heard. This was not a dinner gong but a warning that gas shells were coming over. The Huns, with true Hunnishness, had chosen that moment to drench the area with poison-gas, and we had to put on our gas-masks. Thus what was to have been a unique and wonderful dinner-party became a complete fiasco, for no gas-mask had yet been invented which allowed the wearer to eat and drink a four-course dinner in a dug-out full of poison-gas. After waiting for an hour or two all hope of dinner was abandoned, and the party broke up, but as a consoling parting gift my hosts presented me with a couple of cigars to take away to smoke on some more happy occasion.

The work of the Ambulance was hard; for four or five days and nights we dressed the wounded almost without a break, sustaining ourselves with strong tea and cigarettes. Our stretcher bearers, after bringing back the wounded, would drop asleep while eating or smoking, they were so utterly exhausted. The wet weather which always seemed to come whenever the British army attempted to attack on a grand scale, made the work of the bearers much heavier. Many of the German wounded prisoners appeared to be starving, and ate ravenously of army biscuits and drank endless cups of tea and cocoa. Amongst the prisoners taken

THE SOMME

were several German doctors who seemed much less truculent than the usual German officer, and in more than one case had treated our wounded with kindness before being captured themselves.

One of the advantages a medical officer gained by being with an infantry battalion or a brigade of artillery was freedom from visits of " brass-hats."

In our division we had one indefatigable visitor in the A.D.M.S., Colonel R. J. Blackham, who although he came under the category of " brass-hat " was always welcome. In many ways he was an exception to the orthodox type of army medical big-wig. Never content merely to pay fleeting visits to his regimental aid-posts in the trenches or his advanced dressing-stations on safe and quiet days, he made frequent and protracted calls on all his medical officers and was always ready to stop and listen to any complaints or proposals the M.O. had to offer.

Again, although a regular of the regulars, he had a most open and unconventional outlook on life, military or otherwise, and was always eager to discuss and consider any of our suggestions, however heterodox. Thus it was that the medical staff of the 23rd Division was a particularly happy one, which was one of the principal reasons why the medical work of the division ran all along with complete smoothness and won for itself a high reputation wherever the division went.

Now and again indefatigable sightseers on pleasure bent would come up the line. These, whether of high military rank or distinguished civilians, or merely Members of Parliament, were always a source of anxiety to their unwilling hosts. I had one such visitor however who, if a source of anxiety, was certainly not unwelcome. This was Brigadier-General Seely—as he was then—who suddenly appeared one day at my dug-out at Peake Wood where I had been sent after Fricourt. This advanced dressing-station was situated at the side of the road running between Fricourt and Contalmaison, where it crossed a high ridge. It was in full view of the Boche, who evidently kept a sharp watch on it, for whenever more than a few men passed by together, a salvo of shells was sure to be fired at them. This made the dug-out rather an uncomfortable one, though it was pleasant on a fine day to sit on the roof, from which you got a fine view extending for many miles. But the best view in the world, on the sunniest August day is spoiled for you if your ears are continually on the alert listening for the sound of an approaching shell, and you are unconsciously ready to bolt to earth like a rabbit.

Although the life we led at Peake Wood was, of course, both safe and comfortable in comparison to that of the infantry, yet it did after a while tend to make you nervous and apprehensive unless you were one of those fortunate persons not subject to " nerves " and without a tiresome imagination. It was often noticed that the more a man lived below ground the more he was liable to suffer from agoraphobia—fear of open spaces—so that after a while, when he had to go out of doors, he would scuttle and slink along the sides of walls or banks, and proceed much in the way a child does when playing the game of musical chairs, every entrance to a dug-out or other convenient hiding place being passed very slowly while he hurried across the open places to be near the next bolt hole, in case a shell came.

THE SOMME

General Seely brought with him several officers and an official photographer. He was very interested in our dug-out, which being German was of course much better constructed than any British one. As the end of the visit approached I explained to him how the dug-out was under direct observation of the enemy, and that it was not " healthy " for several persons to stand about there, and I hoped he would take the hint. I then led the party out of the " front door " and was about to say good-bye when somehow or other Beaulieu, the village I used to live in, was mentioned. That started the General off, for he was a great friend of my neighbour and landlord, the late Lord Montagu of Beaulieu, and often stayed at the Palace House. After this we were all photographed together in a group, and General Seely left with a souvenir I presented to him, a very fine German bayonet.

Their motor car had scarcely disappeared round the corner when a salvo of shells exploded exactly over the spot where we had all been standing. Yes, distinguished visitors could be a grave anxiety.

There was not a great deal of work to do at Peake Wood. The large mass of wounded was taken back at night from Contalmaison direct to Fricourt, and I got chiefly odds and ends; men wounded by shrapnel on the roads or wounded men who could walk and had lost their way. One afternoon we had a lot of shelling all round and a good many casualties were brought in to be dressed. One was a German infantryman, a miserable, scared man of about fifty. He was not severely wounded, but had a superficial slash across one shoulder from a piece of shell case.

There was still some shelling going on outside while I was bandaging him, when suddenly we heard the awful scream of a huge shell approaching. The German's nerves were all to pieces, and no wonder; while mine, I am ashamed to confess, for I had not his excuse, were not as steady as they should have been. There was a terrific crash and explosion, the dug-out shook, and the daylight which came down a shaft was blotted out. When the light returned, I found myself lying on the floor closely embracing and as closely embraced by my German prisoner. There is no concealing the fact that it was an undignified position for a British officer to find himself in. It would have been difficult, indeed useless, to try to look stern, brave or dignified as I disengaged myself from the enfolding arms of my patient. Perhaps it was the reaction from acute terror to the absurdity of the situation which made us both laugh and laugh again. Fear makes strange bedfellows; and it is a great leveller, sweeping aside all distinction of rank, birth and race.

By great good fortune Willy Wenze—for that was his name—and I had been undetected in our brotherly intimacy. The occasion was not one for ceremony, so I treated my new friend and old enemy to a mug of hot cocoa, a tot of rum, and some biscuits, then shaking him by the hand sent him back to the prisoners' cage with a packet of cigarettes and a good yarn to tell when he got home to Germany.

Two other distinguished visitors, for I include Willy Wenze in this category, I remember in the following spring of 1917.

The Division had been undergoing an intensive period

of training in the neighbourhood of St. Omer in preparation for some new enterprise in wholesale slaughter. I was attached to an infantry battalion when the orders came for the division to march quickly up to the line. That was the longest and most tiring march I ever remember. Starting at dawn, we marched on and on, along the rough " pavé " roads. Presently word was passed down the column that Mr. Winston Churchill was ahead, watching the troops go by. We pulled ourselves together and soon saw and passed by the distinguished statesman, in mufti, and standing by his side my old friend Mr. Edward Marsh.

Still on and on we plodded, until an hour or more later, again the warning came, " distinguished civilians ahead," and again the tired men straightened themselves up. As they came into view, once again we saw Mr. Winston Churchill and Mr. Edward Marsh. I thought that march would never cease.

At last, late in the afternoon, when men were beginning to fall out from sheer exhaustion, yet a third time the message ran down the line : " distinguished civilians ahead." By now the men were too worn out to care or notice; but as we shuffled by I glanced to the side of the road, and there stood . . . Mr. Winston Churchill and Mr. Edward Marsh. Mr. Marsh I had known as a friend of the family all my life ; Mr. Churchill I had always admired ; but for several days after that nightmare of a march I did not wish to hear or think about either of them. Twice the Division had fought on the Somme and both times in the same sector, Fricourt . . . Contalmaison . . .

My memories of it all have become blurred, leaving

only one or two clear pictures, the rest is a dim impression of filth, ugliness and noise.

At times we—the R.A.M.C.—were kept very hard at work, at others we sat about in dug-outs, damp and stuffy, and read—if we had anything to read—for there was little or no inducement to walk abroad.

I was fortunate in having with me two volumes of Charles Dickens, *Nicholas Nickleby* and *Pickwick Papers*, and I can imagine no two better books nor a kindlier author to take one away from all the unpleasantness of warfare.

I was not the only reader of Dickens in the Great War. Mr. Oskar Teichman in his entertaining *Diary of a Yeomanry M.O.* describes how at the battle of Ras El Nag, in Palestine, he found in a Turkish gun position from which the enemy had just been driven, a copy of *Dombey and Son* lying open on the ground, and several dead Turks lying near. The author observes that a large number of Turks had been to America and suggests that this explains how one of those dead Turkish gunners had been reading the book at the time he was killed.

As can well be believed the birds on the actual battlefields of the Somme were few and very far between. Fricourt had its pair of swallows whose surprising presence left me greatly their debtor. Starlings were always the first civilians to re-occupy shattered strips of Picardy won back by our advancing troops. Whatever they found to attract them I do not know. Had they been carrion feeders it would have been explained, for there were feasts spread out for vultures. But starlings prefer a diet of fruit and insects. Of the first there was

THE SOMME

of course none; of insects there were flies in plenty as well as other crawling ones, which thrived and multiplied on the clothing of living men. As for animals these seemed to have all disappeared, even if trapping had been practicable. Nothing could live in that horrible poison-drenched shell-ploughed waste but man, and his chances of survival were but slender. Even the obsequious trench rat had disappeared. But I did get one addition to my collection in the battle area, which turned out to be a specimen of the very rare subterranean vole, *Pitymys subterraneus*, which burrows to a depth of four and five feet in the earth. It was picked up dead in a trench at Contalmaison by a soldier who gave it to me.

Our second visit to the Somme over, a victorious but shattered division trudged back for a much needed rest and refit. In the back areas of the Somme there were many birds. Partridges in big coveys in August, and earlier in July many quail, which kept up a persistent cry of "weet-weet"—"weet-weet" from morning till night, clamorous sky-larks and numberless crested larks.

Sometimes large hawks were seen, hen harriers and peregrine falcons. The reed-beds which bordered the river Somme were full of strange and familiar notes of birds, of coots, moorhens and dabchicks, of sedge warblers, reed warblers and reed-buntings; not far from Amiens I came upon a pair of beautiful great reed-warblers, very excited and making their odd loud music.

For three days we marched back, a footsore but happy remnant of the fine division we had been a few weeks before. We came to rest in a pleasant cultivated upland country dotted with little woods, above Abbeville. I was billeted in a pretty villa standing in a prim garden bounded by a high wall near the village of Monflières.

Directly I introduced myself to my host and hostess I knew that this was to be a happy billet.

Monsieur Fosse, retired head of police of Abbeville, was a tall grizzled man; Madame Fosse was a dear. When he heard my name, Monsieur Fosse threw up his hands with an exclamation of surprise and delight, and called to Madame Fosse to come quickly. A relative he excitedly explained to his surprised wife. How otherwise could it be . . . Fosse . . . Gosse, Gosse . . . Fosse? Only one letter different, and that one the very next in the alphabet!

Never, during all our time in France, were Bob Church and I more spoiled and more petted than by that amiable couple. Nothing was too good for us, nothing too much trouble for our comfort. Whenever I protested that they really overwhelmed me by their kindness, Monsieur Fosse would reply, " but are we not related ? " as much as to say, " there is nothing more to be said."

At the gate of their garden stood an ancient hollow tree, out of which through a hole high up, smiled down a figure of the Holy Virgin. According to Madame Fosse, there was a very old local tradition that one day, long, long ago, a shepherd was guarding his flock, when suddenly the Virgin appeared in the tree above him. This tree, known as l'Arbre de la Vièrge, was said to be the same original tree of the miracle, and marked the boundary between the manors of Belencourt and de Vauchelles. Beside the tree stood a little chapel, a place of pilgrimage for devotees. I would gladly have spent many weeks at charming Monflières, but all too soon we were ordered away to go, of all places, back to the Somme.

The day before our departure, Monsieur and Madame Fosse gave a dinner party in my honour. Several relatives of his—of ours—and two or three neighbours had been invited.

As the guest of honour I sat between Madame Fosse and a lady whose name I did not catch, but who I remember was enclosed in a very tight-fitting black satin dress, with corsets which creaked as she breathed. Never was such a spread nor such an array of wine bottles. At the end of the meal Monsieur Fosse, rising to his feet, called on the company for silence. He then made a speech which would have raised blushes to my cheeks had not the wine already made that impossible. I wish I could remember the whole of that speech, but what with my natural confusion, the wine I had drunk, and my restricted knowledge of French, to say nothing of the years that have since passed, I recall but a few sentences, though the general tenor remains clear enough.

The speaker began by reminding the assembled guests of that fatal August two years ago, when France, stricken to her knees by the sudden traitorous onslaught of the unspeakable foe, had called aloud for help. Did she call in vain? No! From across the sea immediate answer came from our brave allies, and amongst the first to spring to arms had been his distant relative, Monsieur le capitaine Gosse—loud applause. His cousin, whom they all welcomed amongst them that day, was the head of the English branch of the family.

I would give much to be able to remember by what means my cousin explained how my branch of the family came to migrate to England and when, and why.

Also how he accounted for the slipping of one letter of the alphabet from F to G. I know it all seemed very reasonable at the time and we were all very moved by it.

He begged his guests not to dwell upon the tragedies, the disasters of the War, but to remember and be grateful for the blessings the War had brought with it, not the least of which was the reunion of the so-long-separated branches of his family.

This affecting address made a deep and moving impression on all of us; in fact, the lady on my right in the black dress was so carried away as to kiss me on both my burning cheeks.

Early the next morning we were off once again, but not too early for my dear host and hostess to be down to bid farewell and " bonne chance " to their new found but already departing relative.

Everybody from the highest to the lowest had hoped and believed that the Division had seen the last of the Somme. But it was not so.

Our orders were to return there immediately and soon we were back again in the old sector. For the third time the enemy was driven back, and the victorious 23rd Division eventually pushed on through Martinpuich to Le Sars. Our advanced dressing station was in some wonderful German dug-outs beneath a great heap of bricks and rubble which once had been the Chateau of Contalmaison. Marvellous and elaborate dug-outs these were, far better than any we ever had to show. You went down flights of steps, deeper and deeper, with rooms, some quite large ones, dug out of the solid earth.

At the lowest level of all, far from all sound of gun or shell fire, was a small room in the walls of which were mock port-holes, with mirrors in place of glass, and in other ways made to look like the cabin of a ship.

There was also an elaborate full-sized cheval glass; probably filched from the château which once stood many feet above.

These dug-outs, when we first occupied them, were in a state of great disorder, with every evidence of the hurried departure of the previous tenants. All sorts of things were found when the place was cleaned up. In the cabin were many objects which pointed to a woman having occupied it, such as hair-pins, face powder, a pair of silk stockings and one garter.

There was plenty of work to do at Contalmaison, for the wounded kept pouring down in a steady stream which grew to a flood whenever a battle was being fought up on the ridge above.

One day when we were particularly busy, for the wounded were arriving in their scores, a spick and span military police officer came to see me. He said that amongst the wounded were a certain number who had no business to be there, and had come away from the front line with only trivial wounds, or under the pretext of helping a wounded friend. I told him that if this was the case I did not see how we of the R.A.M.C. could be expected to do anything about it. Our hands were more than full examining and dressing wounds, feeding the wounded and getting them away as quickly as could be managed. The police officer then told me to put under arrest as a deserter any man who I considered was not justified in leaving the fighting line.

At that I really got angry. I told him it was his job as a policeman and not mine as a surgeon to arrest felons or suspected deserters. In any case, I asked him, who was I, working there in a deep dug-out in absolute safety, to say to any man who had been shelled, bombed, gassed, terrified and starved " either you go back into it or else I put you under arrest?" I told him that if he liked to place some of his policemen outside the dug-out entrance he could do so, but on no account would I have one inside.

In the end he did place two policemen outside to arrest deserters and malingerers, but as the place was shelled pretty briskly on and off all that day, I was not at all surprised when I was told the policemen had disappeared; and I heard no more of that.

If I were asked to say what was my chief memory or impression of the Somme, I should reply the rancid smell which pervaded all the dug-outs we occupied and worked in. When the Germans made these dug-outs they provided elaborate and efficient ventilation, but when we occupied them the shafts were blocked up and we worked, ate, and slept in a hot, clammy atmosphere reeking of blood and iodine and stale cigarette smoke.

We had not been long at Contalmaison before the division captured Martinpuich, and the first man of the ambulance to reach the village in search of wounded and to organise an advanced dressing station was the indefatigable Pye-Smith. No danger or hardship could keep him away if there were wounded men to be rescued.

When he returned to the Ambulance after his first exploration of Martinpuich, he brought back news of an excellent German dug-out for an advanced dressing station, and some plunder in the shape of two stuffed birds, a long-eared owl and a rook. These must have been skinned and mounted quite recently by some soldier-taxidermist. Perhaps his was the bloated body which blocked up the air shaft. Probably he had attempted to escape that way when the entrance to the dug-out had become closed by our shells, and being a corpulent man had stuck fast in the narrow shaft and been killed. So fast stuck indeed, that it was only after much difficulty that his body was got out.

On September 24th the Colonel and I were standing outside the dug-out while a party of men were clearing a space for our motor ambulances to turn round in. Suddenly a salvo of shrapnel burst just over our heads and we all rushed to take cover. When I turned round I found the Colonel lying on the ground dead, killed by a bullet which had passed through his steel helmet into his brain. He was buried that evening in the " garden " of the château. The chaplain who conducted the hurried service wore his surplice over his uniform, and like the mourners, kept his steel helmet on, for there was a lot of shelling going on all round.

After our final exit from the bloody stage of the Somme the division moved north, as we hoped and certainly deserved, to a nice quiet piece of the line. That hope was rudely dashed to the ground when we found ourselves once again detraining at the metropolis of the north, Poperinghe. Not that the British soldier disliked that most English of all French or Belgian towns, even then when it had begun to receive the attention of the Hun. It had several attractions, both for men and officers. One of these was Talbot House, a wayside inn where any soldier was sure of a friendly welcome from the energetic, kindly genius who ran it. Another popular resort, for officers, was Skindles, where a really good French lunch or dinner could be enjoyed.

Besides Toc H and Skindles there was a cinema, and a very good one too.

Amongst my father's letters which were found after his death was one addressed by me from Poperinghe to his cat Caruso. All my life some cat or other reigned supreme in my parents' house. The very earliest I can remember was Atossa, a proud aristocrat and professional beauty, a long-haired Persian tabby. She was the gift of Walter Pater, and both in appearance and manner had something reminiscent of that famous writer. She once sat for her portrait to Laurence Alma-Tadema and a statue of her was modelled by Hamo Thornycroft. All this attention tended to make her vain and self-satisfied. When at last she died she was followed by the extremely disreputable and plebeian " Mother of Millions " who reigned for many years, leaving behind her, as may be guessed, many claimants to the throne. The one to succeed was Welland P. Allsop. The initial P. stood for Potbelly, but it was felt when he grew to maturity this name ought to be dropped. On the death of Welland in 1890 the throne was occupied by an impostor, a feline Pope Joan : Joseph Patch Wilson, who during the second year of his reign shocked us all by giving birth to a kitten, although in all fairness it should be put on record that this was his one and only slip from bachelor kingship. Joseph Patch Wilson was presented to us by Sir Harry Wilson, who had recently come down from Cambridge and was living with several other Cambridge men at the Osiers in the Chiswick Mall.

Joseph would correspond occasionally with his old master, and I have before me an unsigned poem in Latin, which I have no doubt is in the handwriting of Sir Harry himself.

The envelope is addressed to Joseph Patch Wilson, Esq., c/o Edmund Gosse, Esq., 29 Delamere Terrace, W.

The poem runs as follows:

> "HENRICUS JOSEPHO
> Josephe, felis felibus felicior
> cunctis, poetæ qui beatus in domo
> lac Londinieuse vase Serico bibis,
> epistulam libenter accepi tuam
> lepore tinctam salubusque Gossicis.
> Speroque, pestis Sarmatarum ni vetet,
> mox adfuturum Delamerio choro.
>
>   ad viii. Kal. Mai."

A learned classic and sometime scholar of Christ Church College, Oxford, to whom I shewed this poem, has translated it for me. Here is his English rendering:

> "HENRY TO JOSEPH
> Joseph, you're a lucky cat
> Lying on the poets' mat
> And untroubled lapping up
> London milk from China cup.

> Happy I your note to get
> Full of Gosse's fun and wit
> Hope soon to come, if naught forfends,
> Back to my Delamereian friends."

Charles Nathaniel reigned in the stead of Joseph Patch. He was a small black and white cat, and took his name from the editor of the weekly illustrated paper, *Black and White*.

Mopseyman, named, I do not know why, after a dog in one of Ibsen's plays, came next, and was succeeded by Caruso, a very handsome Persian, who arrived in a hamper in full song. Twelve years ago, after a long and distinguished reign, Caruso ascended to heaven and made way for James Buchanan, another black and white, and the noblest if worst mannered of his race, who still rules with an iron paw a house in Camden Town.

In some families it may not be the custom to write letters to the cat, or for the cat to correspond with absent members of the family. In mine, I am glad to say, it was regularly done.

The envelope of the letter which was found amongst my father's papers is addressed:

> CARUSO GOSSE, ESQ., M.I.C.E.
> 17 Hanover Terrace,
> Regent's Park, N.W.

and dated Sunday, Oct. 29th, 1916. It runs:

DEAR CARUSO,

I don't quite know which of the family I owe a letter to so I will write one to you. I wonder how you would like to live in this dreary Belgian town in the winter. There are, all the same, many much worse places I believe. This town, which begins with the same letter as does your uncle's name, can boast a delightful club for officers, a restaurant called "Skindles," where a very good French meal can be had, very cheap too, and there are as well two cinemas. The men like this part of the continent much better than further south. They find the people more like themselves, and say they are not out to fleece them of their pocket money, which they declare to be a habit of the brave French. Also they say the Flemish women are very like those they have left behind in England, and last, but not least, the civilians up here speak fluent, though hideous-sounding English.

The principal cinema is in a big empty hall in the town. If you went there on a Sunday afternoon at about—say— 3 o'clock and paid your thirty centimes, you would sit on a bench and watch the pictures and listen to an orchestra of fifty performers, and a very good one too. If you were one of the very lucky ones, you would have your fiancée with you. She would be dressed up in her best, with no hat on her head, and her hair would be well plastered with oil to keep it smooth. Generally two or three rows in the front are crowded by rowdy little Belgian children who have managed to beg a penny off a soldier or else "got round" the benevolent military policeman at the door, to let them in for nothing.

Round three sides of the hall, which are beflagged with the colours of the Allies, runs a gallery; one side for sergeants, charge fifty centimes; the other, with little tea-tables, is for officers, who pay one franc. Opposite the stage is a kind of royal box, where your uncle goes, and pays the exorbitant sum of two francs for a seat there. Nice and neat girls bring tea round to the officers, very well made (the tea) with lovely pastries. The hall is always packed and is well within shell-range; which worries nobody.

Please thank your aunts for the two very welcome

parcels that have lately arrived. Very kind of them to remember me. We have a cat belonging to our ambulance, who never leaves us. When we are on the march, she sits beside the driver of one of the horse-waggons. She is a nice cat, but has very short, thick hair, not like your beautiful wavy kind.

Much love to you all.

Your

Uncle Philip.

At Poperinghe we were billeted in a convent with a very small mess-room, which scarcely held all of us and our attendant chaplains as well.

Unkind comments have been made on the army chaplains and the part they played in France, although most people are agreed that exception should be made in the case of the R.C. chaplains, who remained with their battalions, were known to their men, and who appeared to have been selected for their task. It used to be complained that most of the C. of E. chaplains and those belonging to the nonconforming denominations were seldom seen by their battalions, except when out of the line and then only at a Sunday church parade or a burial service.

Far be it from me to criticise the army chaplains, no doubt they did what they thought necessary and proper. But I do know that all field ambulance main dressing stations became perfect hives of clergymen. Those who attached themselves to the 69th were all hearty, well-favoured young men, the life and soul of the mess, full of jokes and blessed with healthy appetites. Our colonel, although a religious man and a churchgoer, looked upon them with ill-disguised aversion. He used, backed up by his officers, to urge them to seek other and wider fields for their labours, but the broadest hints were generally all in vain. Now and again, as the result of some more than usually pressing exhortation, one of them would leave the dove-cot in search of new pastures, but like the dove would return again to the ark.

It is always dangerous and generally unjust to cast aspersions wholesale on a whole profession. To some people a young clergyman is an object of disfavour. These seem to consider that all priests should begin at middle-life, that the butterfly should not emerge from its chrysalis until mature, and then appear as a full-grown, full-blown clergyman. There may be something in this, but if so, it is a little hard on the young parson.

Even the most extreme fanatic was willing to admit there were certain conspicuous exceptions. There was not a British soldier in France who had not a good word for the splendid work of Philip Byard Clayton, the beloved " Tubby " of Talbot House, and originator, organiser, and inspiration of that world-wide institution Toc H.

One day while we were at the Pension des Bénédictines at Poperinghe, Clayton came to see me on an urgent and serious matter. We had not met since 1914, although we used to see a good deal of each other before the War, when our homes were only a few miles apart in the New Forest.

He had come to tell me about a deserter who had appeared at Toc H, and wanted to discuss with me what should be done about him. It was nothing extraordinary for a deserter to go to Clayton, for he was the recognised friend and confessor of all soldiers who were down on their luck or in need of help or advice. When he first saw him Clayton failed to recognise the scared-looking young soldier, but on hearing his name remembered a boy who was an orphan and had been brought up by two ladies in very reduced circumstances who lived in the New Forest.

It seemed that at the age of sixteen or under he had enlisted, and soon afterwards was sent out to France to the trenches. He had been with his battalion nearly a year, during which time he had been blown up and buried by shells, and seen his friends killed and wounded, until at last, broken in spirit and sick in body, he had bolted.

There was no getting away from it, the lad had deserted. Clayton took me to see the boy at Talbot House, where we found a scared, pale, trembling youth, far more fitted for a hospital than a battlefield.

It was clear that if something was not done about it the wretched lad would be court martialled for desertion and stand a very good chance of being shot. Instead the two conspirators arranged a plot.

I admitted the deserter into our dressing-station as a case of marked debility and shell shock, and put him to bed, where he slept for twelve solid hours.

The difficulty was what to do next. After much discussion, a medical report was made out stating that we had found Private H—— wandering about, that he was not responsible for his actions, and that he had been admitted forthwith to the ambulance, to await despatch to a hospital at the base. The plot was successful, and the lad at last got back to England, whence he ought never to have been sent.

The case of this boy was only one of hundreds of examples of the folly of the Voluntary system of enlistment. Men obviously too old for the trenches would take ten or even a score of years off their ages to enlist, or boys would add several to their teens to get to France. The Voluntary system also allowed men who would be invaluable in their own trades to join units where their special talents were quite wasted.

Some glaring cases of this failure of the Voluntary system cropped up in our own ambulance. After we had been in France for more than a year an order came to send in a list of the civil occupations of all ranks. Perhaps the most incredible was the case of two brothers who had enlisted together in the R.A.M.C. on the outbreak of hostilities. These brothers had worked at the same place and were both skilled rifle-sight makers!

What a system it was that allowed two highly skilled and trained craftsmen, who should have been set to work overtime at their specialized work, to enlist in a non-combatant unit. One day during a heavy rush of work at Contalmaison, when a constant stream of stretcher cases was being brought in, I noticed how efficient one of the nursing orderlies was. In a rush of that sort the lying down wounded were lifted on their stretchers on to trestles, where their first field dressing was removed by the orderlies, while we officers kept moving from one stretcher to another, quickly examining the wounds and treating and bandaging each case before passing on to the next. Each trestle-table was in charge of an experienced nursing orderly. One who particularly attracted my attention by his efficiency and skill was an elderly grey-haired private. I noticed he never required my help, and was thoroughly reliable.

After all the wounded had been got away I made enquiries about him from the sergeant-major, as I thought he should be recommended for promotion to sergeant in the nursing section, and learnt to my surprise that this private was a qualified doctor. I sent for him and asked if it was true he was qualified, and he admitted he was, but made it quite evident he did not wish to discuss with me his reasons for enlisting as a private instead of taking a commission. I reported his case to our A.D.M.S., Colonel Blackham, who offered to apply for a commission for him, but the man of mystery preferred to remain in the ranks.

This visit to Poperinghe was a short one, and we were soon at work again clearing the divisional sick and wounded from the front line, back to our main dressing station at the mill at Vlamertinghe. This mill was a famous landmark and half-way house for all those travellers who passed along the straight but tragic road which ran from Poperinghe to Ypres. Tragic, in the disparity between the number of those who travelled east and of those who returned westward along it.

One evening the orderly corporal came to report that a soldier was in the receiving room who wanted to know if he might sleep at the ambulance because he felt too tired to walk on to Ypres to join the battalion he was going to as a reinforcement. This sounded to me a pretty cool proposal, and I went to see the man, intending in all probability to send him about his business. What

I found sitting on the floor was a miserable looking sallow youth, apparently on the point of fainting. His kit he had thrown on the ground, rifle, bayonet, spade and all the rest of the paraphernalia with which a soldier was weighed down. I felt very sorry for him, but knew that if once the news spread that we took in for the night tired soldiers, the dressing station would soon become as crowded as a common lodging house. While I was looking at him and trying to harden my heart he said " You don't remember me, do you, Captain Gosse ? " But such hundreds and thousands of men had passed through our hands during the last sixteen months, all dressed alike and all looking much alike that at first I failed to recognise him. He soon reminded me however.

It had been at the special hospital at the château at Hersin-Compigney in the preceeding spring that I had last seen him, where only very seriously wounded cases were brought for immediate operation. I now remembered when he was brought in, with a terrible wound in his abdomen from a sniper's bullet. He seemed so near death when we saw him that it scarcely seemed worth while to operate. However the surgeon-specialist H. H. Sampson did operate, found he had to remove one kidney and the spleen, and after lying at death's door for many days the lad made a miraculous recovery. He was still at the hospital when we left, waiting to be sent back to England. This is no medical treatise, so it will be enough to say that a man who has had one kidney and his spleen excised is fortunate to be alive, but must be resigned to leading a semi-invalid life afterwards. By rights he should have been invalided out of the army, or else put to some light employment which would set free an able-bodied man for the ranks. But this was just before conscription started, when every boy or man who had joined up willingly was wanted, and was liable to be pushed back to fill up the ever increasing gaps in the fighting line.

I need hardly say that this credit to the surgeon who operated on him, but discredit to the medical board which passed him fit for the trenches, had a good supper and a comfortable bed for the night, and that steps were taken which I hope resulted in getting him out of the line for good, but a lucky chance it was for him that he happened to fall into the hands of friends who knew him.

Even when there were no battles being fought in the Salient, when there was nothing important enough to be mentioned in the newspapers, a steady stream of wounded passed through the mill at Vlamertinghe, from Ypres to the C.C.S.'s behind Poperinghe. One afternoon an ambulance arrived at the door with two wounded men, an officer and a sergeant.

The orderly who reported them said he thought they were cases to send straight back to the hospital. When I went out to see them I found the officer was my dear friend McKerrow, the beloved M.O. to the Northumberland Fusiliers, and his inseparable companion, his sergeant, both of whom wore every decoration but the V.C. for bravery, including foreign ones as well.

Both of them had been severely wounded in the abdomen, and were in a bad way. McKerrow was under no delusion about the gravity of his wound, and no doubt when I told him I would come and see him next day at the C.C.S. he knew well enough we were saying good-bye to each other. They both died that night, two brave men who had risked their lives time and again going out into No-Man's-Land in broad daylight to give wounded men, English or German, injections of morphia to ease their pain until they could be carried in, under cover of night. I heard afterwards how they came to be hit.

In the Salient every duckboard, corner of a road or track was in direct view of the enemy, whose artillery was able to drop a shell at almost any spot with the greatest precision. No doubt some German forward observation officer, seeing two soldiers walking along the duckboards, had telephoned back to his battery, giving the exact map reading, and given the order to fire. The shrapnel had burst just in front of them and he must have seen them drop, and no doubt telephoned congratulations to his gunners on a very pretty bit of shooting.

Somehow this useless, wanton killing of McKerrow and his sergeant made me more angry than sad, it was such a glaring example of the utter callous stupidity of the whole business of war.

It had been the sight of McKerrow skinning a vole for his little daughter in the trenches by Armentières in 1915 that put it into my head to collect small mammals for the British Museum. Whenever McKerrow and I met, which we did as often as we could, we used to talk about animals and birds, and there was no one in the whole division I liked better or admired more. He was always interested to see my latest captures in the collection, for which he was largely responsible.

Since then the fame or notoriety of my hobby of collecting rats and mice had spread far and wide, even beyond the limits of the Division, as I was soon to learn.

CHAPTER IV

RATS

ONE cold, wet, winter's day the ambulance packed up and, at the rear of the division, marched away from the enemy, the tumult and the mud of the Salient, in the direction of Cassel. Late in the afternoon we arrived at the village of Steenvoorde where we were to be billeted. Bob Church, whom I had sent on ahead, had managed to get me a bedroom at the house of some old friends of mine, Monsieur and Madame Schatt. I had often been billeted on them before. Their house stood in the main street, and their two charming daughters ran one of those amateur shops which were so popular with British officers, where all sorts of trifles from electric torches to scented soap could be purchased at double their proper price.

As a friend of the family I was given the best spare bedroom with the unwonted luxury of sheets in the bed. Rain and sleet were beating on the window when I woke up next morning, so I decided as there was no work to be done to make the most of the sheets, and spend a day in bed. I told Bob if anyone enquired for me to say I was in bed with a bad cold and could not be disturbed.

The morning was passing very comfortably, as I lay between the sheets, smoking and reading, when all of a sudden I became aware of a disturbance outside my room, of loud voices expostulating. A moment later the door was flung open and in strode a small but fierce looking officer. His cap shewed him to be a staff officer of some kind, but as he was wearing a long waterproof coat over his tunic, I could not tell his rank. Now in the army the manner in which a conversation takes place between any two officers largely depends on the relative rank of the speakers. Thus it was I found myself in some difficulty. But the small staff officer quickly came to the point, for after glancing at a paper in his hand he demanded " Are you Captain P. H. G. Gosse?" "Yes," I admitted, though wondering whatever it was all about.

" Well " continued the staff officer, " am I right in understanding you know all about rats?"

Now that, I thought, is a strange question to be asked by a total stranger, still more so when you are lying in bed. I wondered what was at the back of it, and whether it might lead to some nice quiet job or if I was to be court-martialled for a pastime so unbecoming an officer and a gentleman as skinning mice. Like everybody else who had been in the line for any length of time, excepting those rare and to be envied blood-lust soldiers who enjoyed the War, I was all for a safe and cushy post if such was offered me.

But this odd question " You know all about rats?" No . . . I wanted to learn a little more before giving a definite answer. So to gain time I replied, " Well, I know a good deal about birds."

" That's excellent," said he. " You are appointed Rat Officer to the Second Army and will report forthwith to the Director of Medical Services to the Second Army at Hazebrouck," whereupon, without waiting for any further observations from me or bidding me farewell or even expressing any interest in my bad cold, the fierce one right-about turned and marched out of the room.

"So here is a pretty how-d'ye-do," I thought as I lay back again between my warm sheets.

My meditations, however, were soon interrupted by the return of Bob Church, to whom I described what had happened during his absence and asked him what he thought about it all.

"Think about it?" said Bob. "Don't you waste no time, Sir, thinking, we've got a cushy job, and mustn't miss it," whereupon, without another word, my batman fell upon his knees and began with feverish haste to pack my valise, folding camp bed, washstand and armchair and of course the precious specimens, traps and skinning instruments.

In no time we were off in a borrowed motor ambulance to Hazebrouck, where I reported my arrival at Headquarters and was introduced by the fierce one—he proved to be a temporary Major R.A.M.C.—to General Porter, the D.M.S., who formally appointed me Rat Officer to the Second Army. The appointment was to be a temporary one and an experiment, and would not carry with it any promotion in rank nor any emoluments.

He told me that instructions had reached him from higher up to find a suitable officer for the post and that having heard of my activities—that was the word he used, which was accompanied by what looked uncommonly like a wink—he thought I ought to do.

A very pleasant and interesting post it proved to be, while it lasted. First of all there was no precedent to be followed, and King's Regulations contained no mention even of a rat officer, what he should or should not do. This was most encouraging, since almost every form of military initiative appeared to me to be hampered by some rule or formula in King's Regulations.

For more than two years people like myself had been pulled up by King's Regulations, and arguments with quartermasters had always ended by the old hand producing a copy of King's Regulations and finding something there with which to confound one.

Now I had a clear field to work in, with no rules, regulations or precedents. To begin with I was told to draw up a general scheme to shew what damage rats did, and whether they were a possible source of danger to the health of the army, and to offer suggestions for dealing with the plague of rats which swarmed in and behind the trenches.

In such a war as this where two vast armies had been entrenched for over two years, rats were everywhere; not only in the trenches but all over the back areas where troops were quartered. This enormous increase in the rat population was brought about as is always the case by two factors which had upset the balance between the natural enemies of rats and the rats' food supply.

In peace time every man's hand had been against the rat: every farmer took some means or other to keep him in check, if not to exterminate him, while most houses had a cat or a dog which also helped. But when the armies came most of the farmers left, and for some mysterious reason the dogs as well—the French peasants said the English soldiers took them, and not without some justification, for almost every British battalion was accompanied by a small pack of mongrel mascots wherever it went. But probably the most important reason for the increase of rats was food. The British army was supplied with a vast surplus of rations, much more than could be consumed. Food, stale bread, biscuits and particularly cheese, littered the ground. Some quartermasters, to save themselves trouble and to guard against any risk of being caught without enough would indent for greater quantities of rations than they required or were entitled to. This surplus was disposed of in different ways. Much of it went to feed hungry Belgian and French children, at which nobody could complain; as much again was thrown on the rubbish heap, burnt in the incinerators or buried in pits when a battalion moved from its camp.

It is a well known fact that if rats are well fed they breed more often and have bigger litters. Given ideal conditions the number of descendants from one original pair of rats is appalling. It has been calculated that a pair of rats in such ideal conditions will produce eight hundred and eighty offspring in one year, truly a staggering figure.

One glaring example of how our rations were wasted was brought to my notice while I was acting as M.O. to the 9th Yorks, when their own M.O., Rix, was on leave. The battalion had just come out of the line and I was ordered to join the headquarters staff mess at a small house on the Armentières—Sailly road. It was a winter's day and when we arrived at the house we found no fire in the mess room, which was bitterly cold. The colonel sent word to the lady of the house to ask if she could supply us with some firing until the cooks and servants arrived with the mess-cart. In a few minutes Madame entered the room with her apron full of material for making a fire. First she laid in the grate some crumpled pieces of English newspaper and a few pieces of wood. On top of this she built up a sort of open work pyramid of army oatmeal biscuits. On top of these again she placed a few pieces of coal, applied a match to the paper and in no time we had a roaring fire. I did not know until then what a combustible thing an oatmeal biscuit was. But all the same, it did seem a wicked waste of good food. When we expostulated with Madame, and asked her why she used biscuits as kindling, she replied, " ils sont très bons pour allumer un feu."

Having got my instructions from the D.M.S., my batman and I settled down at Hazebrouck in some comfortable billets with a French family, and I got permission to have my meals with them instead of messing with one of the headquarters staff.

I now sat down to write a learned treatise on the natural history of the Brown Rat—*Epimys norvegicus*—going fully into its habits and marriage customs, and dwelling on the enormous destruction it did to army food as well as army equipment.

I also dealt, but not at such length, with the Black Rat—*Epimys rattus*—and pointed out how it might become a carrier of Bubonic plague.

I then proceeded to draw up, but not in detail, several schemes for destroying rats: by poison, by gas and by traps. In theory I slaughtered rats in their thousands and their hundreds of thousands.

I ended my report by pointing out that all methods for the extinction of rats would fail if at the same time proper measures were not taken to prevent the rats getting at food, which I advised should be done by keeping all eatables whether in bulk, or only in small quantities as in dug-outs, in rat-proof cages or cupboards.

When this great treatise was completed to my satisfaction I laid it, not without some feeling of pride, before the General and retired to await his verdict. A few days afterwards I was sent for and informed that my report had been read at headquarters and, with the exception of one part, approved of.

The part objected to was the proposed plan to exterminate the rats by means of poisoned food, which was considered a possible danger to the troops. I was now told to draw up another scheme for a big campaign against the rats in the whole of the Second Army area by means of traps and to give exact details how the traps should be used and by whom. This was a pretty large order, but nothing daunted, I applied for leave to proceed—one always proceeded, never went—to Paris, in order to consult with the French army authorities and learn what they were doing about the rat menace. I had read an article in the *Morning Post* written by Mr. H. Warner Allen, the representative of the British press with the French Army, in which it was stated that in one army corps a reward of one sou was offered for each dead rat brought in from the trenches, and that in one fortnight 8,000 rats were killed and the rewards claimed.

This plausible proposal for a liaison visit to Paris was at once turned down and the next best I could obtain was the use of a car to take me to the Base to interview the Head of all the Quartermasters about supplying the particular type of rat trap I recommended should be used.

It was a pleasant drive from Hazebrouck through Hesdin to the coast. What first struck me when I arrived at the outer office of this high official was the brave display of war decorations. Every military clerk seemed to be wearing at least one ribbon on his tunic. The sergeants had all won the D.C.M. and M.M. with a pretty spattering of French and Belgian ribbons. Most of the corporals wore a military medal, and some a foreign decoration as well. How brave and how clean they all looked after the unclean, undecorated men I had lived amongst for the last two years, where an occasional Military Medal or even rarer Distinguished Conduct Medal was a thing to notice and admire.

Having at length broken through this barrage of heroes I was ushered into the Presence, and stood . . . at attention . . . before the great man himself. After the usual frigid reception—I was getting used to being greeted in this manner and was no longer intimidated by it—I explained my business, and soon found him to be a most pleasant and intelligent man. I put before him the pros and cons for the type of trap I thought best and he promised to let me have—I forget how many thousands—of the sort I wanted; and I returned triumphantly to Hazebrouck.

This habit of the Great I have just referred to, of

receiving junior officers as though they were the very dregs of society, or had just been detected committing some foul crime, I found very disconcerting, indeed terrifying when I first experienced it. But gradually I discovered that most of the Great, and all the less great, began in that way and that really it meant nothing at all, for more often than not they would soon be cracking jokes or at least being quite polite. The secret of success lay in refusing to be bullied, and it was from a big game hunter who ran a school of sniping at Mont des Cats that I learned the secret. His advice to me was to treat a General, a Brigadier, or a full Colonel exactly as you would a lion or any other fierce beast of prey. That is to say, however scared you might be you must not on any account let him see you were frightened, and above all, never for one moment take your eye off him. Once this lesson was learned I found no trouble in dealing with the most fiery of senior officers, even non-combatant ones.

Well do I remember one scene of frightfulness which verified the proverb that every flea on the dog's back has a lesser flea to bite him. On that occasion I was the smallest and the least of all the fleas present. It was one afternoon at Fort Rompu. Suddenly, without warning, there was an irruption of " brass-hats." Our Colonel, Nimmo Walker, was away up the line and I was in charge of the ambulance. Never before had I seen such a galaxy of military doctors of high degree. I am not sure who they all were, but at their head was General MacPherson, known, respected and loved throughout the R.A.M.C. as " Fighting Mac." Following him came the D.D.M.S. corps, with various other medical officers, including the divisional A.D.M.S. and his D.A.D.M.S.

What all the trouble was about I forget, but I was asked a question to which I gave what I thought was the right answer. Instantly the A.D.M.S. reprimanded me, and before all those great men I was humiliated. But hardly had the words passed the lips of the A.D.M.S. when the D.D.M.S. contradicted him and said that both he and I were wrong. But the D.D.M.S. was not to have the final word, for Fighting Mac in a voice which filled the whole building proceeded to "tell off" the D.D.M.S. and then the A.D.M.S. and did so in no half measures. When I thought my turn was coming, I drew myself rigidly to attention to receive my "dressing down" in soldierly fashion, when "Fighting Mac" sprung a pleasant surprise on me by saying "As for you, Lieutenant Gosse, I absolutely agree with what you did and with the answer you gave" and turning to the D.A.D.M.S., told him to make a note of it, and the august group swept out, leaving me shaken but happy.

Several years after the War I was one day talking to an affable-looking member of mildly military appearance, in the billiard room of the Savile Club. I had not the least idea who he was, although we often sat and talked together. Somehow or other his name happened to be mentioned, and I found that this gentle person was no other than the terrible "Fighting Mac." I could not resist the temptation to remind him of the scene of ruthlessness at Fort Rompu, which he laughed over but pretended to believe I had invented.

While organising my rat campaign I had to travel far and wide over the Army area, interviewing all manner of officers from proud brigadier generals to suspicious quartermasters. The latter were by far the more difficult to deal with. Not only were they suspicious—there was nothing about rat-catchers or catching rats in K.R.—but they particularly resented any assumption on my part that their stores might be better if they were protected from rats by wire-netting. Considering that by this time almost every quartermaster's store had become so swarming with vermin as to be a sort of combined House of Commons, Queen Charlotte's Lying-in-Hospital and R.A.C. for rats rolled into one, it might have been thought that any suggestions to improve matters would be welcomed. But this was far from being the case.

Through making these visits I got a very shrewd idea of what it must be like to be a commercial canvasser. The commercial canvasser when he rings the house bell must wonder if he will be turned away without a hearing, or if not, what sort of a person and reception he is about to meet. I had one great advantage over the commercial canvasser in that I could not be turned away without being seen and heard, because all my clients had received warning—probably in triplicate—of my intended visit and instructions to assist me.

Where the fun came in was to observe the manner of the first salutation. A few of the regular R.A.M.C. colonels were frankly rude at the start, while most of the territorial R.A.M.C. colonels were usually the opposite. I think the former classed a Rat-officer with a rat-catcher and that the greeting I so often received was the rat-catcher greeting. Though why anyone should be rude to a rat-catcher I do not know. The few professional rat-catchers I have been privileged to meet, either in business or socially, have all been interesting men with charming manners, but perhaps being members of the same craft or mystery may have helped to put us on a friendly footing.

My whole time was not taken up paying these visits, for as G.O.C. rats, I had to deliver lectures. These began in a quite small way at Hazebrouck, where a school of sanitation for officers had been started and where courses of lectures were delivered by various experts, each on his own special subject. Last but two on the syllabus of subjects, came mine of rats; the two even lower on the list being flies and parasites, the experts on which were familiarly referred to as O.C. Maggots and O.C. Lice. The audiences consisted of officers, some of them regimental medical officers, but for the most part young combatant officers belonging to various infantry regiments, artillery brigades, Royal Engineers, machine gunners, Army Service Corps, etc., in the Second Army. Until my lectures became better known my reception by my pupils was invariably chilly. No bones were made about letting me see that I was wasting their time by talking about rats, time which could and should have been so much better and more agreeably occupied in other ways; some not unconnected with those cafés, half club, half brothel, which provided drink for the thirsty on the ground floor and solace for the bored upstairs. But it was gratifying to the lecturer to observe the gradual change from undisguised boredom to attention, then to interest, until finally the audiences actually became enthusiastic.

RATS

On the days I was to lecture I used to lunch at the Coq d'Or, a comfortable old-fashioned hotel in the Grand Place. In happier days before the War the local Flemish farmers probably met there for their " ordinary." Down the middle of the big dining-room ran a long table. By common consent one half of this table was occupied by the farmers, the other by the British officers who were stopping at Hazebrouck for the course. During one déjeuner à la fourchette, a youthful officer, I think he was in trench mortars but cannot now be certain, asked the company in general what was " on " that afternoon, to which another equally juvenile warrior, a second lieutenant in machine guns, replied " Oh some bloody old fool is going to talk a lot of bunk about rats." I dropped my eyes to my plate but kept my ears open. The subject of my lecture at once became the topic of general conversation, and I soon learned that both the unheard lecture and the unheard lecturer were beyond the pale, but no one spoke more bitterly nor more frankly about both than the machine gunner. Many different points of view were expressed about myself and my lecture, but the unanimous verdict was that it was a scandal that officers like themselves should be compelled to waste their time and rare leisure listening to a silly lecture about rats. Who in any case wanted to be told anything about rats; had they not seen all the rats they wanted to in the trenches, and why could they not be allowed for once to forget about rats?

Half an hour later I stepped on to the raised platform in the lecture room. Exactly opposite to me, in the middle of the front row, was seated the young machine gun officer. Our eyes met . . . in mutual recognition.

He knew that I knew, and I knew that he knew I knew. How uncomfortable he looked, truly I felt sorry for him, for I quite saw his point of view. But he and I were not the only two in that room who appreciated the situation, a feeling of electricity pervaded the hall.

"Gentlemen," I began, "just now while at lunch at the Coq d'Or, one officer asked another what was on this afternoon. The other officer, whom I observe seated amongst you"—here a stern look at the crestfallen lieutenant—"replied 'Some bloody old fool is going to talk a lot of rot about rats.' However," I continued, "I bear him no malice and only hope that he will find my lecture not as dull as he expected nor think me quite such an old bore as he feared."

This opening being greeted with applause, permission to smoke was given, the lecture began, and in no time we were all as jolly as jolly could be. At the end of the lecture, the machine gun subaltern and I had a friendly chat, about all sorts of things, including rats, and parted the best of friends.

This lecture became in time, if I may be allowed to say so, a feature of the War, and the envy of the other armies of the B.E.F. which had neither a rat officer nor rat lectures. Like many other successful concerns, such as Toc H or the B.B.C. or Sir Josiah Stamp, the rat lectures began in quite a small way, to grow and expand into a flourishing undertaking.

At first the lectures were given only to officers, but soon classes were formed for men as well. Gradually I learned to modify the lecture to the two different audiences. I found that some facts and little jests which interested or amused the officers fell flat with the men, and vice-versa. So both clients were catered for. Not the least feature . . . modesty prevents me calling it an attraction . . . of the lectures was the table of exhibits. On this table were arranged specimens I had caught and stuffed of most of the small mammals to be met with in or behind the trenches, as well as models and drawings of traps. To most of those who saw these it came as a surprise to learn how many different animals there were in Northern France, believing as they did that the brown or trench rat was the only beast but man to be found in Flanders. Amongst the exhibits were moles, hedgehogs, common shrews, pigmy shrews, water shrews, white-toothed shrews, garden shrews, weasels, stoats, pole-cats, bank voles, subterranean voles, orchard dormice, wood-mice, harvest mice, rabbits and pipestrell bats. When the fame of the lecture had spread abroad I used to be invited to deliver it—with, of course, the exhibits—to various gatherings. In fact, my lecture became in time to be looked upon as a sort of drawing-room entertainment, and I went about from place to place giving performances much in the way conjurers and ventriloquists do, who give refined entertainments at children's Christmas parties.

By this time, early 1917, schools had become all the rage. Besides schools of sniping, bombing and musketry, there were academies where short courses of instruction were held in bayonet fighting, trench mortars, poison gas, and the construction of latrines and incinerators. Not to be behind the times, the Xth Corps opened a school of sanitation at Vieuxbec, near Poperinghe and sent me there to help to run it. Although not many miles away from the line the village was happily free from evidence of warfare, beyond a few British soldiers and an occasional passing army lorry; while the country round was pretty, with several small but steep wooded hills, delightful rarities in that flat and treeless land.

The staff of the new school consisted of two R.A.M.C. officers and several N.C.O.'s. The senior, my chief, was a cheerful North of Ireland doctor who before the war had been a medical officer of health at Belfast, so that at least one of the staff knew something, and more than something, about the subject we were to teach. Together we started and ran the school, and he was as anxious as I to make the weekly course not only useful but as pleasant and happy as possible for our pupils.

Lectures and demonstrations were given by us both on every conceivable subject relating to public health. By instructions from headquarters the title of my, by now, famous discourse on rats was altered to A Lecture on Zoology in its relation to Sanitation, but I also lectured on lice, fleas, bugs and blue-bottles, trench-foot, its cause and prevention, food, latrines, kitchens, incinerators, grease-traps and cooking. In vain I expostulated against having to lecture on cooking, not merely because I knew nothing about the subject but because a number of our pupils each week were cooks. When I say I knew nothing about the subject of cooking perhaps I do myself an injustice. I knew how to make an omelette with eggs and bread crumbs, a secret divulged to me when a boy by Mr. Harold Cox, and one I had kept jealously ever since. But at a class of cookery you cannot go on day after day, week after week, teaching nothing else but how to make an omelette of eggs and bread crumbs, so I procured a copy of Mrs. Beeton's classic work and crammed up a few simple recipes which seemed to lend themselves to army rations. As a matter of fact we invented several new dishes out of bully beef, Maconochie ration and potatoes, and even made excellent cakes, although nothing surpassed our famous bully beef and biscuit rissoles. All our experiments were tried on our pupils, and some of them were voted satisfactory, and the army cooks returned to their units with many culinary surprises up their sleeves.

The whole of our time was not taken up with lectures and demonstrations. One of my duties, and the one I liked best, was to take the entire class, some fifty men, for a daily march for the benefit of their health. This came under the heading of drill in the syllabus, but it seemed to me incongruous and presumptuous for me, an R.A.M.C. officer and a non-combatant, to drill fifty fighting men on the barrack square, and also I never could remember any words of command other than " Shun ; move to the right in fours, form fours, right, by the right quick march." Beyond this string of words, which any parrot of average intelligence would pick up in a few days, I knew nothing, so that whenever I was in command of a company, section or party of soldiers, it simply had to march away or go round in circles. Having got my little army moving I would march at the head and lead them straight up the side of the nearest hill, where I would give them a short "breather" and then, like the grand old Duke of York, lead them down again on the other side as fast as they could run, getting in a few jumps over hedges and banks to lend excitement.

Of course, there were bound to be one or two of the usual "grousers" who complained at first, but they would soon see the fun of the whole thing and enter into it with the rest. When we got back, dinner would be ready and thanks to Mrs. Beeton there was generally some surprise in store, and the men thoroughly enjoyed the change from the monotonous, unappetising fare they were accustomed to.

The pupils were encouraged to ask questions after the lectures and at the end of the "Zoological" one, the questions often developed into a general conversation on natural history. Now and then one of the men would try to catch me out, and if I was able to score off him instead the audience was delighted.

Some of the soldiers who were country bred used to ask very intelligent questions, or tell me interesting first hand experiences of their own. One day, at the rat lecture, the talk had somehow drifted to hedgehogs and I referred to the popular country belief that hedgehogs sucked the milk of cows. I told them that there was no proof of such an improbable occurrence, and that I had never met anybody who claimed to have seen such a thing happen. At the end of the lecture a tall, rough looking man stood up and said he knew it to be a fact that hedgehogs sucked the milk of cows, because he himself had seen it done. This bold challenge caused an instantaneous sensation, and I invited the man to tell the audience all about it. He said that very early one morning, just before dawn, he and a friend at home in Northumberland were walking along the edge of a meadow beside a coppice. Several cows were lying down and he and his friend saw a hedgehog sucking the teat of one of the cows. I knew well enough the man was only trying to " score off me " so I asked him " what exactly were you and that friend of yours doing at dawn by that coppice? " The soldier, turning red in the face, collapsed into his seat amidst laughter and cries of " poacher," and I got out of it all right and was more than even with my would-be tormentor.

It was a pleasant surprise to find how keen these soldiers were on natural history. At first, I feared they would be bored with anecdotes about birds and beasts, but the majority seemed very interested. After one of the lectures on rats a middle-aged man from a Yorkshire regiment told me how, quite recently, he had entered a wrecked church at Ypres in search of some wood to make a fire with. He found and pulled some down behind the ruined altar, and in doing so uncovered a large bat asleep. After carefully examining the bat he put it into a box, and afterwards laid the box near the fire he had made. After a while, the warmth of the fire—this happened during very cold weather—awakened the bat, which began to scramble about in the box, so the soldier let it out and it flew away.

This little anecdote had a sequel.

Ten minutes later the soldier who told me about his large bat brought up to me another soldier, to whom he had never spoken before but who had overheard us talking about the Ypres bat. The newcomer, after explaining to me that he was " fond of animals " produced a grubby little pocket diary and shewed me this entry for January 2nd, 1917 : " Saw to-day a large bat flying about the streets of Y——. Probably disturbed by shell fire." By comparing notes the two soldiers had found that they both saw the big bat on the same day and about the same hour, and it was a truly strange coincidence that they should have met at my lecture at Vieuxbec.

I fear that there was a sad lack of discipline at our lectures, but all the same the pupils never got out of hand or took advantage of our good nature, and during the whole time the school lasted we never once had to punish a man. Only once was I embarrassed by the heartiness of the applause of my pupils. It was one afternoon when delivering the rat lecture to a particularly bright and sympathetic class. To bring the lecture to a happy termination I told them the famous story of Darkie's rat.

It should be explained that the most popular estaminet in Vieuxbec was the Réunion des Blanchisseuses, ruled over by Madame Perret with the assistance of a big tousled Flemish hoyden called Darkie. This girl, not without good looks of a sort, was a great favourite with the soldiers. My friend, Monsieur Junod, the French interpreter, was billeted at the estaminet and unlike most Frenchmen was a keen naturalist and took great interest in helping me devise and make various types of rat traps. One of these traps was an ingenious contrivance made of wire-netting, and was of some size. Having made it we wanted to try it, to see if it would catch rats in reality as well as it did in theory.

Then it was that Monsieur Junod told me about the monster rat in Darkie's bedroom. How he came to know about this rat I do not know, nor did I press him to tell me, but somehow he had learned that Darkie's slumbers were disturbed by a huge rat which had defied the ingenuity of all ordinary traps. So I entrusted him with our latest invention, which was to be placed beneath Darkie's bed, all ready set and baited.

The experiment met with immediate success, for the very first night the giant entered the trap and the cage was brought round to me the next morning containing a regular colossus of a buck rat.

Of course there were several stuffed specimens on show of the common brown rat, but this one I was determined should be something unique, a super-rat in fact. So when I had removed its skin, instead of filling it with the proper amount of cotton wool, I continued to pack in more and yet more until the skin was so stretched that the rat looked like one of those inflated rubber animals made to support sea bathers. When the skin would hold no more wool, I sewed it up and mounted it. The result was both surprising and alarming.

Towards the close of the rat lecture I used to shew different types of trap and explained how each worked and its good or bad points. On this particular occasion I shewed them the new big wire trap and began to tell the story of Darkie's rat and the interpreter. The mention of Darkie's name was followed by instant close attention, for she was well known to and admired by most of the audience, and many hopes ran high. Then at the critical moment I took Darkie's monster from its hiding place and held it aloft for all to behold and marvel at. This was always a very popular crowning touch and never failed to bring the lecture to a pleasant if boisterous conclusion. But by an unfortunate mischance the General had chosen that afternoon and that very time to bring other generals and their staffs to show them over the school, which was a favourite child of his.

At the precise moment when I was holding up Darkie's rat and the hand clapping and cheering were at their loudest, the General opened the door to allow his guests to have a peep at the Zoology lecture.

The door stood behind me where I could not see it, so that I continued standing with the rat held on high, all unconscious of the other audience in the rear, and it was only when the hilarious laughter suddenly petered out that I turned round to discover the awkward predicament I was in. Generals did not expect frivolity at military lectures.

In spite of this unfortunate occurrence my sojourn at Vieuxbec was a very happy one. I was billeted at the house of the village schoolmaster, Monsieur Berthoud, an old acquaintance, for when we first arrived in France I had been billeted on him at Strazeel and he was now at Vieuxbec. My meals I took with the Town Major, Captain Scrivener, a small, elderly and very precise ex-yeomanry officer. His mess was made up of two very young and enthusiastic signalling lieutenants, who were experimenting with some new piece of magic they referred to as telefunken, a Canadian A.S.C.

officer, whose claim to fame arose from his being able to drive the cork out of a whisky bottle by giving it one hard slap with his hand underneath, and Monsieur Junod, the French interpreter. To this select little coterie I was admitted a member.

Captain Scrivener took his duties as Town Major and Area Commandant with commendable seriousness. To the rest of us it appeared to be a pretty trivial task, but according to the Captain the work was heavy and the responsibility grave.

In his habits he was exceedingly regular. Twice a week he rode to Poperinghe to lunch at Skindles and always returned with the same exciting piece of news "Fritz was on his last legs," and a special bottle of wine would be uncorked to celebrate these encouraging tidings.

Although I was privileged to share the hospitality of his board for several months, Captain Scrivener and I never became really intimate. He was a man of limited interests. To begin with he stated, while watching me unpack my belongings and place my books on the mantelpiece, that he never read books, or indeed read anything but newspaper articles about horse racing. As he was not interested in books, nor I in horse racing, I tried him with another subject, wild birds, and was pleased to learn that birds were a particular passion of his. But on going more deeply into the subject I found that his interest in birds was entirely confined to one species, the pheasant. Not that he had studied pheasants, or ever read a book about pheasants, indeed he proved to know nothing at all about the natural history or habits of his favourite bird. His interest in that noble if half domesticated bird was strictly confined to its wholesale slaughter and artificial propagation for slaughter. To him the English countryside meant a place full of woods and coppices provided by an all-wise deity to harbour vast numbers of pheasants for Scrivener and his city friends to shoot at on Saturdays.

I remarked just now on his regular habits. The Captain maintained it was the duty of a gentleman, and indeed of all of us, to conform as far as the altered circumstances permitted to the routine we had followed at home in peace time. At home, he told us, he always went by train twice a week on Tuesdays and Fridays from Hampshire to lunch at his club in London, and for that reason he made his bi-weekly jaunt to Skindles. But the habit which delighted and impressed all newcomers to the mess was the ritual of the cigarette. Luckily for me I was warned of it in time by the Canadian, or might have done the wrong thing. Naturally the Captain—he was known throughout the district as "the Captain"—sat at the head of the table. In front of him stood a handsome silver cigarette box. After the simple meal was over, the Captain's batman, who he told us had been one of his footmen at home, would open the lid of the box, which was then seen to contain one, and only one, large Turkish cigarette. This the Captain would extract, place it between his lips, his footman-batman then holding a match for him to light it by. The first puff of smoke from the Captain's lips was the signal to the company that they might now light up their " fags," " gaspers " or " yellow-perils."

I was in pretty close proximity to the Captain for

over four months, but we had lived in different worlds, and had not one interest or point of view in common. All topics of conversation flagged except horse racing and the bags of pheasants killed by himself and his wealthy friends. I hope that nothing I have said may be taken to reflect on the good nature of Captain Scrivener; if so, I have done him a grave injustice, for there was no harm in him, but he was just the dullest man I ever met.

At regular and short intervals he would get leave, and I would proudly take over—*pro tem.*—the offices of Town Major of Vieuxbec and Area Commandant. These two posts seemed to me to be sinecures, for the only real work they ever entailed was the weekly paying of wages to some fifty French and Belgian women who worked at the army laundry. It was a noisy business, with no end of loud conversation, expostulation, argument and laughter. My knowledge of the French language, although improving, was not up to tackling this babel of Flemish and Northern French dialect, so I got Monsieur Junod to sit beside me at the table and help me deal with the problems as they arose. And he was the right man to do it, for he knew just how to treat these women, was stern with some, affable to others, and always had a witty retort to their jokes, some of which, even to my unskilled ears, were of the kind we English, in our honest English way, describe as " very French."

The Town Major's mess room was divided by folding doors; in one half we took our meals, while the other half was given over to me for my own use, and there I did my rat-campaign work, wrote letters and skinned my animals. There was not much privacy about my room, and anybody was liable to walk in at any time to see what I was doing. While I was writing a report one day the Canadian strolled in, had a look round, pointed with his pipe at a photograph which stood on the mantelpiece and said " Say, doc, is that old guy your dad ? " and it was.

As I have recounted elsewhere, I at last succeeded in procuring a beech marten for the collection, and on the same morning sat down to skin it. I had never skinned one of these animals before, and owing to that, or possibly to carelessness, I unfortunately cut through the gland which lies close to the root of the animal's tail. This gland secretes a highly offensive fluid, and in a moment the whole room was filled with a noisome odour of beech marten. Although the smell of one of these animals is not so powerful nor suffocating as that of a skunk—I once had an even worse misadventure with one in the Argentine—it belongs to the same category of foul stenches. On seeing and smelling what had happened, I flew to open the window, in spite of the intense cold, to let the smell escape. All too soon luncheon was announced on the other side of the folding doors, and leaving the marten on the window ledge, I joined my fellow messmates at the table.

We had scarcely sat down when " Phew ! " went the Captain. " What a ghastly smell ! " Then everybody began to complain of it. To draw away suspicion from myself I said I thought I too could smell a little something. Then one of the alert young signallers, like a fox-hound on the trail, picked up the scent and followed it as it became stronger and stronger and led the pack into my room, where with loud halloos and yoicks they ran to ground my marten, stuffed and set to dry on the window ledge.

Then a truly unholy row took place. Everybody turned on me and said the most ill-natured things about me and about my hobby, ending with an ultimatum that either I promise never again to skin an animal in my room or else leave the mess and go elsewhere.

This beech marten which was the innocent cause of so much disturbance and bad feeling came to me in the following way.

When I found myself once again billeted with Monsieur and Madame Berthoud, I explained to them about the collection of mammals I was making for the British Museum, and asked Monsieur Berthoud if he thought he could obtain for me a specimen of a polecat or a beech marten; two animals very similar, which I felt sure must occur in the neighbourhood but neither of which I had as yet seen. Monsieur Berthoud assured me he would do his best to get me one, and the very next day, before his assembled scholars, made a speech in which, after informing his pupils that a very distinguished "savant" was staying in his house, he told them to try and procure a fouin, for which he was authorized to offer, as a reward, the handsome sum of twenty francs.

For two days nothing happened, but on the third the trouble began.

As I lay in my bed that morning I was suddenly awakened by an uproar on the stairs outside my door. The noise grew louder, the bedroom door was flung open, and in marched Monsieur Berthoud at the head of a small but excited crowd, while above his head he held in triumph a dead furry animal.

Having handed over the twenty francs reward and got rid of my visitors, I gave out that another specimen was wanted, but that only ten francs would be given for it.

The result of this was that next morning the same noisy scene took place, when no fewer than three fouins were brought to my bedside, to be followed after breakfast by five more. Seeing things were getting serious, I asked the schoolmaster to inform his charges that on no account would any more rewards be given for further specimens.

This answered on the whole, except when I walked abroad, for often in some by-lane or alley of Vieuxbec a polite child would salute me and call my attention to something wrapped in a cloth or in a basket. On being revealed it always proved to be yet another specimen of Martis fiona.

But not only dead animals came under my notice; there was Albert.

Albert was found one cold winter morning warming himself in an empty tin beside an incinerator at the School of Sanitation. A sanitary corporal, who considered he owed me a debt for some trifling service I had once been privileged to render him, brought Albert to me in the box.

He proved to be a tiny garden shrew found in Western Europe, but not in England, his scientific name being *Crocidura russula*.

A cage was made for him and a warm hay nest provided. Albert settled down at once, but soon two difficulties became apparent; his vile temper and his voracious appetite.

If we touched his cage he flew from his nest, squeaking and dithering with rage, to see who it was had dared intrude. His appetite was insatiable. Live worms were the only food he would take; and he wanted one every few hours. They had to be alive, as he would only eat one after he had, like St. George, fought and killed the worm. In twenty-four hours he would eat more than his own weight in earthworms, and they were difficult to find in the hard, frozen ground.

Gradually he was weaned from live worms to eat shreds of bully beef, but these had to be held in a pair of forceps, and a sham fight between the bully beef and Albert had to be fought at every meal.

Bob Church, most long-suffering of batmen, took a more than brotherly interest in Albert; indeed he was both a mother and a father to him and would rise several times each night from his warm blankets to take a piece of bully beef and engage in sleepy mock mortal combat with the fierce battling Albert. Thus Albert thrived and, I like to think, showed a sort of fierce beneficence towards his faithful and long-suffering keeper. Everybody loved him, and even the Town Major, no lover of animals except race-horses, grew fond of Albert.

News of Albert in some way reached the London Zoological Society, and I was informed that the Gardens at Regent's Park had never possessed any kind of shrew, as they were considered impossible to keep in confinement owing to their insatiable lust for live worms. But the difficulty was to get Albert to London, as

I could find no officer going home on leave who was willing to take a pet that not only bit the hand that fed it, but needed feeding and fighting every hour or two in the twenty-four.

Eventually a special leave on urgent private affairs was "wangled" for Bob, who set off with Albert in his strong box and a tin of the reddest, rawest looking bully beef, for Boulogne. He told my mother, whom he visited with Albert on his way through London, that the journey had been a veritable nightmare, as he disturbed his fellow travellers all the way by his frequent and violent attendance on Albert; but the journey ended well, and Albert found a home in the small mammals' house, and had the honour of having his photograph in the "Field," though the photographer spoilt no fewer than a dozen plates before he finally caught Albert still for the necessary fraction of a second.

I had reason to mention a little way back the name of my good friend Monsieur Junod, the interpreter. Unlike so many French interpreters he spoke and understood the English language. Also he understood women. In fact, what Monsieur Junod did not know about women was hardly worth consideration, while some of the things he did know would not bear repeating.

His official duties at Vieuxbec were to settle all questions as to etiquette, difficulties about billeting, claims by farmers for damage; in fact, he acted as liaison officer between the civilian population and the British army.

It was his profound knowledge of the workings of the

mind of woman which once thwarted an unseemly scandal, one which, if left to follow its natural and military termination, might have brought about a weakening of those sacred bonds which bound the French and English nations together.

To explain this affair I must first describe, very briefly, the conditions which led up to this sad scandal in our hitherto happy and innocent village. Like all other villages in Flanders, Vieuxbec possessed several estaminets, though none was held in higher esteem by the British soldiers than the "Réunion des Blanchisseuses." Like other estaminets it was entered by two steps which led down to a well-washed, tiled floor. There were clean-scrubbed tables and chairs for the customers, and a highly polished brazier which burnt all day in the middle of the room. This estaminet was presided over by Madame Henriette Perret—a woman of generous proportions; her age, if one may be so indiscreet, about forty. To assist her she employed two handmaidens—"Darkie," that big, black-eyed, full-breasted romp of a girl, a great favourite with the British soldiers; and a fair, delicately pale blonde, Berthe—pretty, and with still a veneer of maidenly modesty which Darkie had lost long ago, if indeed she had ever possessed it.

The customers consisted almost entirely of British troops who were billeted in the village, most of them infantrymen "resting" for a spell out of the line, or men attending the School of Sanitation; with a sprinkling of odds and ends—men left in charge of a store or a dump; some forgotten altogether, as was the case of an elderly and quite inefficient old soldier who was in charge of an incinerator which was never used. A brutal officer one day swooped down on the village and found this old man, and after a short conversation, crudely called him a deserter. This insult the accused indignantly refuted, declaring that when his battalion marched away a year or so ago he was ordered to tidy up the camp and burn the rubbish in his incinerator, and to remain in charge of it until relieved; and like a true soldier he was carrying out his instructions.

But to get back to Madame Perret of the Réunion des Blanchisseuses. Amongst her most regular customers was a good-looking young soldier, a sanitary corporal. His duties, though scarcely heroic or in any sense spectacular, were of vital importance; and he, having no lust for Teuton blood nor desire for gaudy decoration, was only too pleased to go about his humble duties without fuss or fame.

His daily toil finished—a matter of about one hour—it was his custom to spend as much of the remainder of the day as his money or Madame would allow, sitting in her estaminet, sipping "caffy-avec," a mixture of coffee and chicory into which a little cognac has been added, and chatting, and even flirting a little, with Darkie or Berthe.

But, alas! one day the corporal was able to afford more "caffy-avec" than was good for him, and, emboldened or maddened by this poisonous mixture, he did the dreadful thing. At least, he attempted to.

He made violent love to Madame. Worse, he paid none of those preliminary attentions, whispered none of those sweet secrets that all women have a right to expect from even the most ardent and passionate of lovers. The corporal so far forgot himself and the respect due to a lady of such dignity and position as to attempt to snatch the fruit without first shaking the bough. Madame's feelings were, naturally, outraged.

The first I heard of the matter, which, of course, stirred the village like an earthquake, was from Monsieur Junod. He came to see me in a state of the greatest excitement and perspiration. His face was red, his looks worried; in his haste to consult me he had for once forgotten to don the orange ribbon which he customarily wore, the Ordre de la Mérite Agricole, on his chest. What was to be done? How to stop a court-martial? Military law was most definite as to the punishment to be inflicted on a soldier guilty of this crime against the person of one of our fair unprotected allies.

My own suggestion was that it would be best for him to explain to Madame that the man was drunk at the time, and ask her to excuse him on those grounds. Monsieur Junod was horrified! It would be, he assured me, the worst thing that could possibly be done. This was evidently a case where Monsieur Junod's expert knowledge of women would come in. He had an idea—yes, he saw daylight! He himself would go and talk to Madame, and he believed he could master even so delicate a situation as this one.

The next day I met my friend, who was all radiant with smiles and the orange decoration for proficiency in agriculture.

The affair? Oh yes, he had settled that little business

all right. But it had taken time and tact—much tact. Seated with Madame in her little back room, so lately profaned by the sanitary corporal, the interpreter and she had held converse. They had talked of many matters; about the Town Major; discussed that difficult question as to why all the English officers in France were bachelors; also the rumour that Australian soldiers would be again billeted in the village soon, which would mean much more money flowing into the till of Madame's estaminet. Slowly, very gradually, the interpreter guided the conversation round to *the* affair. Poor Madame! what a terrible thing to happen to a woman of her irreproachable character. Monsieur Junod informed her how shocked and pained all her neighbours were, particularly the women (as a matter of fact, he told me the latter were agreed that it served her right, and they were not at all surprised).

Of course, such an insult must be punished. The man must be taught that a Frenchwoman's honour is sacred. And the corporal; what a pity, too, that so gallant a fellow should die, for, of course, Madame knew the stern, though just, English law for this vile crime— death. He would be tried and then shot at dawn behind the church. Madame asked if some lesser punishment could not be inflicted; for she was really a kind woman and not vindictive. But no; Monsieur had made a close and particular study of English military law, and there was but one punishment. In fact, Monsieur appeared to be also well informed of the family history of the culprit, for he spoke in lowered voice of the corporal's widowed mother in England, so shortly to be childless as well as husbandless. As a matter of crude fact, the corporal, a foundling and a waster from birth, was the child of the Board of Guardians of the Parish of East Ham, which would have been very resigned to their loss had it ever come to their knowledge. Monsieur next became reminiscent. He recalled that gallant affair on the Somme, when the corporal had rushed boldly forward at a very critical situation, bayonet in hand, and killed—he couldn't remember exactly how many Boches, and had afterwards been publicly congratulated and thanked by his Colonel. Madame was interested, for hitherto she thought the corporal had spent his whole military service in the safe and unheroic duties of sanitation—which, indeed, he had. Madame's face began to show a less stern expression, though she was still inclined to let the law take its course.

This was the moment when Monsieur Junod's inside knowledge of women came in. Exactly what he said or how he said it, I do not know. The pith of his argument was this:

Regrettable as, of course, the whole affair was, there was this to be said for the corporal's good taste. Madame herself was famous for her good looks, and who could blame a young, a gallant, and a brave young man for falling violently in love with her? Some men, less particular, might have taken a fancy for Darkie, that bold hussy who tried all she could to attract the men, or that quiet, sly puss, Berthe. But no, the corporal took no notice of those two younger women, and had fallen in love with Madame. Monsieur, who seemed to know everything, was able to tell Madame in strict confidence how the corporal had confided to him that for many months—in fact, since he first saw her—he had been in love with the beautiful proprietress of the Estaminet de Réunion des Blanchisseuses, and how this smouldering passion had, alas, suddenly overwhelmed his reason, with the dreadful result that the poor fellow, so brave, such a boy, must die a scoundrel's death.

But die he must, and rightly too. Madame's honour must be vindicated.

But all ended happily. Madame was generous, the corporal forgiven, and Monsieur's profound knowledge of women was recognised and acclaimed by all.

A few weeks afterwards the Town Major signed the necessary forms, allotting a certain room as a billet, in an estaminet called la Réunion des Blanchisseuses, to a certain corporal (sanitary duties), the proprietor having no objection to the arrangement.

The whole of my time at Vieuxbec was not taken up with lectures at the School of Sanitation, going for country rambles, skinning animals or gossiping with Monsieur Junod. As G.O.C. Rats, Second Army, there was enough and more than enough to occupy my days. Almost every unit in the whole Army area had to be visited, infantry, artillery, engineers, ammunition parks, transport lines, etcetera, as well as all the Field Ambulances. Commanding officers had to be interviewed and given instructions how the rat traps were to be used when, if ever, they were issued. All this while I was designing and experimenting with new types of trap. Any feeling of indifference or hostility there may have been at first to the scheme was compensated by the interest and encouragement I was getting from

England, which was soon explained when I heard from my father what he had been doing.

At this period one of his best friends and his almost daily companion was Lord Haldane, who always lent a sympathetic ear to my father's news about me and what I was doing, and he heard all about the rat campaign. Apparently Lord Haldane had once written a letter about me and my rats to his friend Sir Alfred Keogh, the Director General of the Army Medical Service, who approved so much of the scheme that he forwarded the letter, with a covering one of his own, to Lord Kitchener. What happened after that I do not know, but it was not surprising if my work later came to be regarded in a more serious light and that I was granted almost every facility I asked for.

It was about this time that the authorities were becoming alarmed by the spread of mange among the horses, due to a parasite, one of the sarcoptes. This very contagious disease was spreading from one horse-line to another and brought the condition of the horses to a very low ebb. To prevent this, measures were taken to isolate all infected stables or horse-lines, and all infected horses were treated by being dipped in tanks of strong chemical solutions, but still the disease extended.

Part of my work at this time was to examine large numbers of dead rats, and I noticed that some of these were mangy, and it naturally occurred to me that rats might very easily be acting as carriers of the disease, by passing from one stable to another, and so infecting horses, straw or fodder. As this matter was one entirely to do with the veterinary corps and nothing to do with the medical branch, I was anxious to make quite sure my hypothesis was sound before reporting it. Unfortunately I confided my suspicions to a pushing little R.A.M.C. staff major (not a regular) who, thinking he saw in it something which might bring kudos to himself, behind my back and without my knowledge, wrote a hurried report and rushed with it to a Director of the Army Veterinary Service who, disliking the man and resenting his interference, refused to discuss the matter with him and shewed him the door.

Owing to this self-seeking and tactless busybody I had to go very quietly with my further experiments.

As my father took such a keen interest in all I was doing I told him in a letter my theory that rats infected horses with mange, though nothing about the interfering major. The result was that my father spoke about it to Sir Ray Lankester, who was at once interested and suggested I should make microscopical examinations of the sarcoptes of the rat and the horse, not only to settle the question whether horses contracted mange from rats, but to ascertain whether the sarcoptes contained the bacillus of a rare disease which was then beginning to infect the troops—*spirochætosis icterohæmorrhagica*, an infective jaundice recently discovered in Japan and believed to be spread by rats. If this could be proved, he said I would have made an important discovery. At this time I had no microscope nor any means for carrying out research work, but owing to the efforts of Sir Ray Lankester and Sir Walter Morley Fletcher, the Secretary to the Medical Research Council, I was in due time given the use of a laboratory near Poperinghe. My father, although no man of science and certainly no catcher of rats, left no stone unturned to help me in my project.

Amongst other experiments I was anxious to try, was the effect of different scents in attracting rats to traps. After some trouble he managed to procure and send me small quantities of various essential oils, as cloves, aniseed and caraway seed. But there was another scent I wanted to try, which I had heard was used by trappers in the North of Canada, called oil of rhodium. For many weeks my father tried to get me some of this with no success. He wrote to me that he was told there was not a drop to be procured in London for love or money. During his enquiries he had learned that this oil was made from the root of a convolvulus which only grew in the Canary Islands and that each year the whole crop was sold to a merchant at Leipzig. After trying everywhere he at last applied to the firm of Messrs. Rubeck, the largest merchants of such oils in the City, and on March 23rd he wrote to me:

> "I have succeeded in getting you a bottle of rhodium! I hope you will congratulate me. It is believed to be the only specimen of oil of rhodium left in the City of London."

This winter had been a very cold one, the whole country was iron-bound for weeks, but at last as the days became longer they became warmer, and the belated but longed for spring arrived; and with it the belovèd birds.

Every few days I had to go to Abeel to discuss matters with the D.D.M.S. of the X Corps. I used to go there on foot, walking the three miles through the meadows, along the banks of a winding brook. I am afraid I wasted a lot of time doing so, for there were many distractions by the way.

In the winter I would often flush a woodcock or a wisp of snipe, and once for ten minutes I watched a water-rail skulking along the banks of the stream. By February a few wagtails, the white and the pied, were to be seen and flocks of one hundred or more lapwings. By the middle of March the birds were singing, blackbirds, song thrushes, yellow hammers, meadow pipits and larks, the crested as well as the skylark.

One fine day my friend Junod and I went to explore the wooded sides of Mont des Cats. There were not many birds to be seen, but we had a wonderful view, through our glasses, of a small flock of hawfinches sunning themselves on the top of a bare oak tree. We saw also a pair of tree sparrows, such gentlemen in comparison to their vulgar cousins of the house top, and listened to the delightful clear trilling of a cirl bunting.

It was only a few days before my mother's birthday, and I managed to buy her a present at the monastery which stands—or stood—on the summit of the mount. She had a great fondness for cheese, liked nothing better than to sample a new kind, and was always discovering new cheeses. Whenever I was able I got her a novelty. The rarest I ever gave her was a goat's milk cheese I obtained in Formentera, the smallest inhabited island of the Balearic group. I am sure it was the first of its kind that had ever been exported to England, and for more than one good reason. All across Spain and France and Kent the prize had to travel suspended by a string outside the railway carriage window. My mother was very nice about that cheese, but I think it appealed more to her as a collector of rarities than by its delicacy of flavour.

The Mont des Cats cheese was one of much less potency than that of Formentera, being more like a cream cheese, and passed the base censor quite successfully.

Whenever I heard that the 69th Field Ambulance was in the neighbourhood, I used to ride over to see them. My only other social visits were to a very friendly squadron of yeomanry, the North Irish Horse, who were acting as Corps Cavalry, and who had a mess at Vieuxbec. I often spent the evenings with them playing a simple game they taught me called Blind Hookey or Uncle Sam. This is one of those games which appears so guileless and in which even the worst duffer at card games can join at once and be fleeced, and is, I believe, the one employed by the villain in melodramas to ruin the honest village lad.

One evening when it was decided to stop playing, one more round was proposed and agreed to, and a special prize offered. In one corner of the room stood a deal box in which the squadron fox-terrier bitch was at that very moment in the throes of labour. The prize was to be one of the puppies, the winner to make his own choice. Perhaps because I had lost consistently the whole evening, perhaps because I did not want a dog, the cards turned all in my favour. Just as the last card was played and I had been proclaimed winner, the regimental M.O. who was in attendance on the little bitch, informed the company that the interesting event had come to a happy conclusion, and we inspected the litter of four.

They were an odd lot of puppies, no two appearing to belong to the same breed. This curious fact the doctor explained by telling us that during the period of her courting the squadron had moved from place to place, never remaining more than one day at any.

After very carefully inspecting the litter, I chose the new-born puppy which looked to me most like a fox-terrier. As soon as ever it could be weaned, Bob Church brought it to my billet and undertook the duties of a wet nurse, and henceforward Jim became a member of the family. He went through all the fascinating but all too short stages of puppyhood, and eventually turned out a very nice, smart little fox-terrier and took a very keen and practical interest in the rat campaign.

Amongst other friends I made at Vieuxbec was the local poacher. We first met one day in a little wood. I wondered what he was doing there, and I expect he must have wondered what brought an English officer there. Like so many poachers he was a grave man, with courtly manners and a profound knowledge of the habits of wild animals. When I got to know him well, after some time and francs spent in a small auberge, I asked him if he could get me a rabbit. This may seem a modest request, but these animals, which used to swarm over Flanders before the War, had been all but exterminated. I had never in over two years seen one, nor been able to get a specimen for my collection.

Before long my friend the poacher caught me a rabbit, as well as a pole cat, and several black rats.

It was he who took me to see a cock fight one Sunday afternoon. I had never seen one before and have no desire to see another. The mains took place on the ground, in a ring formed by onlooking Flemish farmers and a few British soldiers. There was a lot of betting in small sums over each one, but it was a brutal sight to see such handsome, gallant birds stabbing at each other with the long sharp steel spurs which were strapped to their legs.

Spring seemed as if it would never come. In the early days of April blizzards still continued and deep drifts of snow lay beside the hedges. The most conspicuous birds were the magpies, which roamed about in robber bands of thirty and forty, and all too many jays.

On April 9th, I heard the first spring migrant, a chiff-chaff, who had come in spite of the cold. Four days later, on one of my official walks to Abeel, I found a nest of a song thrush in which were four eggs. Chiff-chaffs were becoming more numerous every day, in spite of the gales and occasional snow storms. On the 19th the first swallows appeared in the village street, when two flew up and down outside the mess and I heard the first willow wren, so spring had really come at last. From now onwards the weather improved and each day brought its new arrivals and its new joy.

Redstarts, grey wagtails, tree-pipits, and at last a cuckoo came. The last day of April was a red-letter day. It was the first day of really hot sunshine, and I decided to visit the D.D.M.S. at Abeel.

The first newcomer I met was a whinchat, gladly

singing its trilling song, a mixture of harsh and clear notes. Its song brought back memories of Iviza, in the Balearic Islands, which is full of singing whinchats in the spring. During that short walk I must have seen forty whinchats which had probably come in a rush the night before. There were other new migrants as well, a lesser whitethroat and several common whitethroats and cuckoos, which were calling one to another, and easily seen, for there was still not a leaf on the trees to hide them.

In the little stream I flushed a water-rail and a greenshank. As though this banquet of birds was not excuse enough to delay me, there was more to come. As I happened to be lying face downwards on the bank of the rivulet I noticed a small dark object swim rapidly down stream, under water, and wondered whatever it could be. I kept perfectly still, no thoughts of an impatient D.D.M.S. disturbed me, and presently I was rewarded. The dark submerged object was returning rapidly up stream, and when only a couple of feet from my eyes it emerged on a tiny shingle beach, shook itself like a retriever dog, and turned out to be a very handsome water shrew, dressed all in black velvet, and looking as dry as if it had never been in the water at all.

When at last I got to Abeel I apologised to the D.D.M.S. for having been unavoidably detained but did not bother him with details as to what had made me late.

What a day that was. On my way back to Vieuxbec I saw two blue-headed wagtails, which were so tame they allowed me to watch and admire them within a few feet.

When at last I reached the village that evening, there was yet one more treat in store, for several swifts had arrived during my absence, and were flying up and down the street.

This memorable day with birds was to be the last for some time. Next morning a telegram came from General Porter, the D.M.S., to go and see him at Hazebrouck at one o'clock. He was most friendly and after lunch shewed me a most flattering letter from Sir Walter Fletcher, to say that anything I needed in the way of scientific instruments or apparatus would be supplied by the Medical Research Council.

The General also told me another welcome piece of news, that at last the first consignment of rat traps, the sort I had asked for, had arrived, and that I could set about their distribution at once.

Things now began to move with rapidity. The very next day the General came to Vieuxbec with Colonel Stephens, of the Medical Research Council, and after a talk told me he was arranging for me to go to the 10th Casualty Clearing Station at Remy Siding, just outside Poperinghe, to work in a Mobile Laboratory there with the late Adrian Stokes, the bacteriologist.

In the meanwhile I was kept busy from morning to night, allotting the traps to various units and instructing the officers and N.C.O.'s who were to be responsible for them, and who were to supervise the setting of them. It was, of course, a pity the traps had not been procurable and issued at the beginning of the year. Every rat which ought to have been caught in January and February would now be father or mother of one or more families.

But all the same a great improvement had already followed the orders I had initiated for food protection. Every food store was now protected by wire-netting, and in many places where rats used to swarm, scarcely one was to be found.

CHAPTER V

Remy Siding

EARLY in May, I left Vieuxbec and my friends there and took up my quarters at the 10th C.C.S. where I for the first time met Adrian Stokes with whom I was to share the Mobile Laboratory. I had never been in a C.C.S. before. They had an immense mess full of doctors, amongst whom I found one or two old Bart's friends.

The same evening that I arrived I rather shocked the colonel by going out with half-a-dozen mouse-traps my mother had just sent me from Barnstaple, to try my luck in pastures new.

There was a delightful little stream which ran below the hospital, winding between steep banks, covered with willow trees and small bushes, alive with birds.

My mornings at Remy Siding were spent dissecting dead rats which had been sent in from different places, and in the afternoons I visited various camps and billets about the traps. The rat dissecting was not all a bouquet of flowers, for the weather had become very hot and many of the corpses were far from fresh by the time they reached me. Stokes was just then doing some original research work on the obscure endemic disease which had begun to appear among the troops, and went by the formidable name of *Spirochætosis icterohæmorrhagica*, alias, in English, Weil's disease or infective jaundice. He had just made the important discovery that the microbe of this disease was to be found in the kidneys of sick rats caught in the army area.

The common brown, trench or sewer rat, amongst its other unpleasant habits, has that of micturating on any food it does not eat, a habit which resulted in infecting bread, cheese and other eatables which were left unguarded, and so giving the disease to men who ate the infected food afterwards. The discovery by Stokes was one of the earliest practical results of the order that all sick or dead rats were to be sent to the laboratory for examination.

The inquests we held on these dead rats proved that most of them had died from "natural causes," that is, a blow with a stick. But one day a dead rat arrived in a box from Reninghelst, just behind Dickebusch. I knew the M.O. who had sent it, and one glance at the corpse was enough to tell Stokes and myself what had been in his mind when he sent it.

As this dead rat played its part in the Great War I cannot ignore it, and shall be compelled to describe certain technical matters, which shall be done as briefly as possible.

The thing which at once raised our suspicions about this particular rat was the fact that the glands of the axillae and groins were swollen and soft; suggesting to our minds bubonic plague.

It is well known that bubonic plague is carried by a particular rat flea—*Xenopsylla cheopsis*—which swallows the bacillus of the disease when it sucks the blood of a plague-infected rat. When the rat dies and its body becomes cold, the flea leaves in search of another warm-blooded host to live and feed upon. If the flea meets a human being, it sucks his blood and thus infects him with the plague. Hitherto it had been believed that the black rat, *Epimys rattus*, and not the common brown rat, *Epimys norvegicus*, was the species which took part in this triple arrangement.

It was known to the army authorities that several German divisions had just been rushed across Europe from the Russian front, where bubonic plague was endemic, and that one of these was in the line opposite Reninghelst, so that the possibility did exist of a rat infected with plague crossing the few yards which separated the two front lines of trenches and introducing the disease amongst our troops. The danger, though very remote, was not by any means to be ignored, and Adrian Stokes at once got to work.

Firstly he injected into a guinea-pig an emulsion made of the rat's swollen glands. In due time the guinea-pig became ill, developed a high temperature and began to shew definite signs and symptoms compatible with bubonic plague, and died. This was exciting, and further experiments were carried out. A few drops of a preparation made from the dead guinea-pig were injected into another healthy guinea-pig and into a white rat. In due course both these animals also developed the same symptoms, and died, and the microscopical examination of the blood and exudations of the two animals shewed a micro-organism exactly corresponding to that found in the first guinea-pig and in the original rat, and closely resembled the *bacillus pestis* of bubonic plague.

Stokes and I then held a consultation. We did not want to be thought alarmists, but at the same time the matter appeared to be serious, and if eventually the disease did prove to be the plague, it would have been a crime to have delayed reporting our suspicions. So we agreed to carry out one more series of experiments and if these led to the same results, to send in a report forthwith.

So the experiments were repeated with exactly the same results as before, and we set down to write our report to the Medical Director of the Second Army. It was not an easy thing to do, for we were far from certain that what we had been dealing with was plague, so we simply made out a full statement of our experiments and results and left the authorities to draw their own deductions.

For forty-eight hours we heard nothing, when suddenly a full colonel rushed in to ask excitedly what on earth we had been up to, why he had not been told about it, and were we quite mad, and that Sir William Leishman himself, the adviser in pathology to the B.E.F., was on his way from the base that very day to make enquiries.

In due time Colonel Leishman appeared and I doubt if two junior officers ever felt quite so small or such utter duffers as did Stokes and I, by the time he left us.

He began by asking if either of us had ever seen a case of bubonic plague, which we neither of us ever had. Then he looked down the microscopes under which blood and other films had been set out ready for him. After a glance down each he declared our case to be only one of "chicken plague," an obscure disease harmless to man, and then without mincing his words, he summed us both up as a couple of witless alarmists.

Out of the laboratory he strode, leaving Stokes and me looking and feeling two unspeakable fools.

A quarter of an hour later he was back again, saying he wanted to have one more look down the microscopes. This time he made a much longer examination of the slides, and carefully studied Stokes' beautiful charts and reports, which consoled us somewhat for his former brusqueness. After spending nearly half an hour doing this, he went off again without another word or saying good-bye but taking with him our notes and several microscope slides. We had little to comfort ourselves with beyond the fact that at all events his second visit shewed that the problem was not quite so simple as had first appeared. After this we were well chaffed over our case of "plague" and for several days it was the standing joke at the C.C.S. next door, and we also received a sharp reprimand, principally because we had gone straight with our report to headquarters, instead of letting it percolate slowly upwards through the various official channels, by which time, had the case turned out to be bubonic plague, several precious days would have been wasted.

Not long after this episode I got home leave, and went to London. One day at the Savile Club, I entered the smoking-room to find Sir Ray Lankester taking his usual lunch of a glass of whisky and water and ham sandwiches.

"Well, Philip," he called out, "you have done a nice thing!"

"What can that be?" I asked.

"Oh, only that you have cost the country five thousand pounds."

Then I heard from him the end of the story of the rat of Reninghelst.

Apparently after Colonel Leishman left us crushed and humiliated at Remy Siding, he had returned to the base and no doubt on his journey he considered the matter and decided to make further examination of our slides and reports at his own laboratory.

Leishman was not only a distinguished bacteriologist and man of science but a good soldier and a man of the world as well. He must have seen that if by any chance, however improbable, his diagnosis of chicken plague was wrong and this rat really was a case of bubonic plague, the results might be calamitous.

With this in mind he would be wise to be on the safe side, and that no doubt was why the Lister Institute of Preventive Medicine, over which Ray Lankester presided, received an order for the immediate preparation of some fifty thousand doses of Haffkine's plague vaccine.

I was kept very busily occupied at Remy Siding.

At the end of each day there were a number of letters to be answered, instructions to be written to the various A.D.'S M.S. of the Army, and notes to be made of the day's work.

There was so much to do that sometimes I felt inclined to grumble but when I did I had only to remember what my friends were going through at Messines Ridge to feel humbled, and grateful for my interesting job, and get on with it.

Great numbers of wounded were passing through the C.C.S. and when I could spare an hour I used to give anæsthetics to help the overworked staff.

Close by our camp was a Divisional Rest Camp where sick or lightly wounded men were sent so that they would not be lost to their units, which happened if they were sent down to the base.

One day I found six troopers from my old regiment the Surrey Yeomanry there, who had been drafted into a battalion of the Queen's (R.W.S.) regiment. In their honour Bob Church and I gave them a tea party, and we took turns to act as waiters.

They were delightful boys and enjoyed talking over the old days at Dorking which already seemed so long ago, and telling me about their adventures at Messines where they had been wounded.

They consumed enormous quantities of bloater paste sandwiches, tinned lobster, Japanese tinned crab, cake and chocolate, and countless cups of tea. They were as happy as a lot of schoolboys on a picnic and apparently none the worse for their orgy. They were all very much amused at an account which had appeared in the newspapers of how Mr. Lloyd George had been expressly waked up at his home in Surrey in order to hear the explosion when Hill 60 was blown up. We at Remy Siding, who slept on the ground out of doors and were not more than ten miles away, had heard nothing of it.

The areas behind Poperinghe had by now taken on a settled appearance of permanency. A large town had grown up of tents, marquees, big and little huts, canteens and post-offices, intersected by new well-made roads and light railways. The population consisted of English-speaking camp-followers; R.A.M.C., A.S.C. minders of dumps, road makers and hundreds of men employed in the scores of occupations which went to serve an army in the trenches. Gardening had become all the rage, and wherever you looked you saw uniformed men, from colonels to corporals, watering and tending their allotments. Some went in for growing flowers—others, more utilitarian, for vegetables. One of the doctors at the C.C.S. had dug a pit, and was trying to grow mushrooms from some spawn he had planted in a hotbed of manure.

Heavy betting went on as to the date the first mushroom would appear, but no money had changed hands by the time I left.

In the daytime peace reigned, but at night German airmen flew about dropping disconcerting bombs, apparently haphazard.

In addition to the work of the rat campaign I was now put in charge of a new and strange enquiry. This I feel is scarcely a fit subject for a book that may be read by other than doctors or parasitologists, and yet how am I, a camp-follower who tries to tell a plain unvarnished narrative, to pass it by? It is a subject calling for delicate handling, and I fear to botch it with my unskilful pen. Elia could have done it, or Mr. E. V. Lucas, who with his niceness of phrase and delicacy of touch, would write an article in the *Sunday Times* which could be read aloud to any family in Great Britain without raising a blush or giving rise to a hint of indelicacy. But I am a mere blunderer beside those two, and can but do my feeble best. I confess I fear to start, but it is no good to hesitate longer, and so here goes.

The subject of this enquiry was *Lice*. This curse of all armies, this defier of doctors and chemists, *pediculus vestimenti* swarmed in myriads on the bodies and on the clothes of our heroes in the trenches.

In vain were hot baths given; in vain were the clothes baked in ovens or "de-loused" in other ways; lice continued to live and thrive in spite of everything.

The idea of the enquiry came direct from the War Office. Some ingenious theorist had thought to impregnate "gents' underwear" with poisonous chemicals which he fondly hoped would prove so noxious to the filthy louse that it would perish if brought in contact with it. Numbers of vests and drawers arrived and I was given carte-blanche to carry out experiments to test them. First I put up a small camp of bell-tents in an isolated spot. I then asked for and got as a staff one sergeant, two corporals and four R.A.M.C. privates, all guaranteed to be free from the disgusting wingless insect.

Victims for the experiment might be thought difficult to get, as only volunteers were called for. Far from it, the cause of science and the opportunity of a respite from the trenches brought so many willing offers that I was able to pick and choose.

In the end I picked out twenty Scotch soldiers in kilts; no better material could have been found for this kind of enquiry. I also got, though with far greater difficulty, a dozen soldiers quite free from lice. To make their secluded life as cheerful as possible I put up a small canteen, procured a football and a gramophone. We did our own cooking, and what little there was of it, our own laundry.

Fortunately for me it was decided that the commanding officer was not required to sleep in the camp. This is no place to enter minutely into the dreadful things which went on at our camp. My heroes played their parts bravely and willingly. Some of the unlousy were made to sleep in the same blankets with the lousy, others slept in pyjamas, which I had had soaked in carbolic acid, wrapped in blankets which it was better not to inspect too closely. In the day time my brave men wore the special vests and pants sent by the War-Office. It was all very thorough, very scientific and every experiment was carefully checked. Each morning my band of brothers went a long march, I at their head to steer them past estaminets and prevent them from mixing with other soldiers, which might have spoiled the results.

The weather was very hot, but we did our ten miles a day. I had been generous with mouth organs, and when we started from our camp we made a brave show and noise. After a mile or two some of the men began to complain of an itching of the skin. As they became more hot and moist, the music died away, for although a mouth organ can be played with but one hand, it can not be when held only between the teeth. Often I had to permit the more frenzied to remove their underclothes and march carrying these in their hands, but this favour was only granted in the most extreme cases. Apart from the marches they lived a care-free life. There was football in the afternoon, and a concert each evening, to distract their minds from dwelling on the night to follow. They all put on weight, their physique and appetites improved; the same applied, unfortunately, to the lice. The experiment had failed, once again Pediculus Vestimenti triumphed; but as the wise Aristotle wrote : " One should not be childishly contemptuous of the study of the most insignificant animal."

At the end of July this semi-civilian life at Remy Siding came to a sudden end. Rumours of battle were in the air, and all rat-campaigns and even the rats themselves were soon to be left far behind, as the invincible armies of the allies advanced towards Germany.

My own ambulance and division were now in another Army, the Fifth, and to my hot indignation I was ordered to join a strange field ambulance in another division, and this in spite of a solemn promise that when the rat campaign ended I should be sent back to my own field ambulance, of which I was second-in-command. In spite of all my protests, away I had to go, and to add insult to injury, my faithful batman was sent back to the 69th, so that when I reached my new ambulance I had not a single friend there. The colonel of this unit was a very different one from either I had served under in the 69th. On the death of Nimmo Walker his place had been taken by the charming and very efficient Colonel G. H. L. Hammerton, under whom it was a pleasure to serve. The commander of this other field-ambulance was gentle and dreamy but inefficient, and seemed to take little interest in his ambulance and left everything to his second-in-command, with the result that the whole unit was slack and without *esprit de corps*.

What made matters still more unsatisfactory was that being a territorial I had precedence of rank over all the other officers of the field-ambulance except the colonel, which made them just as anxious to get rid of me as I was to go back to my own people.

But I had a friend at court I had not reckoned on.

General Babington, who still commanded the 23rd Division, somehow got to hear of my plight, probably through Colonel Blackham, and wrote a personal letter to the D.M.S. of the army I was now in, asking to have me back, because, he said, " Gosse has so many friends in my Division." How a general who was engaged in fighting battles as General Babington then was could find time to bother about an obscure Captain in the R.A.M.C. such as I, is difficult to understand, but goes far to explain the extraordinary affection in which he was held by all ranks who served under him. The result of his letter was that I returned to my friends, of whom none was more glad to welcome me back than my faithful Bob Church. Without waiting for orders he began to fix up my camp-bed under a tree in the furthest corner of an orchard, by a farm-house in which the ambulance was billeted, and it was good once again to hear him singing, " Oh I am a great success with the girls."

My recollection of the weeks which followed has become confused and blurred with time. I retain indistinct impressions of going with the 23rd Division into the line, of coming out again, of marching away to back areas, and then returning hurriedly to the Salient.

There was much " liveliness " both in the trenches

and in the regions behind. Bright moonlight nights became to be hated, for they meant no sleep nor rest from the Boche airplanes which dropped bombs on camps and billets for many miles back.

One clear picture I can still call up, and there must be thousands alive who remember it as well.

It happened on a clear, sunny day, with here and there a few low clouds, and the arc of the Salient clearly defined by our observation balloons. All at once an enemy airplane popped out of a cloud, flew straight at a balloon and set it on fire. It then flew rapidly all along the line, shooting at and setting on fire half a dozen of our balloons, and then disappeared into another cloud and was gone, leaving behind the unique spectacle of half a dozen observers in the air at once, as they floated to the ground in their parachutes. For some reason or other the sight of these blazing balloons brought back to my mind a story Rider Haggard once told us, at supper at my parents' house. He had been talking about the stupidity of the East-Anglian peasant, particularly those of Suffolk, and as an example of it told us the following tale.

It was in the days when certain adventurous people used to go up in balloons, and one of these found himself drifting slowly over some fields not more than thirty or forty feet above the ground. He had not the least idea where he was, so seeing some labourers at work in a field below him, he hung over the side of the basket and called down, "Hi there, can you tell me where I am?" After a moment or two of silence one of the men shouted back, in broad Suffolk, "You be up in a balloon, lad."

While we were at the mill at Vlamertinghe I was sent to give anæsthetics at No. 3 Australian C.C.S. which was, for an operating hospital, in a fairly forward position. When I arrived there I found I was to give anæsthetics for the distinguished South Australian surgeon Lieut.-Colonel, now Sir Henry Newland, who specialized in operations on the head.

I was only with this cheerful " outfit " for a few days and the principal impression I have is that every hour or two of the day and night all work was stopped, while the whole staff, from colonel to orderly, went off to drink tea.

About this time the persistent rumours of the entry of a new ally were confirmed by the appearance in the fighting area of an unfamiliar uniform. The United States of America may have been a long while making up their minds about coming into the War, but when they did, it was with no half-measures. Slow to anger, when roused at last they were more ruthless than any other of the belligerents.

In all the other armies, the fighting men, the infantry and field artillery were put in the vanguard, and in the rear came the medical corps; the camp-followers. But such was the grim bloodthirstiness of this new army that the front rank was formed of American Army surgeons and the fighting men followed behind later on.

Two or three were allotted to each British division, not only to spread terror amongst the Germans, but to gain instruction and to relieve British medical officers for other duties. Two of these American doctors reported to us at the mill at Vlamertinghe before being posted to our divisional infantry. One, Major Browne, was a Southerner; the other, who came from a city in the Middle West, was named, I think, Rabbit, or it may have been Barrett; my memory on the point is not clear. He was a very hearty man, took a commendable pride in his " home-town " and was an inveterate sightseer. He never stirred without a copy of Baedeker's guide to Belgium in his hand, and was determined to make the most of his first visit to Europe. Filled with this desire he pressed me to go with him, then and there, to visit historic Ypres. I declined his invitation, telling him bluntly that I had seen all I wanted of Ypres, and that nothing at all except duty or definite orders would induce me to enter that woeful and perilous place again. I strongly advised him to leave Ypres well alone, assuring him he would get plenty of opportunities to visit that city later on.

But nothing I could say would deter him, and off he went directly after lunch, guide book in hand, to explore Ypres, promising to be back in time for dinner. He returned earlier, in a motor-ambulance, having seen Ypres, lost his guide book and his left leg.

When the American army surgeons were posted to our infantry battalions, they proved a great success and were much liked by our men.

Major Browne I got to know quite well. He was the type of Southerner you read about in American novels, tall, dignified, with charming manners.

His great-grandfather had been Governor of Alabama seventy years earlier, when my grandfather had landed at Mobile with no possessions but a few Canadian dollars, a butterfly net and a letter of introduction to a planter at Dallas. There my grandfather had set up a small school for the children of the better-to-do planters, and spent all his spare time collecting and painting butterflies, until owing to his views on slavery he was given a polite but unambiguous hint to go elsewhere. Afterwards he wrote an interesting little book *Letters from Alabama* in which he recounted his adventures, and described the birds, flowers and insects he had seen there.

I used to reproach Major Browne with the unkindness of his ancestor who had driven mine from the country.

After a few weeks at Vlamertinghe we marched with the rest of the Division to a pleasant district somewhere in the neighbourhood of Cassel. The autumn weather was at its best, and although we never stopped more than two nights at the same place we all enjoyed the change from the Ypres neighbourhood. Our work was principally to set up small temporary hospitals where men slightly ill or whose feet prevented them marching came for a few days' rest and treatment.

Our ambulance now boasted a silver band, some thirty strong, very strong, and behind it we marched hither and thither like the troubadours of old. On the long, dusty, tiring marches when our band would have been an inspiration and a help, it was dumb, but whenever we approached a village it burst into music, the drummer banged his big drum and the martial strains of " Colonel Bogey "—their only tune—brought the population to their doorsteps; girls waved, dogs barked, and happy children marched by our sides, until the last house was passed. Then the music stopped, and we trudged

on in silence until another village hove in sight, when
" Colonel Bogey " resounded once more.

Eventually we reached the country behind St. Omer,
the farthest the division had ever been from the trenches.
Nothing could have been more lovely or more peaceful,
the little meadows, the tall hedges basking in the August
sunshine.

Marching from Frémont to Est Mont a sporting dog
which had joined us flushed a bevy of quails, which flew
over our heads. In a quarry near le Comminal, in the
Forest d'Eperlique, there were some sand martins,
and in a small wood near by, I saw several green wood-
peckers.

A few miles farther on I saw a British officer in uniform
walking slowly along beside a tall hedge. On one
arm he carried a small hawk. The hawk was probably
a merlin and the quarry no doubt thrushes and blackbirds.
As we were on a divisional march I could not fall out
and talk to him about his hawking as I should like to
have done. I often have wondered who that officer
was and how he managed to bring a trained hawk to
France.

It was during our wanderings when I was billeted
in a small cottage at l'Eperlique, that I committed my
crime.

Unlike most of my French hosts, the peasants who
inhabited this cottage were uncouth and unfriendly.
But the room I slept in had one curious and unexpected
feature, for the walls were lined with books from floor
to ceiling; all bound alike, in rough blue boards, backed
by old vellum, on which were traces of ancient handwriting. Naturally I examined these, and found they

had all belonged to Jean Baptiste David Van Vineg. His name was written in almost every volume. The books were thickly covered in dust and evidently the present owners took neither care of nor interest in them. I made several attempts to find out about them but my hosts knew nothing, or at all events had no wish to discuss them with me, or in fact to meet any of my attempts to be friends.

Amongst these books I found one charming little duodecimo volume of natural history stories for children, illustrated by a coloured frontispiece depicting a pink Adam standing naked in the Garden of Eden, surrounded by all sorts of surprisingly coloured animals, birds and reptiles, and there were many quaint wood blocks as well. Its title ran " *Buffon* des petits enfants, ou précis élémentaire de l'histoire naturelle. Edition ornée de 80 figures."

Inside the covers Monsieur Van Vineg had written his name with many flourishes, in four different places and with many different spellings. This little volume lies open before me as I write, and I herewith make full confession.

I stole that book; and wish I had not. I tried to persuade the owners to sell it to me, but they refused.

It was a dreadful thing to do, and every time I have taken the little volume off its shelf during the sixteen years since my conscience has pricked me.

I think on looking back it is the only thing I ever stole except matches and writing paper, and if other thieves have suffered with their consciences as I have, robbery as a profession must be a wretched one. I feel now that I can understand what goes on in the minds of those otherwise respectable married ladies who live in the suburbs and going up to London for a day's shopping, are suddenly seized with an uncontrollable desire for some article they see in a shop and steal it.

Again and again did I put Buffon back on the dusty shelf, but again and again I pulled it out and longed to possess it. I have got no pleasure out of it, and wish I could return it to the rightful owners. Sometimes I think I will send it by post—anonymously—to the maire of Eperlique, but probably the village is too small to boast such a dignitary. Nor do I know if the present occupiers of the cottage are called Van Vineg.

At other times I have had serious thoughts of taking the book to France and setting out to find Eperlique and then if I could recognise the cottage again, I would knock at the door, quickly hand the book to the person who opened it, and without a word of explanation leap into my car and drive away.

If these lines are ever printed and if, which is most improbable, they should be read by a Frenchman, I beg him to write to me to say how I can get rid of this pestilential War souvenir.

It is now the fashion to return all spoil and plunder to their rightful owners and I would like to do the same with mine.

Although this was my only act of plunder during the whole War, I had to suffer from the suspicion of theft for another deed which was perfectly above board.

In the summer of 1916, when the division went south to take part in the battle of the Somme, we spent a night on the way at the shattered city of Albert, famous for its leaning Virgin. The house we occupied had been considerably knocked about. The whole of one outer wall of one of the bedrooms had been blown out by a shell and half the roof was missing. While wandering about this dilapidated building I managed to climb into the loft. There I found exposed to rain, wind and sun, a heap of books, lying mildewed on the floor. To a bibliophile this was a sad and distressing spectacle, and I knelt down to search for anything worth while rescuing. These books were not of any particular interest or value but I found and kept two old volumes of travels which had escaped damage.

One day, after the War, I happened to mention this incident to Lord Haldane who, being a lawyer and Lord High Chancellor of England, pulled me up sharply for using the word "rescue" to describe my act of salvage, and with a twinkle in his eye suggested a harsher word instead. Though I hotly denied the reproach, he was not to be convinced of my innocence and I thought it best to allow him to remain in ignorance of the affair of the little book from Eperlique.

And so it often happens, one steals and is unsuspected and undetected, while for an honest act of rescue one is pointed at with an accusing finger as a thief.

Before the end of the month we were once more back in the Salient, with our main dressing station at Dickebusch now become an "unhealthy" and most unpleasant spot. During the day time it was shelled by big high-velocity guns, while at night Boche airplanes dropped great bombs hither and thither.

Naturally I went off to visit the lake near by, now almost covered with reed beds, from which came the calls of various water birds, amongst which I recognised those of the great crested grebe.

One bright moonlight night, during heavy bombing all round our camp, amidst the crash of exploding bombs, the roar of low-flying German planes and the barking of our anti-aircraft guns and machine guns, I heard the lovely wild cry of curlews flying high above in the dark sky.

Except for the birds in the lake, the curlews, a few yellow wagtails and one cooing turtle dove which for some reason had not yet left for the south, there was nothing at all to recommend Dickebusch, and we were not sorry when we left it to return to the neighbourhood of St. Omer.

This time we went further north, with our headquarters at the village of Lederzeele, which stood close beside the Canal de l'Aa, and was surrounded by a net-work of water-ditches. Without my knowing it, my "War-diary" was almost at an end. Here are the last two entries :

> September 5th, 1917. Lederzeele. On march yesterday from Steenvoorde saw a "hawk" soaring in circles high up : only once flapped its wings, slightly. A buzzard?
> Caught alive 1 large green frog.
>   1 medium sized „
>   1 bronze   „
>   1 salamander

The very last entry of all runs :

> September 11th. Many wheatears in fields round Lederzeele, migrating. Many warblers amongst the leaves of the root crops. Caught bream, perch and roach in the Watten canal.

While we were at Lederzeele I was sent to act as M.O. to my old friends the 9th Yorks; by then, alas, a very different battalion from the one I had known when we all came out to France more than two years before. Of the original officers but two remained, Major H. A. S. Prior and the Quartermaster. Late in September the battalion packed up and began to march back again to the bloody Salient. As we went along and I was riding beside the colonel, a motor despatch cyclist overtook us and handed an envelope to the colonel, who after opening it and reading the letter, handed it to me with the words " lucky devil."

The despatch was an order for Captain P. H. G. Gosse to proceed to England and then to the East.

Perhaps I would be well advised to keep to myself the thoughts which passed through my mind on reading those orders.

My first impression was one of profound thankfulness at leaving France and joy at the prospect of going to the East, one of the unrealized dreams of my life.

But this state of jubilation was soon dashed by other thoughts, when I remembered how only two months before, when I was posted to a strange ambulance in a strange division, I had protested at being taken away from my own ambulance and my own division, and how at last, owing to the extraordinary kindness of the General himself, I had got back amongst my own friends. I felt I ought to protest again just as loudly as before to be allowed to remain with the 23rd Division in France. I could not keep back the reflection that although I had been for over two years in or about the fighting line, I had owing to the rat campaign spent some six months in safety and comfort, while the rest of the ambulance had been in the thick of it. In the end I did nothing, made no protests, but boarded a lorry going to Dunkirk.

That last night, by way of farewell to France, the town was heavily bombed; the next morning I went on board a steamer and set out for England.

CHAPTER VI

INDIA

I LEFT France with my imagination all aglow with visions of the East. The gateway to the mysterious Orient was Blackpool; a singular starting-place for a pilgrimage to the land of Akbar the Great, the " Guardian of Mankind."

The R.A.M.C. depôt and training camp had been moved from Tweseldown to the bracing Lancashire holiday resort, about which I do not remember very much. One picture stands out clearly enough, of big men in their shirt sleeves eating. These were munition workers taking their holidays, and their days of relaxation seemed to be spent like the lives of cows, in one everlasting meal. Every other house was a lodging house and the parlour windows stood wide open, giving passers-by a clear view of their inmates. At whatever hour you passed, from early morning till late at night, you saw those coatless men, eating, eating.

Orders soon came for me to embark at Devonport, and on the way through London I managed to pay a fleeting visit to Oldfield Thomas at the Natural History Museum, who presented me with a letter of introduction to W. S. Millard, the honorary secretary of the Bombay Natural History Society, a letter which was to prove of the greatest value when I reached India.

INDIA

On October 9th we went on board a liner at Devonport, one of four taking reinforcements to India and returning troops to South Africa and Australia. We remained lying at anchor for two days, and every signal or tugboat which came to us from the shore filled me with fear lest at the last moment my going to India might be cancelled, and I should have to go back again to France. On the 11th definite orders came for the convoy to up anchor and sail, and then I felt really safe; but at the final moment I received a fright.

The last launch to come alongside brought an official envelope addressed to me. My name was shouted up and down the ship, and I felt certain that I was to go back, at this, the eleventh hour. The envelope was handed to me, and reluctantly with a sinking feeling in the stomach, I opened it. It was a letter from Colonel Blackham, my late A.D.M.S., to say how sorry he was to lose me from the division and to wish me every good luck in India or Mesopotamia. I breathed again; but took the precaution to hide in my cabin until the ship was really under way.

No one wants to read a description of a journey on a liner; all such journeys are dull and monotonous whether the traveller be on board a transport or in a luxury liner on a sunshine cruise.

On our ship we carried a large number of R.A.M.C. officers, all of whom, with two exceptions, had served for a considerable period with regiments or field ambulances in France, and I learned for the first time that owing to the break-down of the medical arrangements in Mesopotamia, under the Indian Medical Service, a large number of R.A.M.C. officers were being sent out, preference being given to those who had seen active service in the line in France.

For several days no one knew where our first port of call would be, but a rumour persisted that it would be on the West Coast of Africa. On the strength of this I searched the ship's library and found a copy of Mary Kingsley's *West Africa* which I read right through, to be prepared for the best, or worst.

After sailing for about a week we came in sight of high mountains and were told that we were to call at Freetown in Sierra Leone, so I began to search for someone who had been there who could tell me what to do and what to see during our short stay. I soon found an officer who had spent nine months there and was returning from leave. His advice was damping, for he told me there was nothing to do at Freetown and nothing to see, and advised me to remain on board ship and not go ashore. But I had met his sort before and was determined to land and see all I could.

This uninquisitive type of Englishman is all too common, who will tell you that in any part of the world he has visited there is nothing to do or see; in fact, that it is dull, when all the time it is he who is dull and not the place. This type is not by any means a product of this century, it has always existed. The prize for being the most incurious traveller of all time must surely go to that sea cook Father Avery.

In April, 1635, Sir William Courten's little fleet set sail from Gravesend for India, China and Japan. On board one of the ships, the *Planter*, was a very old man called Avery, but there was also aboard one of the world's greatest sightseers, Peter Mundy, a Cornish-

INDIA

man, son of a pilchard fisherman of Penzance. Peter Mundy spent his whole life travelling, and throughout it kept a minute diary, crowded with observations of everything he saw which appeared to be interesting.

After sailing from place to place for more than three and a half years, during which she touched at many ports no Englishman had ever visited before, the ship returned to Erith on December 15th, 1638.

In his journal on the date that they arrived back at Erith, Mundy wrote: "Among our company were two old men not to be forgotten. The one Antonio Gonsalez, a Portugall, who was taken by Sir Francis Drake, was with him in the West Indies when he died, married an English woman, and now homeward bound grew blind, a good honest, poor old man. The other was Father Avery, our cook, who came in to the ship at Gravesend, and although we touched at sundry ports, the ship lying near the shore, boats and skiffs continually going to and from the ships, yet he was not known to set his foot on land (although he was in good health) from the time he came aboard at Gravesend, as aforesaid, until the ship arrived at Erith, where he came to his long home, being carried ashore there to be buried, who died aboard as the ship came up the river." The world is still full of Father Averys, but I think the old sea cook of the *Planter* will ever remain the world's worst sightseer.

At last our little fleet entered the beautiful harbour of Freetown, backed by the great mountain range of Sierra Leone, covered from base to summit by jungle.

In eager readiness to go ashore I got out the sun-helmet which had been issued at Blackpool. Inside the brim I discovered a circular piece of paper gummed in, on which was written " This is to wish you a safe return and the best of luck from Miss Mary Walsh, 38 Emma Street, Accrington." Dear Mary Walsh; I wonder if she received all the picture post-cards I sent her from West, South and East Africa and India.

The moment leave was given I jumped into a native boat and was rowed ashore.

Once on land I slipped away from my friends who were setting off in search of drinks and wandered about the town. The only tropical towns I had known had been in Brazil and the difference was striking. Everything in Freetown was spotlessly clean; no smells, no beggars; the natives all smiling and polite. During my wanderings I came across a little public garden, grotesquely styled Victoria Park, but obviously the original Garden of Eden. Flying about amongst the trees and flowering shrubs were some gorgeous birds. Azure blue flycatchers, with long fan-shaped tails and snow-white breasts, brilliant scarlet tanagers, and small finches with bright red heads and shoulders, and green wings and tails. Metallic green sugar birds were gathering nectar from large yellow trumpet-shaped flowers. Huge butterflies and moths of surprising colours sailed hither and thither.

After a while I left the lovely garden and scrambled up the steep hillside behind the town, along a path as red as any Devonshire lane. Above the town were flocks of English birds, wheeling round in hundreds, swallows, house-martins and swifts. I was in love with the place and began to wish I had applied for West Africa and need not return to the ship, which was to

INDIA

sail in a few hours. As it was I was the last passenger to get on board, and was very nearly left behind, having almost forgotten to send Mary Walsh a picture postcard and only remembering just in time.

The crowd in the ship was now even greater than before, as we had taken on board thirty officers of the West Africa Field Force who, having concluded their own little war, were on their way to join the expeditionary force in East Africa. I was fortunate in my cabin companion, who was a young Irish doctor, David Hadden, who had done well in France, having won the unusual distinction of the Military Cross with two bars. He had a quick temper, was impetuous, loyal and altogether charming, and we became close friends and were together all the while I was in India.

We were due to arrive at Cape Town early on November 6th and it was bitterly cold when at dawn I went out on deck and got my first sight of the towering black mass which was Table Mountain. As the sun rose the city could be seen sheltering beneath the mountain with mile upon mile of white sand dunes bordering the sea. We were to leave our ship here to board another which was to take us to Durban, and Hadden and I lost no time in getting ashore.

We could not make any excursions far afield as no one could say on what day or at what hour we might be ordered to embark. Hadden and I made one expedition to Camps Beach on the coast a few miles from the city, which could be reached by tram-car. The white beach and the high, bare mountains were very fine. Of course, I kept an eye out for birds but there were not many; the only common one being the Cape wagtail, a sprightly little fellow with a neat black collar and tie.

The three principal objects of note at Cape Town were the Yacht Club, a good book shop, and the Nelson Hotel.

We all were elected temporary members of the Club and much enjoyed the privilege; the book shop in Adderley Street was well stocked with old as well as modern books, but the famous Nelson Hotel we discovered to be the haunt of "brass-hats" and what I believe Mr. Max Beerbohm once described as "the merely rich." We preferred the Yacht Club.

There were many birds to be seen, the commonest being little Cape turtle-doves, laughing doves, weaver birds and tiny sugar birds. The boldest and most conspicuous of all was an introduced foreigner, the Persian nightingale of the poets, but known to ornithologists by the more prosaic title of red-vented bulbul.

After several pleasant days the order came for us to leave Cape Town, and we embarked on board the *Llanestephan Castle* which was to take us as far as Durban. She was a new finely appointed ship, but was very crowded with reinforcements for the East Africa force, or people like ourselves bound for India.

For company the ship had albatrosses, sooty shearwaters, and Cape chickens. On November 14th we arrived at Durban, which seemed very warm after the cold of Cape Town. All of us, officers and men, were sent to a camp of canvas bell-tents, which was pitched in a peculiarly unfortunate locality, in a bare, low-lying triangle formed by railway lines. The weather was hot and muggy but dry, and the camp was deep in

INDIA

fine dust while the food was quite uneatable. Then next day the expected rains broke and quickly turned the camp into a lake of mud. As there were no floor boards in the tents the conditions soon became unbearable. We were told by others who had tried that all applications for permission to find drier quarters had been turned down, therefore Hadden and I took it upon ourselves to procure four rickshaws, pile all our kit into them and drive off in search of better quarters, which we found in a small cheap hotel, where we stayed unknown to the authorities, as long as we were at Durban.

The men, who were in a miserable plight in the submerged camp, were rescued by the kind-hearted inhabitants of Durban, who took them as guests into their houses until the camp became habitable again. We were very glad we left camp when we did, for on reporting ourselves next morning we found that our tent had been blown down in the night by the gale.

The great solace of our stay here was the Durban Club of which every officer passing through the Natal capital automatically became an honorary member.

As there were at times several hundred officers passing north or south that hospitality was of no small order.

The club was a handsome two-storied building, with columns holding up deep cool shady verandahs, and had a large courtyard or patio, filled with palms and flowers.

But the hospitality of the club did not end here. The first time Hadden and I entered it for lunch we crept modestly, as new or temporary members of any club should do, to sit with our fellow travellers at one large table in the dining-room. Scarcely had we sat down when various old members got up and came over to us, saying it would never do for us all to sit together, and took us off to their different tables. Nothing could have been more friendly or hospitable. The member who claimed Hadden and myself, drove us in his car afterwards to visit a sugar plantation and factory at Mount Edgecombe.

Later on when we were in India, we often compared the attitude of the pukka military, to whom we " temporary gents " were of the untouchable caste, with the warm kindness of these South Africans, not only at Durban but at the Yacht Club at Cape Town.

The ship that was to take us on the last stage of our voyage to India was a huge North Atlantic liner, the *Empress of Britain*. She was packed with troops. Deck below deck, down into the very bowels of the ship, soldiers were wedged in like the pieces of a jig-saw puzzle. As only a part of them could take exercise at a time, the rest were made to huddle themselves together in any odd hole or corner, in order to give deck space to the exercisers. On December 4th the *Empress of Britain* berthed alongside the quay at Bombay, and with the other R.A.M.C. officers I went at once to report to the D.A.D.M.S. Embarkation at his office on the Alexandra Dock. The job allotted to me was to go that same afternoon as M.O. in charge of a train-load of British troops to Bangalore, in the south of India. The moment this was settled I jumped into a gharri and drove round to the Bombay Natural History Society's headquarters which were in the offices of Messrs. Phipson, in the Apollo Bunder, and where Mr. W. S. Millard found time not only to direct the well-known wine company of which he was senior partner, but to discharge the duties of Honorary Secretary to the B.N.H.S. as well. I sent in my letter of introduction from Oldfield Thomas and was immediately shewn into the office. Millard was seated at his desk, and behind his chair was a large cage built round a window. The sole occupant of this cage was an enormous hornbill, which had lived there for five and twenty years. This giant bird, the size of a turkey, had a monstrous bill and looked all the more absurd as it hopped about the ground like a sparrow. Also it had eyelids like a human being, adorned by long curved bushy black eyelashes and whenever I see a photograph of some famous actress wearing artificial eyelashes, I always think of Millard's office pet.

The bird took a keen interest in all that went on in the room and was apt at times to get so excited as to give forth booming grunts which seemed to issue from the very bowels of the earth, drowning all conversation between the senior partner and his client. To prevent this and gain silence a small boy squatted all day on the floor beside the cage, and whenever the hornbill became obstreperous, gave him a light tap on the back with a switch, which never failed, for a short while, to quieten him.

Another favourite specimen of the small zoo at the Natural History Society was a large and handsome chameleon, of saturnine demeanour, its sombre black coat being relieved by a few ashy spots. Opposite its cage stood a cigarette tin containing live grasshoppers. Whenever Millard took up the tin and began to fumble with the lid, the chameleon turned a vivid green with excitement and greed.

As I had several things to do before starting on my journey, my first visit to Millard had to be a short one and I had no time to see any other of his live pets. As I left he handed me a small slim green volume which he said I should find useful in identifying the common Indian birds. I slipped it into my pocket, said good-bye and hurried away.

On the troop train I had a saloon carriage all to myself and thoroughly enjoyed the experience of travelling through a new country. After passing across the flat land that surrounds Bombay the train began to climb the Western Ghats mountains. Presently it pulled up at a station amidst wild mountainous country intersected by deep valleys filled with dense jungle. I was so enraptured by the country that I then and there decided that if ever the opportunity came I would return to stay there, and I wrote down the name of the place, Khandala, in my notebook.

When I awoke next morning we were well beyond the mountains and travelling through hot flat plains. From dawn to dusk as the train rumbled south I sat on the floor of the carriage with my legs dangling out of the open door, watching the passing country and the birds which seemed to have taken up their places on the telegraph lines on purpose to see our train go by. Some of the birds I recognised from pictures or stuffed specimens seen in England, but many were quite unknown to me and would have remained so had it not been for Millard's little book. This was called *The Common Birds of Bombay* by " Eha " and with it I

INDIA

was able to recognise most of the birds we passed. The author, Edward Hamilton Aitken, whom I had never even heard of till then, had an unusual gift for describing in a few words not only the appearance of every bird, but also any little habit of flight, movement, song, or other particular characteristic.

I became so enchanted by this book that directly I got back to Bombay I went straight to a bookshop and bought all " Eha's " other works, which proved to be even more entertaining, particularly those about India, *The Tribes of my Frontier*, *A Naturalist on the Prowl* and *Behind the Bungalow*.

Now and again the train stopped at a station and we got a meal. At one small wayside station where we stopped to water the engine, an elderly Indian lady was washing herself at the public drinking fountain. She was adorned by quantities of rings and bangles and wore a flowing garment, a sari of bright orange colour. The manner in which she took her bath and changed her dress under the direct and close observation of six hundred Tommies filled me with admiration.

First she squatted beneath the trickling tap and while the water ran down all over her, she kept up a brisk rubbing of her body and limbs beneath the soaked sari. When this was finished, a tiny brown boy brought her a dry garment, which she put on over the wet one. Violent wriggling movements then took place beneath the dry garment, until the wet sari fell to the ground at her feet and she stalked off in a dignified manner in the dry one, followed by the small brown boy carrying the discarded wet one. It was an astonishing performance, one requiring practice, coolness, and natural dignity.

At the end of three days and two nights I was able to hand my charges over at Bangalore with only a few minor casualties, the result of eating fruit bought against strict orders from vendors on the railway platforms.

Bangalore looked so inviting that I refused to return to Bombay by the next train, but went instead to stop a couple of days at the Cubbon Hotel, a lovely old-India bungalow set in a fine garden a few miles outside the city.

When at last I got back to Bombay I learned that I had been posted to the King George's War Hospital at Poona, a place considered to be a first-class station, and better still that I was to go there with David Hadden.

Until we found suitable quarters Hadden and I put up at an hotel which shall be nameless, a dirty badly managed place with indescribably unpalatable food. We were almost the only male guests, as most of the others were officers' wives; and it did not require our medical knowledge to recognise that the majority of these ladies were in what is described by policemen as a " certain " and by newspaper reporters as an " interesting " condition.

We were quickly falling in with the ways of the country and during the hot afternoons we went to our bedrooms for a siesta.

One day while I was lying on my bed after lunch trying to sleep, several natives burst in without knocking and in a state of great excitement. I could not make out what all the bustle was about or what they wanted, but got up and followed them to a room at the other end of the passage. Without ceremony I was ushered into a bedroom to find a young woman who was, without question, about to be brought to bed. Faced with this alarming prospect I at once sent for a gharri, assisted the lady into it, and in my best Hindustani ordered the driver to go to the Civil Hospital "jildi," that is as quickly as ever he could drive his two starved horses.

That evening when Hadden and I entered the crowded dining-room we noted that the ladies all round bowed and smiled to us. After dinner was over and we were sitting in the verandah, several came up and spoke to us. They said how kind I had been to little Mrs—— to get her off to the hospital in time; and what a sense of relief and security it gave to many of them to have us two doctors living in the hotel. They asked if we had been in general practice at home, and had much experience in that sort of thing.

As soon as Hadden and I were alone we discussed this unexpected development and left the hotel the first thing next morning for safer bachelor quarters.

The hospital to which we were attached had just been built. It consisted of a number of large and airy one-roomed thatched bungalows surrounded by deep verandahs. The whole hospital covered a wide area, and was supplied with almost everything necessary to a hospital except patients, of which there were none for a long while.

The nursing staff, excepting the matron, who was a very charming English lady belonging to the regular army nursing corps, were Australian, most of them amateurs who had joined up for the duration of the War and very indignant at not being sent somewhere to nurse their own countrymen.

They were a light-hearted, affectionate crowd of

young women, who managed to get all the fun they could out of life, and had the usual Australian contempt and disregard for all rules, regulations and discipline.

One sister and one nurse were allotted to each empty ward, and one medical officer as well. Although there were no patients in the wards each doctor was strictly charged to be at his ward, or in the sister's little room off it, for three full hours each morning. Thus many warm friendships were made, and some hearts broken, for the devil, or perhaps it was Venus, the goddess of love, found the wherewithal for idle hands to do. As for myself I was appointed to the less romantic post of sanitary officer to the camp.

The colonel in charge, having heard of my appointment to the Xth Corps School of Sanitation, could hardly be blamed for thinking I possessed some special knowledge of that subject. As it happened it did not matter. There was no sanitation. Everything sanitary that had to be done was accomplished before we arrived each morning at the camp. Enough to say that sanitation in India is carried out, not by pipes, and cesspools, but by incinerators.

Thus my daily work of inspection consisted merely of a pleasant round of calls at each ward, partaking of tea, biscuits and cigarettes at each, and occasionally trying to patch up a lovers' quarrel, or lending a sympathetic ear to a tale of woe. After a few days of this I was sent for to go to the orderly room, to face the irate colonel.

In great anger he demanded why the camp was in such a filthy condition. I was staggered, and asked him what in particular he found fault with. He replied that that very morning he had seen three cigarette ends lying on the ground, and repeated that the state of the camp was a disgrace and ordered me to see that such a thing never occurred again. After that the following daily routine took place.

A procession started, headed by myself; next came my sanitary corporal, and the rear was brought up by a naked Indian sweeper of distinctly untouchable caste, who balanced a wide wicker basket on his head. In this order we would sally forth and quarter the bare and arid compound, marching and counter-marching, prying, peeping, searching for the accursed things. Then suddenly I would catch sight of a cigarette end and halt.

First of all I would approach the loathsome object, point towards it with my cane, and then pass on. The corporal would follow and do likewise, and last of all the sweeper would go up to the foul thing, seize it with his toes, transfer it with surprising dexterity to his hand, and so to the basket still balanced on his head, and the column would then proceed in search of other cigarette ends. But, regrettable as it is to admit it, advantage was taken of me by my colleagues.

At first a cigarette end was a very rare find; we were quite glad to get one occasionally. But I soon began to notice that the numbers greatly increased. Then one day I got an inkling that something was afoot from the laughter that came from behind the *chicks* or cane curtains shading the verandah of one of the sisters' rooms. I had just found, and was rather pleased than otherwise, a whole handful of fag-ends outside this ward, but as we were moving away I heard giggles. Then it was that

I found out that the idle inhabitants who smoked cigarettes and drank tea behind the *chicks* amused themselves by scattering cigarette ends outside for the fun of watching my party come along and discover them. They meant no harm by it, and really it was no more than what we do in winter time when we throw bread crumbs out of the window and watch behind the curtains for the little birds that gather round to pick them up.

Five of us, all in the R.A.M.C. and all "temporary gents" or territorials, clubbed together to take a bungalow. We had a jolly one in a garden, belonging to a Parsee race-horse owner. It stood just outside the botanical gardens at Ghorpuri, and well away from the town. It had many small ponds behind it and was known locally, as we found out later on, as "Fever Hall."

The place suited me down to the ground. Besides being a good way from Poona and the military, I only had to step over the low wall of the compound to get straight into the country, with its paddy and millet fields, its date groves, and its rocky hills. I was now able to settle down in earnest to collect animals, as the hospital still had no patients in it, so that the whole day was free except for a few hours each morning.

I soon found it easy to awake in the dark and, after dressing by lamplight, would creep out of the slumbering bungalow, clad in a sleeveless khaki shirt, shorts, stockings and my green Majorcan alpagatas with thick canvas soles. In my hand I carried a twenty-eight bore collecting gun, round my neck hung my binoculars and over my shoulders a smaller canvas bag for cartridges, traps and specimens.

INDIA

As I clambered over the low wall behind the bungalow, dawn would be breaking to the accompaniment of a loud clamour. This was not the morning song of birds, but reminded one rather of the distant roar of a football crowd, and was made by scores of natives who all together began loudly to call their cattle. Soon this noise ceased, to give way to the sound, so characteristic of hot Indian days, of the creaking wooden machinery by which water is raised from the deep wells to irrigate the paddy fields.

The first thing to do was to gather up the traps set over night. These had been set near together in one locality, as a small spring trap is easily overlooked and lost.

Even when such early visits were paid the ferocious ants only too often had got there before me, and left nothing of the small beast in the trap but a few pieces of skin and bone.

What birds there were, of marvellous colours and in such numbers! The earliest risers, after myself, were the Satbhai, the Seven Brothers. This babbler is never spoken of in India in the singular, but always as the Seven Brothers, for they are only seen in small parties, never alone, hurrying from bush to bush, continually chattering in a friendly way.

Rollers flew about with a flash of azure blue as they spread their wings. The perky little black and white robin, with his tail cocked ever skywards was, like our own robin red-breast, very friendly and inquisitive, and always wanting to find out exactly what I was about when stooping down setting a trap. In the moist green paddy fields, white egrets and brown cattle egrets stalked solemnly about, peering in their short-sighted way for frogs.

Some of the birds were later risers than I. I used to tip-toe past one old kite so as not to wake him, as he slept perched on a low branch, with his head drooping, eyes closed, and his beak buried in the feathers of his breast.

My favourite walk of all was along the banks of the Mutha canal, which supplied the water-works of the late and regretted Sir Jamsetjee Jeejeebhoy, Bart.

The word canal calls up a picture of a straight waterway with still or very slowly moving water, perhaps none too clear, and a tow-path on one side of it. The Mutha canal was not at all like this. Between high banks on which grew green trees, palms and many sorts of green flowering shrubs, clear water ran in a swift stream. The trees shaded both the path and the stream and made it cool even in the hottest weather when the neighbouring fields were burnt brown. Fishes, big and little, darted to and fro.

One morning, as I was walking along the banks, I saw, some hundred yards in front of me on the brown earth path what looked exactly like a heap of grass newly cut by a lawn mower which the gardener has emptied from the box of the machine. But the whole green heap seemed to be in movement.

Warily I approached nearer until with my field-glasses I solved the mystery. What I had taken to be a heaving mound of grass proved to be a mass of emerald green bee-eaters, which were lying close together, higgledy-piggledy, enjoying a dust bath. Some were lying on their bellies, others on their sides, and all were flapping their wings with vigour. There must have been thirty or more birds together on one small patch of ground.

A common bird at Poona and one of the most active was the long-tailed green Indian parrakeet, with a rose-coloured ring round its neck and a piercing cry. Small flocks of these were always to be seen and heard in the date groves or the millet fields. Some of the handsomest birds which haunted the canal and the Poona river were the black and white kingfishers. They always hunted in couples. They did not fish from a perch as do all other kingfishers, but hovered over the water like a kestrel, with their long beaks pointing vertically down, and mandibles slightly open, giving sharp cries all the while. Then all of a sudden one of them would spy a small fish and fall like a bullet, head first, striking the water with a splash, to rise an instant later and fly away with a struggling fish in its beak.

Later on in the year, when the millet crops were ripe, the fields teemed with small seed-eating birds such as finches and buntings. In order to scare away the birds the farmers built tall platforms, shaded by palm leaf roofs, where women and children reclined all day long, shouting and beating on gongs. But they might just as well have slept, or remained at home, for the birds took no notice whatever of their clamour, but continued to gorge themselves with millet seeds until their little crops bulged and they looked as though each had swallowed a golf ball. The commonest of these raiders were the little munias, the silver-bill of bird fanciers, the lovely rose-finch, the blackheaded bunting with yellow body and the yellow-throated sparrow.

Although their religion does not allow them to take

an animal's life, the farmers seemed only too pleased when I came their way with my gun and urged me to slay the plunderers.

It is a significant fact, and one which I would like to have explained by some learned theologian, that birds seem to prosper in heathen lands and wilt in Christian ones. I believe that wherever Christianity has not penetrated birds are numerous, unmolested and fearless of man. Before the Anglo-Saxon race brought religion and civilization to the then benighted continent of North Africa birds swarmed there. To-day they are few and far between, some species being near to extinction, and societies have been founded by bird-lovers to try to preserve what are left from the gunner and the bird-snarer. In Italy, too, where priests and churches abound, and where the people are deeply religious, they kill and eat small birds, even swallows and robins.

Many pleasant hours were spent—not wasted—hanging over the low walls of the wide, deep wells. Far down in the cool twilight could be made out a big frog or a toad floating on the surface, a prisoner undergoing a life of solitary confinement. In the words of Eha " the live-long day it is doomed to float on the surface of the water, vacantly gazing at heaven, with supplicating palms outstretched and fat thighs helplessly pendulous in the clear water." Another life-prisoner of the wells was the water-tortoise, and in some of them were shoals of small fishes, the size and shape of minnows.

As the sun rose higher in the sky and the day became hotter most of the birds disappeared to sleep in cool, shady places. All except the persistent little coppersmith and that curse of India, the Keol, a huge black cuckoo with a long tail, a green bill and a wicked blood-shot eye. Throughout the hottest day, from early morn till dusk, its penetrating, persistent cry is heard, in a rising crescendo "Who—be—you?—who—be—you?—who—be—you?—who—be—you?" until the sufferer would gladly wring the neck of this devilish harbinger of spring, so well nicknamed the brain-fever bird.

If the early mornings of India are enchanting, the evenings after a broiling-hot day are also delightful. When at last the scorching sun dips towards the horizon and the shadows lengthen and blessed coolness comes, birds, beasts and man awake from their torpor.

In Tropic lands the twilight is short and, as in all countries where life is spent out of doors, everything that is done is accompanied by noise. One of the noisiest at this hour before sleep is the so-called common myna. Linnæus gave this sprightly bird the name of Acridotheres tristis, the sad grasshopper-hunter. But the great Swedish naturalist can never have known the myna in his native haunts. A grasshopper-hunter he certainly is, but sad, never. Perhaps the adjective sad was to describe the colour of his quaker brown suit. At dusk great companies of these mynas used to congregate in the cactus thickets causing a tremendous uproar as they settled down for their night's repose and wished each other good night. A thousand throats would chatter all together, sounds like the beating of a hundred little gongs would be heard from beneath the cactus roof. Then sudden complete silence, broken presently by a clear, unhuman laugh. Then all the gongs would begin to beat again and the hubbub and din would be renewed, the clamour seeming to be echoed beneath the canopy of cactus bushes as in some underground vault.

These groves of cactus bushes were favourite roosting and nesting places for birds, not only for the mynas, but for the rosy pastors, also noisy bed-goers with their orchestra of jingling silver bells. The little gray doves were fond of building their small frail nests among the cactus; probably the cruel sharp needles which grow on the leaves made a safe protection from enemies for sleeping birds and nestlings.

When the last of the mynas and pastors had settled down and it was almost dark, great fruit bats—flying foxes as they are sometimes called—would pass silently overhead, with slow unbatlike strokes of their big wings, all bearing in one direction. If you followed them they would lead you eventually to some tall, wide-spreading banyan tree whose fruit, small hard figs, had become ripe. The news of this had somehow spread abroad, and from far and wide the fruit bats would come to spend the night climbing among the branches eating, fighting, squabbling and squeaking.

With the sudden onset of darkness a new chorus set up. Next to Fever Hall were the Empress Botanical Gardens, from which the public was excluded at dusk. In them were ornamental ponds, with giant waterlilies and tall rushes and frogs. Monster giant frogs and small light-green frogs, which attached themselves to the equally green smooth leaves of trees; yellow frogs, frogs of all sizes, shapes and shades, but having one common accomplishment, that of vocal boisterousness. As soon as ever it was dark the gardens rang with a hullaballoo of discordant croakings, snores, groans and grunts, accompanied by loud whoops, howls, screams and shrieks. Only once did I hear a greater uproar of frogs, when with a friend I got lost one night in a marsh in Chile. Although the public was turned out at dusk by the attendants and the gates of the gardens were shut and locked, this did not prevent us from visiting them at night. After dinner we used to climb over the wall which separated our compound from the gardens and, armed with electric torches and nets, hunt for frogs, snakes, fish, and anything else we could catch.

In order that no one should be idle I persuaded my friends in the bungalow to help me with my collecting. Although none of them had any real interest in natural history, such is the infection of enthusiasm that they were soon hard at it.

David Hadden was put on to butterflies and moths, and used to get very heated in pursuit of a butterfly with his green net in hand. Arthur Hawes was appointed reptile collector, and on one occasion came with pride into my room to show me the treasure that he had caught and brought alive in a box. I peeped in and there was a live and very active specimen of that deadly snake the krite. A. V. Ledger was in charge of fishes, and although he never succeeded in catching one, was most useful, as he was able to make nets and supplied each of us with one. Our other inmate at the bungalow was an elderly major, whom nothing would induce to take to collecting, and indeed I think he regarded the rest of us as being just a little mad.

When we set up house we were presented with a list of the names and addresses of the military who would expect us to drop cards into the little boxes which are found on every bungalow front gate.

Reluctantly Hadden and I hired a gharri, and spent the whole of one afternoon driving from house to house, depositing our cards. But we need not have worried that we would be drawn into the social life of Poona, for not one call was returned, nor a single invitation received. The visited were all "pukka Sahibs," while we were only "chota Sahibs"; that is to say of little account. But what a contrast to Cape Town and Durban!

The caste system in India is by no means confined to the native inhabitants. There are, or were, two clubs in Poona. One was the Gymkhana, a club for men and women, where lawn tennis was played, dances given, and drinks served without difficulty or waste of time. The other, a much grander and more select institution, was the Club of Western India.

I did not hanker after either, as I knew I should be much happier in the open fields and jungle. But a good friend who had influence at the C.W.I. offered to put Hadden and me up for temporary membership, and we did not like to refuse. In due course we were elected. It was said to be one of the best clubs in India, and I can well believe it. It was a handsome building with great, cool rooms, and stood in a large garden. It had an air of great exclusiveness, was full of palms, generals, rules and regulations; notices were frequent with "Don't . . ." or "Hush" written on them. The latter injunction was certainly well observed by the regular members, for not one of them ever addressed a word to either of us until a year later, on a memorable occasion which will be referred to in due course.

INDIA

A story was told in Poona that one evening a temporary member of the club, who like ourselves had gone to India from France, went there to dine dressed in the ordinary khaki drill uniform, having no other kit. It was said that after he had sat down at one of the small tables in a corner of the room as far away as possible from the regular members who were all in evening dress or mess uniform, the butler was sent to place a screen round his table, to hide the horrid spectacle from his fellow members. Probably the tale was quite untrue, but the fact remains that such a story could be told, and passed on joyfully from one to another.

Some of the temporary officers, who had seen much fighting in France and perhaps been wounded or were suffering from the effects of gassing or being blown up, resented very much this social boycotting by the regulars, but it did not worry me. The club was a very pleasant place in which to write letters or read the newspapers.

Most of my spare time, and we had plenty of it at first, was spent out of doors collecting specimens and enjoying all the wonderful things to be seen. Every morning before sunrise I was up and out with my field-glasses and gun, visiting my traps. Then back to "Fever Hall," where I would skin my specimens and write up my notes. Then a hot bath and a good breakfast. After this we would all mount our hired bicycles and ride over to the hospital to drag out the three hours of idleness.

One of the difficulties of collecting in a tropical climate is that the skins, particularly of the small insect-eating birds begin to decompose very quickly. At first I was getting so many specimens that I made myself quite ill with overwork at skinning, as I took on an average half an hour to make a good bird's skin, and rather less time to make a small mammal's. So I arranged with kind Millard to send my bearer, Kerudin, who was quite willing, to Bombay for a week to learn skinning at the Natural History Society.

Kerudin turned out to be a very neat-fingered taxidermist and proved invaluable, as he left me much more time to be out of doors hunting for specimens, while he stopped at home skinning. I also initiated him into the mystery of trapping, at which he soon became adept, and to encourage him rewarded him with one anna for every animal he caught. I was collecting the birds for the British Museum, and the mammals eventually were to go there, but not until they had been examined and classified for the India Mammal Survey, which was making a complete and extensive enquiry into the mammals, great and small, of the Indian Continent.

My collection of mammals was afterwards worked out by the late R. C. Wroughton and Miss Winifred Davidson, and two reports were published on it in the Journal of the Bombay Natural History Society.

Already by the middle of February I had skinned one hundred and eighty birds and sixty small animals, and also had preserved in spirits a large number of parasites and other zoological odds and ends.

With March the weather became really hot, and I went down with a severe attack of dysentery. By a curious arrangement which I never understood, all sick officers were sent to the Civilian Sassoon Hospital at Poona, in spite of there being two large new army hospitals, one our own King George's and another at Kirkee.

They were very kind to us at the Sassoon Hospital. The nurse in charge of the wing I was in was young, pretty and gentle, but she ruled her riotous patients with tact and firmness. Her home was in the Nilgiri Hills, where her mother owned a tea estate, but when the War broke out she had left it to become a hospital nurse. The majority of her charges were subalterns of various regiments, with one or two captains and majors. As most of them were convalescent and only waiting to go before a medical board before being granted sick leave they were full of high spirits and devilment.

This question of sick leave was the one absorbing topic of conversation amongst us. The merits of the various places to which convalescent officers were sent were discussed at great length; but all of them were in the north, at the hill station, in the Himalayas. For my own part I knew where I meant to go when my time came to appear before the medical board, and that was Khandala, the place I had seen from the train.

As I became better my bed was moved out of the small private ward on to the verandah, which was far nicer, with sky to look at and birds to see in the hospital compound. The ever kind Millard sent me some books about the Indian mammals, so I told Kerudin to bring me the specimens we had already skinned and with the help of the books I was able to identify most of them, and to learn a lot about them and their habits.

My bed was at one end of the verandah and for company I had ghekos, small lizards with big heads and superchilious expressions, which run about the walls of all Indian houses by means of suckers on their toes and make familiar clucking noises from time to time. I had another friend, a large green lizard a foot long, which every now and again would fall from the roof with a heavy flop flat on its belly on the stone floor. It never seemed any the worse for this experience, but after watching me with a glittering bright eye until I moved a little would dash off into the garden.

The common Indian mynas were tame and cheeky and soon took to joining me at meals, standing round my bed, waiting for such scraps of food as I cared to spare them from my tray.

Also there were bats of several kinds. Bats had been my greatest difficulty to collect. The only way I had been able to get specimens was to shoot them—or at them —with my collecting gun during the short dusk before night. What with their sudden twists and turns I very seldom hit one though I wasted large numbers of cartridges; and cartridges to fit my small gun were hard to procure and ruinously expensive.

There was one sort of bat which lived in the *chicks*, the rolled sunblinds made of split bamboo, which I was certain I had not seen elsewhere. All day long squeaking and rustling went on in the blinds above my head, and I was determined when I was strong enough to try and catch one or two.

Meanwhile there was nothing else to do but lie patiently and read, look at the sky, enjoy the meals and listen to the gramophone. The blast of this accursed invention of the devil was dinned into one's ears from morning till night, ceasing only when the other patients went into the dining hall. It seemed to be understood that anybody had the right to put on a record whenever he felt so inclined. The choice of tunes fell between three records, each an ear-splitting melody of the ragtime variety. Being bed-ridden there was no escape for me from the maddening noise, which I suffered as long as I could. But there is a limit to all things, and the day came when I determined that the pandemonium should cease.

So while my fellow patients were at their dinner I got out of bed, not without difficulty, for I was still very weak, and tottering down the verandah quickly removed the sound-box from the noise-machine and crept back to bed, where I hid the thing beneath the mattress. Ten minutes later I heard the diners returning and I lay back, with closed eyes, simulating slumber. A cheery voice asked, "What about a little tune?" and another voice called for "You are my yum-yum baby," a terrible record which had been played at least twenty times a day for the preceding fortnight.

Then the trouble began. Everybody accused everybody else of having taken the sound-box, which each hotly denied. A general search was made for the missing thing; not a chink or corner was left unexplored, except the bed of the sick sleeping officer at the other end of the verandah. The native servants were sent for, accused, examined, cross-examined in English, Hindustani and Marathi, but all in vain. Nor did the nurse on duty know anything about it, the thing was declared a mystery and remained one until the sound box was found the day after I left the hospital.

As it began to dawn on me that I would be an inmate of the Sassoon hospital for a fairly long while, I started to worry about my collecting which had been brought to an end.

Every morning Kerudin used to come and ask for orders and bring me my letters. So one day I told him to set my traps each evening and when he came to the hospital in the morning to bring everything he had caught in the traps the previous night for me to examine, he was then to take them back to Fever Hall, skin them, and tie on the labels which I would write up when I examined the freshly trapped beasts. This arrangement worked very well. Each morning the smiling Kerudin entered my room with a sack thrown over his shoulder; salaamed, enquired after my health, and then poured the contents of the sack on the floor beside my bed, where I could see and admire them.

It was the one exciting event in each otherwise dreary day. You never knew what would appear. An average catch might include a couple of musk shrews, a banyan squirrel, an antelope rat, a tree-mouse, or a white-tailed rat. "Din" would then hand me each corpse in turn, and I would take its measurements and note them, with sex, date and locality of capture, on a label and attach it to the animal's leg. When this was done, "Din" would put them all back in his sack and return home to skin them.

This routine had gone on quite satisfactorily for about a week, when a rather unfortunate occurrence took place. The time for "Din's" visit was arranged to coincide with the hour at which the Matron breakfasted. She was a nice woman for a matron, but I felt sure she would not understand this business or be sympathetic about it.

Then one morning as I was lying in bed expecting Din to arrive with the night's catch I heard the voice of the Matron in high expostulation in the passage outside my room. A few moments later the small, scared-looking Din entered my room followed by the tall and angry Matron. The sack was on his back and was more bulky than usual. The Matron informed me she had caught this stranger walking about her hospital with a sack on his back and he had refused to tell her what was in it; all he would say was that it belonged to his master. I assured her it was quite all right, that this was my bearer who had brought a few things for me from my bungalow. The Matron, rather wanting in good taste, demanded to see what was in the sack; she suspected it was fruit, which I was not allowed to have. I hastened to assure her it contained no fruit, nothing in fact for me to eat, just a few little personal belongings. But the strong-minded disciplinarian was not to be put off and insisted on seeing for herself what the sack contained. As there was no help for it I told Din to empty the sack on to the floor. It was the best night's catch he had ever made! Not only were there rats, mice and shrews in plenty, but something new to the collection. It was the last object to fall on to the heap. What the repulsive thing was I had not the faintest notion. It was as large as a big tom cat, and was stark naked, its blue crinkled skin being quite hairless. It was one of the most interesting and exciting captures we had made, but I wished that its arrival had not coincided with that of the Matron, for it really did look out of place in the clean ward.

There followed a very painful scene; the Matron raged, I pleaded and expostulated. At first she was for calling the hospital sweeper to throw away our specimens into the incinerator, an act of vandalism which, of course, I opposed with might and main. In the end she agreed that Din should be allowed to take the corpses home again, but only on a promise from me that I would never again have any more brought into the hospital.

In case any reader wishes to know what the repulsive creature proved to be, it was nothing more nor less than a toddy cat suffering from mange. Kerudin had caught it in a gin the night before in the nullah behind the bungalow. When I asked Din what the animal was, he called it a *biju*. I looked this up in my Hindustani dictionary and found it meant a ratel. I pointed this out to Din, who then said the animal was called by some people an *ood-bilaou*, which in Hindustani means an otter, which was worse than ever. He explained the animal's baldness by the fact that it lived on dead men, and that this so heated its blood that its hair fell out.

After the storm was over and the irate matron, Din, and the misunderstood quadrupeds had departed, I turned the matter over in my mind and decided that a promise wrung from me under such compulsion had not the value of one given willingly. So the cause of science being sacred, I told Din the next day to come as usual with his catches, not by the front door of the hospital, but through the hedge that bounded the compound. After that lamentable scene I used to listen for a low whistle from outside, when I would slip out of bed, cross the verandah and find Din hiding with his sack amongst the bushes. Hurriedly I would measure the catch, write the labels, and then creep back to bed while Din returned the way he had come.

The hospital seemed to be run by ladies belonging to some religious sisterhood, so on Easter Sunday most of us attended service at the hospital chapel. The officiating priest was a Hindu, and was very supple when it came to the genuflections.

The Christian festival happened that year to coincide with the date of a great Hindu festival. I made enquiries about it of my nurse, who had been born and bred in India, and as far as I could make out the great god Gampati once went to pay a visit to Mai, the goddess of love and children. But Gampati dallied on the road, and " caught the eye " of some good-looking but less high-born goddesses, with the result that he was so long on his journey that Mai, after waiting fourteen days for him, became annoyed and took her revenge on Gampati by casting her favours on sundry local and minor gods. And indeed there seemed to be going on in the bazaar next to the hospital a very orgy of debauch, immorality and noise.

In any case Gampati showed no sense of shame nor remorse, for early on Easter Sunday he emerged from his temple and marched in a long procession which meandered about the city. At the head of the procession was a large band armed with European brass musical instruments. The tune they played, not an inappropriate one either, was " For he's a jolly good fellow."

We were glad when Easter Sunday was over, for Gampati's temple was close by, and the beating of drums and the squealing of pipes continued till after midnight.

When at last I was strong enough to get up, a fellow convalescent, a cavalry subaltern, and I arranged a bat-hunting raid. Armed with a butterfly net and several tin boxes we examined the top of every *chick* on my verandah. As I was not strong enough for climbing my daring and agile companion did it for me by balancing himself on a chair placed upon a table. As a result of this raid we caught half-a-dozen bats, two of which had hideous corrugated faces. When, later on in London, these came to be examined by the late R. C. Wroughton for the Indian Mammal Survey they proved to be a species unknown to science. In my honour this new bat was christened *Tadarida Gossei*, or Gosse's Thick-tailed Wrinkle-lip bat; a delicate compliment which I much appreciated, and by which my name is immortalised and of which my descendants may well be proud. How much do big events result from small ones! Had I not eaten a rotten banana I should not have got dysentery, nor have gone to the Sassoon hospital, and Gosse's Thick-tailed Wrinkle-lip bat would have continued to be born, marry and die in the *chicks* of the Sassoon Hospital, unhonoured and unnamed.

As I grew stronger I was able to take a more active part in these bat forays and in time we raided every *chick* in the whole building, thereby adding some rare and interesting specimens to the collection.

The boldest birds of all at the hospital, bolder even than the common mynas, were the Indian house-sparrows. They shewed no fear of man, no respect for privacy, nor a scrap of decent feeling. Two rival pairs decided to build their nests just over the head of my bed. Every morning I was awakened by their chatter, or by pieces of straw which fell on my face. Now and again the four birds ceased from their fights and attempts to build, and perching in a row along the iron bar at the foot of my bed, they would loudly thrash the matter out; a sort of peace conference which always ended in renewed fighting.

I was by now so far recovered as to be allowed to go out of the hospital for drives. I used to go to the C.W.I. where one could be very comfortable and was quite certain not to be disturbed or excited by one's fellow members. It was there one day that I met by appointment, T. R. Bell, the Chief Conservator of the Forests of Bombay. This meeting put me yet again in the debt of Millard, to whom I already owed so much.

Five minutes in the company of the Chief Conservator were enough to learn that I had met a man after my own heart. A keen naturalist, who had spent the best part of his life in the Bombay forests, he knew every bird, beast, plant and insect which inhabited the jungles of which he was in charge. His home was on the Malabar coast in Kanara, just south of the Portuguese colony of Goa, where he at once invited me to stay with him if I could get away. He told me his bungalow was surrounded by untouched jungle which swarmed with all kinds of wild animals and birds, and that whenever friends came to stay with him he advised them not to bring their dogs with them, as the panthers had a habit of coming on to the verandah and carrying them off. He also told me about an uninhabited island,

Pigeon Island, twenty miles off the coast, and promised to send me there one day to make an exhaustive collection of its flora and fauna. I had never before met such a man, for he agreed to go collecting with me in the Laccadive Islands, and ended our first meeting by presenting me with a signed permit to shoot when and where and what I liked, for scientific purposes.

At last the day came for me to go before the medical board. After the interview they granted me four weeks' sick leave, and asked me if I had any particular choice of a hill station. When I said I would like to go to Khandala they seemed somewhat surprised, for none of them had heard of that hill station as a health resort, but all the same, they agreed to it, and to Khandala I went.

CHAPTER VII

KHANDALA

ON April 8th we arrived at the longed-for Khandala. One of my friends from Fever Hall, A. V. Ledger, came with me for the first week, and of course we brought our bearers with us. The hotel we found to consist of a collection of ramshackle buildings, only one of which was two-storied. Most of the bedrooms were tumble-down shanties, without windows and having floors of beaten mud. Being the only guests Ledger and I were given, at a low rate, the best room in the hotel, the whole upper floor of the two-storied bungalow. It consisted of one large airy room, with four windows and five doors opening on to a balcony which ran round the building. From this there was a superb view of the mountains above and the deep jungle-filled valleys below. As soon as ever our servants had unpacked our luggage I was out with my traps and collecting-gun. At half-past five next morning we were awakened by a rush of wind through our great room and hurried to dress and go out. The first trap I visited, set amongst the roots of a huge tree, contained something quite new: a large soft-furred rat with a white belly, which proved to be Blandford's white-tailed rat. The lure she had succumbed to was chapatti, delicately flavoured with oil of aniseed, a bait which I found very deadly in India.

Immediately below the hotel I came across a small torrent which leaped and tumbled down the side of a steep gorge and which turned out to be a favourite resort for all sorts of birds. Before following the stream down the gorge I sat still and watched the rising sun light up the tree tops of the forest which lay beneath me. It was all deeply silent except for the sound of the little waterfall which fell over the precipice, and the occasional cry of some bird in the thick jungle.

Now and again a large grey bird of prey with black wings floated above my head. Suddenly the stillness was broken by loud whoops and chattering in a treetop, where I could see the branches being shaken. Keeping very still and watching the waving branches through my field glasses, I soon made out a family of langur monkeys feeding off the leaves of the tree, and presently I discovered the cause of all the noise.

Sitting comfortably with his back against the tree trunk was an old big male langur with a black face and a grey beard which stuck truculently forward. He seemed to be guarding his family while they ate their breakfast. Most of the time he kept up a regular chattering, like a magpie. I could see his mouth open and shut while he did so. Every now and again he would give forth a loud deep whoop, which was answered by another langur somewhere far away in the deep ravine below. The sound was such as might be produced by blowing into a gourd or hollow box. It was an impressive sound at such an hour and in such surroundings, and the echo of it was tossed hither and thither from one side of the ravine to the other.

After sitting there for half an hour I followed the stream by scrambling down the precipice into the deep valley, which was filled by dense jungle. The silence was broken only by the distant rumble of the waterfall above, the occasional whoops of the langur, and a furtive rustling among the large dry leaves which lay in a deep layer on the ground. At first I was rather apprehensive of this rustling, for I thought perhaps it was made by a tiger stalking me, which I sincerely hoped was not the case, as I was armed for defence with nothing more lethal than a small collecting gun and cartridges loaded with dust shot. But presently I spied out the rustler, which was only a hen spur-fowl, a wild bantam with a red face scratching amongst the leaves and clucking to her tiny fluffy chicks, just as a dunghill hen does in a farmyard in England.

The following days were spent very happily, and as I grew stronger I was able to make expeditions further afield. The place abounded with birds, great and small. There were two kinds of bulbuls, one with a jaunty crest and a red seat to his trousers, water wagtails with striped wings, cimeter bush-babblers in noisy companies, shrikes, black-chats, night-jars and small birds of all sorts of colours and song. Indeed it was a paradise for birds.

Of cuckoos there were two varieties, as well as numbers of drongoes or king crows, with their scissor-like tails. These sat bolt upright ready to attack any other bird which came near, without regard to its size.

Azure-blue flycatchers darted about and green barbets spent their days tapping high up in tall trees throughout the heat of the day. Big India pies, blue and grey with long striped tails trailing behind them, flew away to hide in the thick branches. Doves and pigeons laughed and cooed.

There was one particularly lovely thrush, smaller than our song thrush, with a reddish crown and a cream white throat and breast boldly speckled. Sometimes in some cool shady place, near water, I would hear a rich deep whistling. It sounded just as though the whistler was a man intently occupied with something, a series of sounds disjointed but very lovely. By keeping quite still the whistler could be seen; it was a large dark-blue thrush known to Anglo-Indians as the " Whistling schoolboy."

Sometimes I flushed a covey of bush quails, and each little bird would fly off in a different direction to drop into cover and crouch for a while in silence. Then one or another would utter its soft call-note, to be answered from different directions and the little party would soon be united again.

One of the first things to interest me at Khandala were the palm squirrels. Although to look at, they appeared exactly like the very common palm squirrel of Poona, the local race had a different voice. The Poona ones when angry, which they often were, or excited, which they almost always were, gave forth a harsh gibbering cry, with no variation of tone. But these Khandala squirrels had sweet musical voices, a bird-like whistle—" oo-wet, oo-wet," which continued in a regular rhythm, starting with several rapid notes

KHANDALA

but becoming slower towards the end of the refrain. Again and again I was deceived by the song, for song it was, believing it to be a bird's. Eventually I distinguished through my field-glasses one of these squirrels in the very act of singing, and procured it. To my unskilled eye this specimen did not differ from the Poona squirrel, but afterwards when it was examined at the British Museum it proved to be an unknown species and was christened *Funambulus Thomasi*, Thomas's Forest Squirrel, or literally, Thomas's Forest Rope-dancer, in honour of my friend Oldfield Thomas.

In the jungle not far away from the hotel there was a tribe of wild and nearly naked aborigines, who dwelt in wigwams made of branches of trees and lived by hunting. I thought that these hunters might be able to get specimens for me, so through the Goanese manager of the hotel I was introduced to the chief. After some bargaining the chief agreed to hire me his whole tribe for a day's hunting, and I was to go with them armed with an old twelve-bore gun I had picked up at Poona. I had also procured in the bazaar at a fabulous price one hundred cartridges to fit the gun.

At five o'clock on the morning of the great day the local shikari and I set out on foot to climb the saddle between two mountain tops. On the other side we met fifteen naked savages, armed with bows and arrows, who were to act as beaters and drive past me the game which I was to bowl over with my gun.

At the first drive several mouse-deer, or Indian chevrotain passed within easy shot of me and I missed every one. Soon after this despicable exhibition of marksmanship, loud shouts arose from the excited beaters, signifying that some further game was afoot and a moment after, not more than twenty paces from where I stood, there trotted slowly past me a ruddy mongoose. Now, I thought, I will show these contemptible blacks what a white sahib can do, so I aimed carefully, fired—and the ruddy mongoose trotted on, not deigning even to mend its leisurely pace. The savages gathered round me, all chattering, and my lack of knowledge of their language did not prevent me from comprehending the contempt in which they held me.

Perhaps I may add that this particular mongoose was not the common species, *Mungos mungo moerens*, but *Mongos smithi*, the Ruddy Mongoose. I mention this fact in order to clear myself of any hint or accusation of giving way to temper or vulgar abuse.

The situation had by now become critical. I had never professed to be a skilled shot, but I could hit an ordinary running rabbit and not disgrace myself when out with other guns. While we were all standing about, a little trusting dove came and perched on a branch not fifteen yards from me. The excited shikari cried out, "Master, master, look!" and pointed at the dove. I had already begun to suspect that the cartridges and not I were the cause of my bad shooting, so, amid the breathless silence of the tribe, I levelled my piece, drew a bead on the innocent, and pressed the trigger. A tremendous explosion, a cloud of black smoke, and away flew the little dove, scared but uninjured.

I now felt no doubt whatever that the old rascal from whom I had bought those cartridges had swindled me, so I handed my gun to the shikari and for the rest of the day I joined the beaters.

The next drive was through some jungle of straight bare canes. We soon roused a mouse-deer which went off like a streak of lightning, twisting and turning in and out among the canes, when suddenly it fell head over heels with an arrow through it. A wonderful piece of marksmanship.

Shortly afterwards up jumped another chevrotain, to fall dead, pierced by no fewer than four arrows.

We turned up many more mouse-deer during the day, but as we already had a male and a female I would not allow any more to be killed, much to the disappointment and bewilderment of the tribe.

At the close of a glorious if tiring day I paid the chief the prearranged sum for the services of himself and his followers, and promised to pay him well for any animals big or small other than mouse-deer which he could procure for me.

Now and then during my rambles in the jungle I used to come across the naked children of these hunting Indians. They were very wild and shy, but I used to make friends with them by putting down on the ground little gifts, such as picture postcards from England, and then walking away to watch the result. Gradually inquisitiveness overcame their fear, and the bolder would approach and pick up the gifts and take them back to the more timid children. I wonder what they made of photographs of the Pump-room at Bath, or the parade at Eastbourne, with waves breaking over it.

One evening I was in the act of setting my traps in a

gorge in the jungle, a stony dried-up river bed, when a big handsome jackal trotted close by without seeing me. I quickly brought my gun up to my shoulder and raised the hammer. The faint click of this brought him round instantly. So quickly, that he did not seem to stop and turn, but rather to have changed in a twinkling from a care-free animal proceeding at a steady loping gait going away from me, into an alert beast standing stock still staring at me. His sense of hearing must have been most acute to distinguish the slight sound of the gun hammer, for there were many other sounds, the rattling of the big dry leaves in the evening wind and the noise of a waterfall not far away.

The jackal left unscathed, for I am a moral coward.

One of my most exciting captures in the traps at Khandala was also my last. I had a large steel spring trap, one of those pitiless contrivances with sharp teeth, strong enough to hold a fox. I had set it in a ravine below the old English cemetery. When I went to look at it the following morning I found in it a fierce jungle cat, with spotted fur and pale-gold coloured eyes, caught by one leg. After killing the poor brute I began to climb up the steep cliff, carrying the dead cat and the trap. The sun was now become very hot and as I climbed I began to feel downright ill, but managed to get back to the bungalow, when I set about skinning the animal.

I had a splitting headache and everything in the room seemed to go round and round. I felt that at any cost the job must be finished, and at last the skin was off,

KHANDALA

stuffed and set up. What happened after this I do not know, for I lost consciousness and for several days I must have been very ill. Ledger had gone back to Poona before this, but my faithful Kerudin nursed me, and a kind Indian doctor from the village came to see me each day and give me medicines.

When the worst of the attacks were over I went back again to the Sassoon Hospital, before my convalescent leave was up, to be treated for malaria.

I was glad afterwards that I had resisted the temptation to give up the attempt to skin the jungle-cat, for it proved to be a Rusty Spotted Jungle Cat, which caused quite a stir in mammalogical circles, not because it was an unknown species, but because it was supposed to be entirely confined to the extreme south of the Indian continent, and had never before been reported from elsewhere.

Before leaving Khandala I sent word to the chief of the hunters to bring me whatever he could before I left by train next day. When everything was packed up and ready for our departure from the hotel, I crept away with the steel trap down to a pond, into which I threw the accursed thing, as Sir Bedivere did Excalibur, so that it could never again be used.

Almost to time the Poona train pulled into the Khandala railway station, but still no signs of the hunters with their trophies. Kerudin, having put me into a first-class carriage, went off to find for himself a place in the third-class.

As the guard was about to blow his whistle the chief appeared on the platform. I waved and shouted for him to hurry so he broke into a run, and as the train began to move away he handed me a small brass pot covered by a banana leaf neatly tied on with grass-stems. I threw him a rupee, the size of the prize did not seem to demand more, and we were off. What could the brass pot contain?

Gingerly I undid the grass-bound cover, and lifted the leaf lid, wondering if some live thing would spring out. But all that emerged was a terrible odour of mortifying flesh. The result of the hunting tribe's zeal was now disclosed. At the bottom of the pot lay the corpses, in an advanced stage of corruption, of a mother mouse and her three little offspring.

My next stay at the hospital was a short one, for under quinine treatment I was soon well enough to go back to Fever Hall.

Shortly afterwards I received a letter from Lord Montagu of Beaulieu to say that he was leaving Simla to embark for Egypt, and asking me to meet him at Bombay.

I got leave off, and went to stop with Mr. and Mrs. Millard at their lovely bungalow, on Malabar Hill. Their garden was as beautiful as their house, and was said to be the most interesting and the best kept garden in the whole of India. Every kind of tropical flower was in bloom. Orchids of all sorts and endless varieties of ferns grew in shady places.

Lord Montagu was never a man to be idle, whether at home at Beaulieu or abroad. He liked to see everything there was to see and to meet interesting people. The Millards asked him up to dinner, and he and his hosts got on well together for he was at his very best. He was full of all sorts of confidences " which must go no further, my dear lady," that really were no secrets at all, but this style of recounting gossip is always flattering to the hearer, and effective. He had only one day for sight-seeing and it was arranged to visit the government laboratories at the old Government House at Parel.

Next morning I called for him and with his arm round my neck, as was his friendly wont, he introduced me to a bevy of generals and other high officials as " Philip, my oldest and dearest friend " ; which certainly put the generals and myself on an easy footing for that one day.

Off we went, generals and all, to the hospital which stood a few miles outside the city. It was fitted up with fine laboratories, where anti-plague virus was made, and we were shown all sorts of interesting things ; a microbe which would and did—we saw it do it—kill a bowl full of small fishes in ten minutes, and we had demonstrated to us the life history of a parasite which spent part of its life in certain snails, then in fishes, and lastly in men. We also met Major Kunhardt, who knew more about rats, particularly plague rats, and how to kill them than any living man. Naturally we two got on like a house on fire, and talked endless rat " shop."

We were then taken to see the live snakes from which was collected the venom for making " venine " used for saving the lives of people who had been bitten by cobras or Russell's vipers. There was a special native who carried out this most dangerous work. After we were all seated in chairs in a big hall, a tin box was brought and placed on the floor in front of us. Then the Indian, who was practically naked and armed only with a stick, opened the lid of the box and out coiled a big cobra, which immediately raised its head, spread its hood and began to make vicious strikes at the Indian. But the man was too quick for it and got his stick across the snake's neck, which he then held in place with his bare foot. He then seized the snake's tail with his left hand and worked the other up to the reptile's head. Having got a good hold of it, he lifted up the cobra and forced open its jaws, exposing a pair of wicked poison fangs. The Director of the Laboratories, Colonel Glen Lister, then took a wine glass over the top of which some rubber was stretched, and putting the cobra's open upper jaw over this rammed it on to the rubber so that the long poison fangs went through, and the yellow poison could be seen dripping down to form a small puddle at the bottom of the glass. He then squeezed its parotid glands to get out the last drop. Before letting it go the snake was fed by a funnel and rubber tube, the latter being passed down its throat and a good sized egg-flip poured down, since cobras will not feed themselves in captivity and this is the only way of keeping them alive.

We next had a Russell's viper brought out, a great thick vicious brute that attacked the man each time he went near it and he could not get the stick properly on its neck. Several times the viper nearly had him and at last to our relief he let it go back into its box. The Colonel told us it was the first time he had ever known this man give up. He had been bitten already three times but anti-venine was always ready at hand and beyond losing a finger he was none the worse.

KHANDALA

After this we got into our motors and went to a leper colony not far away. It was very sad to see the poor creatures being slowly eaten away. There was one wretched white man amongst them who looked after a small gas engine. The little doomed community, we were told, was practically self-supporting.

I had not been back at Fever Hall for very long before the attacks of the malaria I had contracted at Khandala became so regular and so severe that I had to return once again to the Sassoon Hospital. There is little to tell about this stay, which was a much longer one than it would have been had not one of the patients developed smallpox, for which reason we were all put in strict quarantine for a month, however fit we might be.

The weather had now become very hot indeed and almost unbearable in the afternoons; the hospital being placed in the middle of the city, what little sultry wind blew only covered the place with dust from the roads.

The view from my bed was not a cheerful one. The two principal and most prominent objects were the corrugated-iron mortuary and a tree which appeared to be lifeless and waiting to be admitted to the deadhouse.

The best, indeed for a while the only pleasing thing to gaze at was the blue sky. But the gaunt leafless tree had a surprise in store. Without warning, and quite unexpectedly, it resurrected, and shewed signs of life; not by green leaf buds, but gorgeous flowers of flaming orange, which covered it like some giant azalea bush. It was the famous Golden Mohr tree, of Madagascar.

For me, lying in bed, this spectacle of blazing orange colour entirely changed the drab outlook to one of indescribable loveliness. Owing to the quarantine, time hung heavily, for no visitors were allowed, not even the Indian hawkers of carpets, brass ware and all the other bazaar goods. Before we were placed in isolation these hucksters used to come in the afternoons and spread their stock out on the verandah, and the time passed pleasantly for the patients and profitably for the higglers as the bargaining went on. It took time before any bargain was clinched, but what was time to us or to the bazaar wallahs? Perhaps your eye spied out a brass god, and you enquired the price. " Fifty rupees, Master," might be the answer, with a flicker of an eyelid. In return you offered ten rupees. The merchant put on an expression of pained surprise, left the brass god and drew your attention to other objects. If you knew the rules of the game you pretended to have forgotten all about the brass god, and sooner or later the vendor would take it up and tell you he would *give* it you for forty rupees. You scoffed at the idea and turned away, and the merchant then asked you to name your price. This time you would go up to—say—fifteen rupees. And so the bargaining dragged on. To have shown symptoms of great desire for the object would have been fatal. At last, as at an economic congress, there was apt to come a stage where a deadlock threatened to bring the whole business to an end.

The merchant having now come down from fifty to thirty rupees, you raised your offer to twenty. A state of stalemate had arisen and you began to think the brass god would never be yours. Then came in the sporting gambling spirit inherent in every son of India. Throwing aside at last his mask of indifference the merchant would cry excitedly " Master make toss ! "

This meant that you took and spun a coin and if it came down heads, you won, and got your brass god at your own price of twenty rupees, but if it was tails, then you paid the huckster his price of thirty. This form of barter had points in its favour, and it was gratifying to us that the Indian was always ready to allow the foreigner to toss the coin and trust him to say if it was heads or tails. A cynic might spoil it by observing that in any case the brass god was probably not worth more than ten rupees.

The hot days dragged slowly by without visitors or bazaar-wallahs and for once in my life I really was bored. The one event I looked forward to and enjoyed was watching the breaking of dawn and the sun rise. Each morning was just like every other morning, but the last one always seemed even more wonderful than any that had gone before. As the first rays of the sun touched the crown of my golden tree all sorts of birds would fly up there and sit preening their feathers and enjoying the warmth.

There might be as many as fifty rose-coloured pastors crowded together amongst the upper branches, each bird facing the morning light as though worshipping the god of its happiness and life. Most of them sat quite still, though from time to time one or another would bend down his head and adjust a feather that had got out of place.

One morning in particular I remember. The sky was a pale blue with a silver moon high up that looked transparent and appeared as if the faint blue of the sky could be seen through it. From time to time a pure white egret, or two in company, flew slowly and steadily overhead in the direction of the river; and in this light they too appeared, not opaque, but of thin transparent ivory, like the moon.

Most of the birds seemed content to sit quite still and enjoy the sunshine, but not all. The crows and the black cuckoos could not remain quiet but kept flying about in a restless, nervous way, from one branch to another. Why they did this I do not know. They disturbed the sun-worshippers by pitching clumsily and heavily amongst the devout congregation, which was broken up, to gather together again elsewhere.

As the sun rose higher in the sky the birds began to get livelier and very talkative, particularly the coppersmith, a sturdy little green barbet with a ruby throat, who was always one of the first to strike up. He would choose his site for the day on the very topmost twig of the tree, and sitting bolt upright settle down for a long day's "tap-tap-tap," on his little make-believe copper pot. I suppose he rested sometimes for meals, but I never noticed him away from his twig nor did his monotonous hammering ever seem to cease.

As the day advanced most of the birds had completed their devotions and were busy in the tree-top. The rose-coloured worshippers became an ecstatic chorus, to judge from the sound like the jingling of a myriad tiny silver bells.

There were the gorgeous little sugar birds, wee pellets

of life, all metallic blue and gold; very noisy, and busy hunting from one flower to another, never stopping to finish the honey in one flower, but darting on to another as though greedily afraid that one of their comrades in the little family troupe might get there first and find an extra big drop of nectar.

CHAPTER VIII

THE NILGIRI HILLS

SOONER or later all things come to an end, even quarantine for smallpox, and towards the end of May, I was granted six weeks' sick leave and left Poona with Kerudin, my collecting outfit, and a permit to travel first-class to Ootacamund via Bangalore. The generous authorities even granted me a sleeping-berth on the train as well, all free of charge.

The monsoon was overdue and the heat terrific. The view from the railway carriage window was very different from what I had gazed at on my first journey to Bangalore five months before. Now the flat country we passed through was burnt brown, with scarcely a green leaf to be seen. I was fortunate in meeting with a delightful travelling-companion, a Captain Dacey, who knew all about Ootacamund, and warned me that I should find the place full up, and advised me to go to Coonoor until I had found some lodgings. Owing to the War, Anglo-Indians who would in the ordinary course of things have gone home to England for their leave now went instead to one or other of the Indian hill stations.

When we reached Bangalore at seven o'clock one morning I found that my train to the Nilgiris did not leave until seven the same evening, but the kind Dacey insisted on taking me to the United Service Club and standing me hot baths and meals.

All that night and the following morning we travelled through the sweltering plains of Coimbatore until at last we began to ascend the foot-hills of the Nilgiris. As the train puffed and wormed its way up the steep valleys the views became more and more wonderful. For several hours I hung out of the carriage window peering down on torrents far below at the foot of perpendicular precipices, or gazing up at forest-clad mountain tops and every hour as the train climbed higher the temperature fell lower, so that I had to keep putting on one garment after another to keep warm.

In the late afternoon we reached Coonoor and I got out and was pulled and pushed up a steep zig-zag road in a rickshaw by four men, Kerudin following more sedately with the luggage in a small covered cart pulled by a diminutive bullock.

The Glenview hotel did not belie its name, for it was perched at the summit of a conical hill with magnificent views on every side.

The next morning I was out and about exploring the evergreen jungle which surrounded the hotel. I had thought nothing in the world could be more romantic or beautiful than Khandala, but now I had to admit to myself that the Nilgiri Hills were even lovelier. Khandala was superb in a fierce, rugged way, with its bare mountain tops, but in late spring, before the monsoon broke, everything had become burnt up, except in the deepest ravines. But here at Coonoor the mountains were covered to their very summits by dense green jungle, or shola, formed by dwarf flowering trees, while the valleys were of a deep mysterious blue.

The atmosphere too was softer and certainly damper than at Khandala and reminded me of Ventnor in the Isle of Wight just before a thunderstorm. All sorts of trees seemed to flourish, for besides the indigenous shola there were many species of pines, as well as eucalyptus trees, many of them of great height. Everywhere masses of flowers bloomed, yellow, pink and blue. Tropical ferns throve in the hot damp valleys, from great spreading tree-ferns which grew along the sides of the rushing mountain torrents to tiny feathery maiden-hair ferns which hid themselves in cool shady places. Here and there on the steep sides of the valleys the shola had been cut down to make room for plantations of tea or coffee.

On the second evening I got to work and went out into the gorge just below the hotel and set all of my eighteen mouse traps.

One of the fascinations of collecting, whether it be field-mice, books about pirates or toby jugs, is the occasional prize which, when least expected, rewards the patient seeker.

When I left the hotel early the following morning to look at my traps I was full of hope and excitement to learn what treasures awaited me in those " woods and pastures new." But as I went from trap to trap to find each one empty my spirits fell lower and lower. Could fate be so unkind as to deny me even one example of a Nilgiri mouse at my first venture? But when I reached the last trap of all, behold a prize, for it contained the dead body of a mouse unlike any I had ever seen before!

It was a small mouse, covered on the back and sides by long, dense, very dark brown fur sprinkled over with a tinge of copper, and it had a waistcoat of mahogany colour. I had no idea at the time what sort of mouse it was with which I had opened my Nilgiri campaign, nor if it was rare or common.

Later on it proved to be only the second specimen known to science of the Nilgiri Wild Mouse—*Leggada famula*. The previous one also had been caught at Coonoor twenty years before by the late Charles Gray, a planter and keen local naturalist. His original specimen, a very poor one, was a male and as mine, a female, was in perfect pelage—as the mammalogists term it—and an excellent skin in every way, the species was redescribed by the British Museum from my capture.

This tendency to boast of my small successes in the mouse-collecting line must be severely held in check, but one other I plead to be allowed to mention. This other mouse was also captured at Coonoor and was a first cousin to *Leggada famula*. I trapped it in a clearing in the jungle and it was as red as a fox and had a pure white belly. My capture of it released the poor little thing from the necessity of living out its life under the lugubrious name of *Leggada boodugo*.

Many pleasant hours at Coonoor were spent sitting on the verandah after dinner. The nights were cool and strange exotic sounds and scents arose from the deep ravine below. For company I had three civilians, a judge, the head of an Indian college, and a retired indigo planter.

Here at last I met with men who, like Millard and Bell, did not look upon India as a pestilential place of exile, nor regard all Indians as damned niggers. These three civilians seemed to be fond of India and interested in its past history and its future, and were wise in the ways and customs of its native races. I was able to ask about things of which I was ignorant, about the different castes and caste marks, the temples and religious ceremonies, and a hundred and one subjects which I had not been able to find out about at military Poona.

In spite of its tropical setting Coonoor, like all these southern hill stations, was intensely English. The whole of the European population was of the same upper-middle class; planters or retired Indian civil servants, or else widows who preferred to end their days in this lovely place with its kindly climate, where they could live well within their incomes and have plenty of servants, instead of returning to eke out their pensions among strangers in dull boarding houses at Hove and Cheltenham.

Most of the houses were cottages or small bungalows which stood on ground levelled out of the mountain side and had gardens filled with English flowers, rambler roses and tall-growing fuchsias, and as often as not there was a small babbling mountain torrent near by.

After a few lazy days at Coonoor I went by train to hunt for lodgings at Ootacamund, which had a more bracing climate. Although the two places are only nine miles apart as the crow flies, the train took two hours to climb the fifteen hundred feet, but of what account was time on such a journey for which I would gladly travel half-way round the world?

"Ooty," as it is always known, is a large rambling hill station, full of trees and flower gardens, and surrounded by high bare rounded hills, not unlike parts of the Wiltshire downs.

I hired a gharri by the hour and drove to several addresses I had been given of people who took in paying guests, but found that every one was full.

Then, while driving along a winding road over which arched tall trees between high banks covered with ferns, we came to a whitewashed cottage half hidden by rambler roses. On the white gate was painted *Fox How*, and by the gate stood a big pine tree on the trunk of which was nailed Madame de Merville. At least a board was, with her name on it.

I called to the driver to stop and with the boldness of desperation walked in and knocked at the open cottage door. A pretty old lady came to the door, Madame de Merville herself, to whom I put my piteous case and begged her to take me in. She invited me into her drawing-room and was very nice about it, said she did sometimes take paying guests, but that at present both her spare rooms were occupied, and added she was very sorry. She then went on to tell me how she kept her own cows and fowls, and as I could then eat nothing else but milk and eggs, this made yet another reason, I told her, why she should not turn me away.

She complained that the wild pigs and porcupines were playing havoc with her garden and that a panther had been " bothering " her cows in the meadow.

This was more than I could bear and I told her quite candidly that somehow or other she had got to find room for me and that I refused to return to Coonoor without her solemn promise to let me know immediately she could put me up. My persistence was rewarded, for the very next day a telegram arrived telling me to come at once, and the same evening I was installed in a bedroom at Highbury House, a mile away from Fox How, where I took all my meals.

It was impossible not to get fit and strong at Ooty, with its bracing air and the good fresh milk and eggs, and before long I was able to walk and climb hills for hours on end. Soon I was out all day and began to get together quite a representative collection of birds and small animals.

Thanks to Bell, I received from the forest officer a permit to shoot in the Reserved Forest and other Government lands for the purpose of collecting small animals, though this permission did not cover the shooting of game.

This permit was very useful, for the game laws were, and quite rightly so, strictly enforced. The forest officer, when I explained about my collection, and how it was not to be a private one but to go to the British Museum, told me that one of his duties was to pay out rewards given by the Madras Government for the destruction of vermin, or what was classed as such, and that he had a quantity of skins on which rewards had been paid, and said that I was welcome to go over them and keep any I wanted. I jumped at the offer and was taken into a shed which was full of skins. These I carefully inspected, picking out a few of the best and most interesting, such as jungle-cat, leopard-cat, small Indian civet, stripe-necked and Carnatic mongooses, common and clawless otters, sloth bear, South Indian jackal and Indian wild dog. I was very glad to get these skins as it would have been impossible for me with my limited time and small traps to have captured such animals myself.

I had another introduction from the ever kind Millard to the Director of the Ootacamund botanical gardens. These were very fine and well arranged, but what interested me most of all was the collection of medicinal plants, which ranged from the chincona from which quinine is made to the English foxglove, from which digitalis is extracted.

I got to know many civilians at Ooty, who were all most friendly and hospitable. At the house of a member of the staff of the Governor of Madras I was introduced to charming and pretty Mrs. James, the wife of a staff major. When she heard I came from Poona, she began to reel off the names of all her friends there, soldiers and their wives, and was very surprised to find I knew none of them. I then explained to her as nicely as I could that, being only a temporary officer, or at least a territorial one which was almost as bad, I did not know any of the service people of Poona otherwise than officially; on the barrack square so to speak.

She was highly indignant at this, and hardly credited it, so I told her about my friend David Hadden.

An order was issued one day that a few commissions were available in the regular R.A.M.C. open to those holding temporary commissions. The only one of us to send in his name was Hadden. He was essentially cut out to be a soldier; smart, intelligent, very keen on the soldiering side of the profession, and, being the son of a doctor in general practice, had a very strong and natural disinclination to enter general practice himself after the War. Also he had done very well in France as Medical Officer with a battalion, and had the extremely rare distinction of winning the Military Cross with two bars.

Our commanding officer, a lieutenant-colonel in the R.A.M.C. was a very efficient officer and we all liked him, but he never invited any of us to meet his family or to his bungalow. In due time Hadden received his commission, became a captain R.A.M.C. in the regulars, and a few days afterwards was invited to dine with the colonel at his house. Not one of us " temporaries " was ever invited.

Before leaving Ooty, Mrs. James made me promise to call on her friends Major and Mrs. Geoffrey Martyn as soon as ever I got back, as they would be delighted to know me and would ask me to meet lots of other nice soldiers and their families at Poona. What came of this introduction to the Martyns will appear later.

Wishing to see all I could of the Nilgiri Hills during my limited time I arranged to go and stop at the hotel at Kotagiri. To get there one travelled by rickshaw with four men to pull and push it up and over the high mountain range. I was so well by now that I walked up all the hills and only used the rickshaw when the men could run with it, on the level and downhill. The rickshawmen, although physically poor specimens to look at, jogged along at a good steady pace, and were none the worse for the twenty mile journey over high mountain passes.

As soon as I was installed at the Blue Mountain hotel,

THE NILGIRI HILLS

I opened the Kotagiri campaign by trapping in my bedroom, one Indian house-mouse, one musk-shrew, one Indian house-rat, and catching two toads, a bat and a lizard, these all on the first night; a zoological exploit which ought to give a pretty fair idea as to the type of hotel it was. I might have made an interesting collection of all the live things which shared that bedroom with me. If I had it would have comprised, besides mice, shrews, rats, reptiles and bats, many sorts of insects winged and crawling.

I particularly use the past-tense, for this all happened sixteen years ago, and the hotel has passed through the hands of several proprietors and managers since my visit, and I am told that if any zoologically minded person hopes to achieve what I did, he will be sorely disappointed.

One other feature of the Blue Mountain Hotel was very good indeed, the view; but no man can subsist indefinitely on a view, however good, nor on the livestock in his bedroom, however varied it may be, so I was glad to accept one of the many invitations I received from the planters of the neighbourhood.

The hospitality of the Nilgiri planters was positively embarrassing. If I had accepted all their invitations to stay with them, I might be in the Nilgiri hills to this day.

I will not pretend that I left the Blue Mountain hotel with many regrets. I took away with me, in my specimen boxes, the best it had to offer its guests. In a rickshaw made to carry only one passenger I travelled along a narrow track which wound its way through the shola, up hill and down dale, until after going some eight miles the path ended at the Rookery Estate, Kilkotagiri, the home of Mr. and Mrs. J. B. Vernède.

The long, low bungalow stood on the side of a steep hill and in front of it range after range of mountains extended, those nearest a brilliant green, the more distant blue or purple. Five thousand feet below could be seen, across a hedge of sky-blue plumbago, the sweltering plains of Mysore, which changed their colours all day long like a chameleon. It was almost unbelievable and totally indescribable in its beauty.

My host was a famous shikari and spoke five different local dialects, while his daughter, aged nine, was also a mighty hunter of butterflies and such-like small game. Everything was done by these kind people to make my visit pleasant; several coolies were at once taken off their work in the tea and coffee gardens to hunt specimens for me, and many a time as I stepped from the house on to the verandah I would see a black man standing waiting for me. After salaaming politely, he would approach and offer me something he had caught. It might be a Russell's viper, a couple of iguana lizards, or a bird's egg.

Kilkotagiri was a paradise of squirrels. In the very tallest trees in the virgin forest the handsome Bombay giant squirrels, with chocolate back and yellow belly, gibbered and threatened intruders from above. Sometimes high up in the trunk of a big tree you would see a hole, and if you tapped hard on the trunk with a stick an angry face might pop out of the hole and peer down at you, as though wanting to know who you were and what you meant by disturbing a Madras flying-squirrel during his afternoon nap.

THE NILGIRI HILLS

The smallest of them all was the tiny Malabar pigmy palm-squirrel, an active and agile mite, exceedingly difficult to distinguish amongst the thick leaves.

There was also another palm-squirrel, larger than the last, resembling the Khandala squirrel which sang so nicely and was named after Oldfield Thomas. But the Kilkotagiri kind had a different voice and a less musical song; it proved to be an unknown species and was christened *Funambulus Gossei*—my very own rope-dancer.

One day a coolie brought me something alive in a little wicker basket. When I gingerly lifted the lid I found inside a tiny baby hare of the South Indian blacknecked race. It cannot have been more than a few days old and seemed very tame. It was too young to feed itself so I had to turn nurse and bottle-feed it. At first I gave it warm diluted buffalo's milk through a pen-filler. It took instantly and eagerly to this process of weaning and grew larger and absurdly tame. At night it slept in a little bed of dry grass in a basket beside me, and used to wake up very early in the morning and scratch against me, apparently in order to rouse me to get up and give it its bottle.

We soon became great friends, the little hare and I. Wherever I went he went with me, both in the Nilgiri Hills and afterwards to Madras. But on the long, hot railway journey from Madras to Poona I had to feed him on whatever milk could be bought at the stations en route, and I think it was this that upset him, for he became ill and died before we got back. I missed him very much for he was a small but very good companion. In the sleeping saloon on the train he used to run about the floor and when tired would jump up on to the bunk and go to sleep close beside me.

One day a messenger arrived at the Rookery to report that a rogue elephant was damaging the peasants' crops some miles away and asking Vernède to come and shoot it. So we started at early dawn next morning on foot to the plains several thousand feet below. Some natives met us there and led us to a place where the herd had lately been feeding and we easily followed their tracks by the torn-down branches of trees and uprooted saplings.

Vernède, who had shot many elephants, informed me that he never fired at one at a longer range than fifteen yards but preferred only five. He was armed with a rifle which looked a very insufficient weapon with which to kill an elephant; in fact it seemed to me little better than a rook rifle. From time to time as we roamed about in the sweltering bamboo jungle, Vernède would apologize to me for the disappointment I must be feeling at our failure to catch up the herd and come to grips with the rogue elephant. I thought of the five yard range and looked at his absurd toy of a rifle and told him not to worry about me, as I was quite enjoying the walk. The day's outing, though exhausting, was highly satisfactory, though whether the rogue elephant or the hunters gained by the failure to make contact I do not know.

My sick leave had now come to an end and as I was never in better health in my life I could not well apply for an extension. Since nothing had been said about the route by which I should return to Poona I took a somewhat roundabout way, starting in the opposite

THE NILGIRI HILLS

direction and going via Madras. I wanted very much to see the Fort St. George of the old East India Company, and also to visit the famous aquarium there.

It was extremely hot in July at Madras, but very interesting. Amongst other things I visited the Museum, where specimens of native craftsmanship were exhibited. A novel feature of this Museum I should like to call to the notice of the directors of our English museums, particularly the director of the Victoria and Albert Museum. At the Madras Museum, anyhow in the section I visited, every object in the show cases could be bought and was marked with its price. This custom lends an added interest to museum visiting. I made several small purchases of models and specimens of brass work for quite small sums.

When I arrived at the Aquarium the official inside the pigeon-hole at the booking office informed me of the devastating news that it was purdah day and only ladies were admitted. I could scarcely claim admittance under this category, but I told him how I had come the whole way from England expressly to see his world-famed aquarium and had to return next day, and how bitterly disappointing it would be if I had to leave the country without seeing one of the glories of India.

I could see that the attendant was not unmoved by my words, and then in a flash I remembered and slipped a couple of rupees across the counter. These he took and disappeared through a door. Soon sounds of expostulation shrill and feminine could be heard coming from the direction of the aquarium, and then the attendant returned to say that I might enter, as there were no ladies there.

In the small hall the tanks were few but the fishes in them were very beautiful and interesting and enough to make the journey to Madras well worth while. There were fishes of every colour and shape, some lovely, others fantastic, and I remember one unpleasant eel which had pale blue eyes and the appearance of being made of chewed leather.

CHAPTER IX

PUKKA POONA

ON my return to Poona about the middle of August, I found a great change. Instead of the bare stony hills and the parched fields I had left six weeks before, the whole country-side had been turned a fresh emerald green by the rains of the monsoon. But I was shocked at the appearance of the inhabitants of Fever Hall. They were all pale and thin and looked ill, and I soon found out the cause, which was nothing else than bad food. The question of housekeeping had all along been a difficult one. Each one of them had in turn tried his hand at it, but the fare became worse and worse. In our ignorance of the country and the ways of Indian servants we had agreed to the butler's suggestion that we should pay him a fixed sum per head and leave it to him to feed us, engage and pay a cook and supply everything down to wood for the kitchen fire and oil for the lamps. This arrangement, which had sounded so simple, promised to save us from all the worries of housekeeping. What actually happened was that the butler underpaid the cook, and a bad one at that, and bought in the bazaar the very cheapest rubbish to feed us on, smothering it in strong curry powder. It was curry for breakfast, curry for lunch and curry for dinner, and belly-ache all night.

Coming straight from the Nilgiris and its wholesome food I made a great to-do over the disgusting uneatable fare at Fever Hall, and the then acting housekeeper, Hawes, at once and thankfully resigned his post and I was unanimously installed in his place. By way of a start I sacked both the butler and his poor relation the cook, and engaged a new butler, Wharri by name, a dignified Mohammedan with a black beard, and a well-recommended Goanese cook.

To the uninitiated the cook appeared to be a pure-blooded Indian coolie, but as he wore a topee on his head he could claim to be of European descent. In fact our new cook was reputed to be a major in the Goanese militia and to come of a very good family; as well he might, since his full names were: Manuel Joao Domingo Francisco de Xavier Jesus de Gama. No man, however dark his complexion or humble his station in life, could fail to be of gentle and European birth with a patronym like that.

Each morning Wharri and I discussed the day's bill of fare. It was a tiresome and irritating proceeding, for there was not only the language difficulty, but the utterly incomprehensible oriental mind of Wharri, and to Wharri, no doubt, my own equally inscrutable occidental one. Anyhow the new system worked well for a time and we got pure food and plenty of it, properly cooked by Manuel de Gama.

There were however drawbacks even to this method. It was annoying to have to order daily small amounts of everything and check the cost of each item in Wharri's account, and there was also the expense.

To give only one example: I have before me one of

Wharri's daily household accounts. It covers the whole of one side of a sheet of foolscap paper, and contains thirty-two separate items with the price of each. When it is remembered that the Indian rupee was worth one shilling and six pence, an anna one penny and a pie about the third of a farthing, the reader of these lines, particularly if she be a housewife, will appreciate the trouble I had brought upon myself.

The list is far too long to give in full, but here are a few of the entries as a sample of the rest, in the order in which Wharri wrote them down:

Soopa	3 annas.
Underpart Beef	8 annas.
Kiddney	2 annas.
New green stuff	9 pies.
Frut	4 annas.
passly and salry	6 pies.
orranges	5 annas.
curry stuff } cocknut }	2 annas.
munkynut	1 anna.
char col	1 anna, 6 pies.
Firwood	12 annas.
oil : 2 botles	4 annas, 6 pies.
Coolis : 2	6 annas.

This is but a sample of the daily list which had to be gone through and checked, and on every item, however small, Wharri had received an infinitesimal commission from the vendor at the bazaar, where he spent his mornings shopping and bargaining.

I soon wearied of this retail way of housekeeping, which in any case was very expensive. For example we bought one day's supply of firewood at a time for the cook's fire for twelve annas and paid the coolie six annas to bring it to the bungalow from the bazaar. I upset Wharri very much by purchasing a whole bullock-cart load of firewood for twelve rupees, and paying twelve annas for having it brought up. In the old way this firewood would have cost us fifteen rupees and about six rupees for the coolies who brought a little quantity each day.

Everything was purchased in the same way, even things of which we used small quantities daily, such as charcoal, salt and curry powder. Under the new regime I bought all the necessary articles in bulk, kept them locked up and served out what was wanted each morning. This method was troublesome but much less so than the daily wrangling over each account, and our household expenses fell by nearly fifty per cent. Even then I have no doubt advantage was taken of my ignorance of housekeeping and the ways of India. The erudite Eha, himself born and bred in the country, complained of the difficulties of these household accounts. Writing about the boy or butler in his delightful book *Behind the Bungalow* he says:

> "There is a mystery about these accounts which I have never been able to solve. The total is always, on the face of it, monstrous and not to be endured; but when you call your Boy up and prepare to discharge the bombshell of your indignation, he merely inquires in an unagitated tone of voice which item you find fault with and you become painfully aware that you have not a leg to stand on. In the first place, most of the items are too minute to allow of much retrenchment. You can scarcely make sweeping reductions on such charges as: 'Butons for master's

trouser, 9 pies' (less than one farthing); 'Tramwei for going to market, 1 anna 6 pies'; 'Grain to sparrow' (canary seed!) '1 anna 3 pies'; 'Making white to master's hat, 5 pies'; and when at last you find a charge big enough to lay hold of, the imperturbable man proceeds to explain how, in the case of that particular item, he was able, by the exercise of a little forethought, to save you 2 annas and 3 pies. I have struggled against these accounts and know them. It is vain to be indignant. You must pay the bill."

One of the first things I did after returning from the Nilgiri hills was to keep my promise to Mrs. James and pay the call which was to gain for me the entrée to the exclusive military circles of Poona. I was determined to do the thing properly for was not the reputation of all of us "temporary gents" at stake? So I went to the unheard of extravagance of having a new suit made by the only European tailor in the city. Hitherto all our clothes had been made by the dirzi, Gampat, a round smiling little tailor, who always wore a tape measure, the insignia of his profession, round his neck, and who came to measure us at the bungalow.

As soon as ever the new suit was finished, I dropped my visiting card in the little box chained to the gate of Major Martyn's compound, and within a day or two received a polite invitation to tea.

When the auspicious afternoon arrived I left Fever Hall resplendent in my new suit and wearing on my head a bran-new Cawnpore Tent-club Topee, a thing like a huge meringue, and stepped into the two-horse gharri, for although the two bungalows were not more than half a mile apart it would never do, I thought, to arrive on foot.

Mrs. Martyn's drawing-room was already full of other guests, who had been invited to meet me. I was first of all introduced to a lady who at once asked me if I thought Freddy would get his " K " next time and didn't I think it too bad he had not been given it at the last birthday honours. I did not know who Freddy was, nor what a " K " was either, so I gave a sympathetic non-committal answer. By keeping my ears open and putting one thing and the other together I learned during my visit, what a " K " was, but not the identity of Freddy, who should have got it last time. In the profession of arms, if you have been good and given no trouble, you are rewarded in time by the C.B. (military). Then if you go on being good long enough and rise very high in rank you become a knight, a K.C.B. I had never heard the expression a " K " before, though possibly it is a common one.

I am going rather minutely into what took place at this party because it was bound to have a very important bearing on my military career.

The next visitor I was introduced to was an elderly lady who asked me, very earnestly, what games I played. While we had tea I talked to another lady, young and married and the mother of two small children. She was fond of big-game shooting and told me a graphic story of how she once shot a panther which proved to be pregnant and had two living cubs inside her body, the same number as she herself had babies. She was very naïve in telling me about it, and I am sure saw nothing incongruous in the incident.

After tea the guests sat round the room and gradually the general conversation broke off and only my hostess

PUKKA POONA

and I were left talking while the rest listened to our dialogue. This took the form of question and answer, with Mrs. Martyn sitting on one side of the circle asking questions, while I answered from the other.

The conversation, if such it can be called, will best be represented as follows:

Q. Do you play polo, Captain Gosse?
A. No, I don't play polo.
Q. Did you hunt while you were at Ooty?
A. No, Mrs. Martyn.
Q. I suppose you ride?
A. No; you see I haven't got a horse.
Q. Then you don't go in for pig-sticking?
A. No.
Q. What do you think of our golf course?
A. I don't play golf.
Q. Do you play lawn-tennis?
A. I used to play a lot before the War.
Q. What about cricket?
A. I've not played cricket since I was at school.
Q. Were you at Eton?
A. No.
Q. I suppose you motor a good deal?
A. No; it's very expensive in India and I can't afford to.
Q. Do you fish for mahseer in our river?
A. No; I haven't got a rod, and they cannot be bought even in Bombay.
Q. Do you do a lot of racing? As you live almost on the race-course I expect you do.
A. (Brightly) No, I've never been to a race-meeting in my life.

Q. Perhaps you play bridge? Such a splendid way of passing the time.

A. No, I'm a duffer at all card games.

Q. (In a voice in which I thought I detected a note of despair.) Possibly you shoot?

This simply could not go on. An ominous silence reigned amongst the expectant ring of listeners, waiting to learn if I shot, and wondering, if not, what in God's name I did do.

Had I the moral courage, I asked myself, to answer that I did not shoot, either tiger, panther or even black buck? No I simply dared not, so I murmured, " Yes, I do shoot a little."

With a sigh of relief Mrs. Martyn turned towards her husband, the staff-major, and called out across the room in a clear voice, " Geoffrey dear, he *does* shoot."

Little did that gathering of sportsmen suspect that the biggest game I had shot in India was a bat!

However, this news of my being a shot, a shikari, did good. It put me on a sound footing with the others and things became distinctly easier, for these soldiers and their wives did, I am sure, want to be nice and friendly, if only they could light upon some common interest.

All might, and I believe would, have gone well after this discovery that I was a big-game shooter if only the subject of fox-hunting had not cropped up again. I do not know what infernal impulse prompted me to it, and it was very stupid of me.

The major, who had not hitherto spoken to me, said he was very surprised to hear me say I had not been out with the fox-hounds while I was at Ooty, and asked me if I did not think fox-hunting a ripping sport. Then it was I did the fatal thing. I think it must have been the reaction after the tension of the cross-examination, together with the general solemnity of the gathering that gave me an uncontrollable desire to brighten things up, and I told the major that I rather agreed with Oscar Wilde's definition of fox-hunting.

Everybody at once asked what that was, so I told them how someone once asked Wilde to define fox-hunting, and he replied, " the unspeakable in pursuit of the uneatable." This witticism was received in stony silence. It was an idiotic thing for me to say, and quite the wrong time and place to say it. Anyhow I knew now that any secret ambitions I might have had of entering into Poona military life were over and done with for good and all.

So I returned to the jungle, for which I was better fitted than for the drawing-room, and resumed my collecting and long rambles. I found very few birds which I hadn't got, for I had already more than two hundred and fifty specimens and almost as many mammals. Also, truth to tell, I had become rather tired of collecting. To capture, skin, and stuff five hundred animals means a lot of hard work, and I was conscious of an increasing aversion to killing things.

Perhaps it was this, on top of my late social failure, which prompted me to apply to be transferred from India to Mesopotamia or Persia, I did not mind which, but with no success. Fortunately there was now work for all of us to do. The so-called Spanish influenza reached India about this time and was spreading rapidly amongst the natives and the British troops. King

George's hospital was soon full of patients, and the most serious cases, those which developed pneumonia or bronchitis, were segregated into one large ward, of which I was put in charge. It was a very responsible post and a depressing one, for a large proportion of these cases, all young English soldiers, died, in spite of everything that was done to save them. All the usual remedies and drugs, such as injections of strychnine and inhalations of oxygen proved useless.

Whenever a soldier in one of the other wards was found to have developed symptoms of pneumonia or bronchitis he was immediately transferred to my ward, and I found out that amongst themselves the soldiers looked upon this as equivalent to a death sentence.

During the height of the epidemic I spent a large part of each day at the hospital, and always visited my ward last thing at night.

One morning as the sister and I were making our round we stopped at the bedside of a patient who was very ill indeed with pneumonia in both lungs and rapidly sinking. He was a private in a Somersetshire Territorial regiment, and I read on his case-sheet, hanging over the head of the bed, that in civil life he had been a porter on the Great Western Railway. Bending down I asked him where he lived and he whispered back that his home was at Stogumber, where he lived alone with his mother. I had not heard the name of Stogumber since I was a boy, when we used to travel by train between Taunton and Dunster, and it recalled to me the voice of a porter at one of the stations on that line who used to call out the names of the stations in broad Somerset dialect, and how as children we always looked out for this man and his recitation.

In the forlorn hope that it might revive the dying railway porter to hear the names of the railway stations near his home, I repeated them, in their order, as far as I could remember them, and in as good " Zomerzet " as I could master.

They went as follows : " Norton Fitzwarren, Bishops Lydeard, Crowcombe, Stogumber, Stogursey, Williton, Watchet, Washford, Blue Anchor, Dunster, Minehead."

The effect of this recital on the sinking patient was striking. At the name of Stogursey he raised his head and whispered in a tone of contempt " Stogercy b'aint got no station " and fell back again exhausted. But when I left him he had lost some of the dull leaden expression on his face, and for the first time I had hopes that perhaps after all he might prove a miracle and recover.

A few hours later, when I was again in the ward, the sister asked me if I would mind calling over those stations again, as it seemed to have done the railway porter good. Of course I did so, but remembered to leave out the miserable Stogursey which had no railway station. At this performance the patient smiled. For several days his life hung in the balance, so twice daily, night and morning, I repeated my chorus and eventually by slow degrees my patient recovered. I firmly believe he owed his recovery, not to medical skill, drugs, or even nursing, but to the sound of the familiar names which he used to call out so often in days gone by.

Now that there was plenty of work to be done I gave up all collecting, but on Sundays I used to go away on my bicycle for the whole day, leaving Fever Hall after an early breakfast at six o'clock, with some sandwiches and oranges in my pockets and of course the field glasses. My favourite route was along a road which led towards the mountains, and when it became a mere track I would leave the bicycle to take care of itself and clamber on foot up the mountains, which were now green with fresh grass.

Although there was no cover to speak of there were plenty of animals and a few birds. Now and again I disturbed peacocks and peahens, which looked rather ridiculous as they flew away for dear life, with their long tails streaming behind them. Sometimes I came across small herds of black buck, or an occasional Bennet's gazelle, or chink. There were many black-naped hares, as well as long-tailed Indian pies, with their sweet flute-like whistles. Wild pigs were pretty common. Once I surprised a sounder of these, a huge black boar and his big sow with their family of very small piglets. They were in some high grass and as they rushed away in terror, the parents leading and the young following and leaping in the tall grass to keep up, they reminded me of two dreadnoughts steaming through a choppy sea followed by a flotilla of torpedo boats being tossed about by the waves.

One sight I was very interested to see, because I had read of it in Eha. It was a small sly fox busily engaged in catching and eating some flying ants as they emerged from their hole in the ground.

Eha writes such an amusing description of this by no means uncommon Indian occurrence, that I give here an extract out of his *Tribes of my Frontier*:

He has been discussing the white ants, "the arch-scourge of humanity—the foes of civilization and blight of learning—who prepare for their summer campaign by mustering their hordes, and going forth to sack our libraries, ravage our museums, desolate our godowns and eat our boots." After describing the mounds several feet high made by the white ants he passes on to the subject of the emigration of these pests, when they appear with wings and feebly flutter away.

"I remember sitting with a friend and watching them one fine monsoon day as they issued from a hole in the ground. The hole was so small that they struggled out with difficulty, one at a time, though a number of sturdy workers were behind pushing them. At first a lizard was posted at the mouth of the hole and licked them up as they came out, but we drove it off and mounted guard ourselves to see fair play. Every point of vantage on the trees around was occupied by a king-crow, or one of those strange birds the swallow-shrikes. As each young adventurer drew itself through the narrow gateway, arrayed like a bride in its long gauze wings, it bade a tearful farewell to the friends of its childhood, and, rising upon the breeze, started upon the voyage of life. I do not know what rosy hopes were at that moment blushing on the horizon of its young life, but a king-crow shot from his station and wiped them all out with one loud snap of its beak. In half a minute a second rose on its feathery wings and sailed away towards the sky, until a swallow-shrike seemed to glide over it and it disappeared . . . thus, one after another, each in happy ignorance of the fate of its predecessors, they went forth to seek their fortunes, and the fortunes of all were the same. I doubt if a single one came to a happy end."

From time to time a medical officer was required

to accompany a troop-train to some other part of India. For some reason this duty was looked upon with disfavour by most of the R.A.M.C. officers except Hadden and myself, who agreed in thinking that the more of India we could see at the expense of the Government the better, and we took turns to go in the place of others.

Most of the trains which carried troops from Poona went to the South of India, generally to Bangalore or Secunderabad. Thus it happened that during the year I was in India I never visited the Punjab or any of the more famous places in the North of India, such as Lucknow or the sublime Taj Mahal. This was a disappointment, but anyhow saved me from making the slip that an American lady globe-trotter made.

She had " done " India in a ten-day rush, and afterwards when she returned home to the States a friend asked her what had impressed her most in the whole of India. After a few moments' thought the lady replied that the most beautiful and the most romantic sight she remembered seeing was the Aga Khan by moonlight.

My recent and unsuccessful attempt to enter the social life of Poona had not been altogether without result. Thinking the matter over afterwards, I began to feel that perhaps I had been wrong not to mix more with my fellows and play games with them, and that I spent too much time alone with the birds in the jungle. Poona was now very gay, as it always was when the Governor of the Presidency and his household and staff took up their residence there for the season, so to make amends for my past, I joined the gymkhana, bought a tennis racket and drank chota-pegs. Mrs. Martyn had reminded me that the race-course was just opposite to our bungalow. Hitherto whenever a race-meeting was held I had fled in the opposite direction until it was over.

It happened that Fever Hall belonged to an Indian race-horse owner and was provided with numerous loose-boxes, which we let during the racing season to a trainer who kept his string of race-horses there. Owing to this fact we were supposed to be full of valuable inside information as to "form," and were always being asked to give tips on really good things "straight from the horse's mouth," if that is the proper term. It was certainly a sad waste of opportunity, for not one of us cared about "the Sport of Kings" or betting, and no doubt if we had we might have got information at first-hand and made—or lost—quite a lot of money.

Now all this was changed. Dressed for the part I attended my first race-meeting; mingled with the crowd; put my money on a horse, and then forgot the name of it. Much as I hated a crowd it was all very amusing and interesting because of the medley of races and costumes. Every Indian is an inveterate gambler and the staff of our bungalow were quite demoralised during the racing season. They were never at hand when needed, and when not at the races were to be found in the stables in earnest conversation with the grooms, or as they are termed in Bombay, ghorawallas. When the racing came to an end we were left with a disillusioned retinue of servants, amongst all of whom not five rupees could have been scraped together.

Lady Willingdon, ever energetic in a good cause, decided that a pageant should be held at Poona to raise funds for some deserving object. Multitudes of people were to dress up in fancy costume and march about the race-course while great crowds paid their money to look on.

Under ordinary circumstances nothing in the world, not even the mandate of Her Excellency herself, would have induced me to consider taking part in such a spectacle. But since I was still smarting under the cross-examination of Mrs. Martyn and the poor shewing I had made on that occasion, I offered to take part in the pageant.

I attended before a committee of ladies, who after looking me over decided I would make a good Russian. But I objected. For one thing I found the Russian costume, though no doubt excellent in Russia, not at all suited to the Indian climate, and for another, I was not at all enamoured of the Russians in 1918. After some discussion I agreed to be a Croat, for the Croatian costume was not only picturesque but very light and cool, though I was not at all sure whether the Croatians were on our side.

As the day of the pageant drew near my courage began to fail me. I had honestly meant to see the thing through, but somehow the thought of marching round and round the race-course dressed up in a stiff white skirt made of gauze, with my legs in pink tights, and a gaping mob . . . well, I simply could not face it, so with deep apologies to the committee I returned the costume, and to ease my conscience attended the pageant, dressed up in my own . . . best . . . clothes and when I saw what I had so nearly taken part in, I shuddered.

I did the thing handsomely and properly; spent my money at the side shows in the bazaar, until an intense longing overcame me to escape, change into comfortable clothes and go far away from it all into the jungle.

As I was making for the exit, I espied a pretty little Parsee girl seated at a stall. She appeared to have no customers and with the sight of her sitting there all alone the thought occurred to me how pleased Lady Willingdon would be if I spent my very last rupee—no matter on what—for the splendid cause.

I saluted the little Parsee lady and found she was selling copies of a small book, but had met with little success so far. I bought a copy which I slipped into my pocket and when it became difficult to find any excuse for stopping longer I bade her farewell and returned to the bungalow and a bath.

As I emptied the pockets of my jacket I found the little book which I had entirely forgotten. The title *How he Got Over* gave no hint as to the good things to follow, but the brief and modest preface informed the reader that the author, Rustum Mehta, was only seventeen " and as such, dear readers, you will judge this first humble attempt of mine." The modest autobiography continued, " I am born of Parsee parents—have not been to England, and consequently have drawn the picture out of inspiration, and what little I have seen of English life in this country."

The story opened at Rashleigh, a charming suburb of London, " considered to be one of those excelling in beauty, climate and scenery . . . in sight of a range of majestic hills, covered with green tall trees, look like one mantale spread over them." After reading this delightful little volume one hoped that Rustum Mehta never would visit England, for the disillusionment would be cruel.

The versatile author had himself drawn the three illustrations, and we can hazard the guess that he also chose the titles to them. The frontispiece was a portrait of the heroine, Miss S. Smith. The second illustration depicted a lively ball-room scene, " He led the girl in the centre of the hall and whirled round it." The third, and unfortunately the last, was a picture of the hero, Captain Whist, escaping " After having thrown all his things, he slided down."

I am probably the only happy owner of this literary and bibliographical treasure in England, and only wish I could share its joys with others.

Having once emerged from my life of retirement and thrown off the trappings of the austere recluse, I stopped at nothing in the way of worldly pleasures. I went to merry fancy-dress balls at the Gymkhana dressed as a pierrot and joined in giving cheerful dinner parties to the Australian nurses at the Kirkee Boating Club. This was a very pleasant place indeed to dine. The tables, large or small, were placed on the lawn, the brilliant stars of India shone in the dark sky above, while below the silent river flowed.

One day I received a letter of reproof from my father. In it he complained that although I wrote to him of rats and bats I had never once mentioned cats. And when I came to ponder over the accusation I had to acknowledge the truth of it. It had not occurred to me till then how small a place in the life of India the cat held. I sat down at once to rectify the omission and pointed out how the Hindoo did not worship the cat nor, as far as I could find out, hold it in the high respect which it deserved. How different from the Egyptians who regarded the cat as a deity. In India, the elephant is held in high esteem and quite rightly so, while the monkey, a very inferior animal to the cat, in spite of what the biologists may say, is looked upon in Southern India as particularly sacred. The peacock as well is held in veneration and may not be killed or molested. But the cat of Hindustan seemed to belong to the untouchable caste, an unclean animal like the cloven-hoofed pig.

As a matter of fact, I met very few cats in India, to speak to I mean. I loved one very dearly at Kilkotagiri and after I left I felt her loss keenly, although she was a heartless and accomplished flirt. My feelings towards her can be best expressed by quoting the lines of the late Miss Maria Edgeworth:

> "My mind, still hovering round about you,
> I thought I could not live without you;
> But now we've lived three weeks asunder,
> How I lived with you is the wonder."

It was an odd coincidence that my father should have written to me about cats when he did, for I had just been reading Mark Twain on the cats of Bermuda. They seem to have been a remarkable race of cats. Their names alone prove it; for what a magnificent old tom must Hecta G. Yelverton have been, or Sir John Baldwin, and what a heroic veteran of the feline family "Hold-the-fort-for-I-am-coming Jackson." India had no cats of that calibre.

MEMOIRS OF A CAMP-FOLLOWER

In Poona one very rarely saw any kind of cat at all, or at the most a tail disappearing hurriedly round a corner. But there was one I used to see occasionally in the town, sitting on a high arch safe from rude pariah dogs. I always addressed it in those high-pitched squeaky noises supposed to be so attractive to the ears of cats whenever I passed by and I rather think it appreciated the little attention.

This cat's home was a large pretentious building belonging to a wealthy Parsee and called "Loveley Hall," while next door to it stood a very small and unpretentious bungalow named "Happy Hall." I often wondered if someone was having a sly dig at his rich neighbour.

The only other cat I knew at all well—and now that we are on the subject of cats it is as well to get it done with—was one at an hotel at Secunderabad. She was a nice small white cat with a kink in her tail and was very sentimental when alone with you. I was sure she had something on her mind she badly wanted me to know about, but every time she had worked herself up to the point of telling me all about it somebody was sure to enter the room and so the secret was lost.

The subject of cats leads one on to that of rats. One day I received a letter from Major Kunhardt, the Bombay plague expert, telling me about the work being done by Dr. Chitre, on the Poona Plague enquiry and enclosing a letter of introduction to him. I lost no time going to call on the Indian doctor and found him carrying out some interesting experiments.

Since the black rat is the carrier of plague it has

to be destroyed and as far as is possible exterminated. There are many ways of doing this, the two principal being by traps or poison. Dr. Chitre had constructed a rat-proof chamber, that is to say it was proof against the escape of rats, and peep-holes had been let into the walls through which observers could watch the imprisoned rodents.

For my benefit three hundred plague rats had been liberated in the room, where a dozen rat-traps of different types had been set. It was very interesting and exciting to watch through the spy-holes the manner in which the rats approached or entered the various traps. But while we were looking on only the young and foolish rats blundered into the traps, the older and more experienced seeming to be suspicious. At the end of the demonstration I proposed to Dr. Chitre that we should put a fox terrier into the pit and watch what he made of the three hundred rats. The doctor did not fall in with my suggestion; in fact, he seemed a little displeased by it.

It may have been remarked by any reader who has borne with me thus far that there has scarcely been a mention made of the War in the latter part of this book which concerns my sojourn in India. This silence has not been deliberate. For one thing the memory of the war to anybody who had recently taken part in it in France and had been in or about the fighting area, was a foul nightmare of horror, and as far as possible to be forgotten. This was not difficult because the war was seldom referred to at Poona, and often it was really difficult to believe that the Empire was in the titanic throes of a life and death struggle, while we played games, drank chota-pegs and gossiped. Those who had been in the fighting scarcely ever spoke of their experiences, even to one another; the subject was still too close and was deliberately ignored.

There were a number of professional soldiers at Poona who had seen no fighting and certainly shewed curiously little interest in the war, except so far as it interfered with their daily life, and who made no secret of their longing for the return to the good old days. But it must be remembered that most of the regulars we temporary soldiers met at Poona were far from being typical of the real Indian army. The best had gone to fight on one or other of the battle-fields, where they still remained, above or below ground, while those who had been left behind to be cantonment magistrates, town majors or to do other administrative jobs were those who could be dispensed with from the serious side of soldiering.

On Wednesday, November 12th, 1918, the news leaked out. True, a rumour had spread through the cantonment on the evening before that the armistice had been signed, but as nothing official was announced the report was not taken seriously. On the Wednesday morning the glorious news was in the local newspapers, and descriptions given of the rejoicings which had taken place in other parts of India. But Poona waited, calm, composed, unmoved.

Here and there regrettable signs of spontaneous boisterousness did bubble up. Some common soldiers, territorials and the like, had cheered and sung patriotic songs in the cinema, and others had attempted to form an impromptu procession. But the official eye had looked askance on these manifestations of joy and they had petered out.

We must be strictly just to the headquarters staff; they did make one gesture. On Wednesday, November 12th, the day after the armistice was signed bringing the World War with all its slaughter and suffering to an end, G.H.Q. at Poona published an order which belied the accusation that they didn't care. If, as I believe, it was a sign that they too rejoiced, they had their own method of showing it.

It came in the form of a typewritten order from the General commanding at Poona and was to the effect that a class for the instruction of temporary R.A.M.C. officers only, was to be inaugurated forthwith. The classes were to be held at 7 a.m. daily, for the instruction of these officers in the care and saddling of mules. This piece of news met with the hilarious approval of all combatant officers of every branch of the service, who recognised how useful this knowledge would be to the R.A.M.C. officers when they returned to their homes and private practices.

There was a good deal of indignant comment amongst the rank and file at Poona over the want of enthusiasm at headquarters and some correspondence on the subject appeared in the columns of the *Times of India*. One correspondent wrote on November 18th:

> "I have been wondering whether you can solve a problem for me. Why is it that Poona is never in the running where public celebrations are concerned? The news *re* the signing of the armistice crept into Poona about 8 o'clock on Wednesday morning, November 12th. I say crept because there were a good many people who were not

certain it was true when they went to bed on Tuesday night. ... I took a walk around Poona on the Wednesday morning it was announced in the paper and only noticed one Union Jack, this was on the house of a Captain in Kahn Road."

Two days later the following appeared in the same paper; under the heading " Lethargic Poona."

"There is no cause, however forlorn, which need lack a champion in India. We have received another letter strongly protesting against the idea that Poona has been wanting in a display of enthusiasm over the Allied victory.

"It is quite untrue, as our correspondent remarks, that there were no outward and visible signs of Peace in Poona. I have it on very good authority that at the C.W.I. on the day after the news crept out, a pukka member was seen to nod and murmur ' good evening ' to a temporary member. Again at the bar of the Gymkhana, at about 8 o'clock the same evening, the crowd was counted and reported to be nine rows deep instead of the usual seven."

After referring to the by now famous mule-saddling class for R.A.M.C. officers the writer continued:

"If to outsiders it appears that Poona is apathetic over the good news, it must in fairness be remembered that Poona never knew there was a war going on. Just think what would have happened if Poona had been French!"

The greeting by the regular member of the C.W.I. referred to in the above letter, when he muttered " good-evening " to a temporary one, may not appear to the uninitiated to be excessive or extravagant. But circumstances do very much alter cases, and this slight token of recognition was as if on that same Wednesday a temporary member had entered the smoking-room of the Athenæum Club and the Dean of Saint Paul's had leaped up from his armchair and heartily slapped him on the back.

It is just such a club as the C.W.I., exclusive and frigid, which Mr. James Laver describes so wittily in his enchanting poem " Cupid's Changeling or the Lady's Mistake," published this year by the Nonesuch Press. He hits off so exactly the feelings of a new or temporary member of a really haughty club that I have begged and received of the poet permission to print the following lines :

> " Alas ! 'tis not the payment of a sub
> That makes a man a member of a Club.
> No ! many years must pass before he knows
> The Clubman's calm self-satisfied repose ;
> Yea, many years before he can expect
> A nod, a smile, a word from the elect.
> Till then he walks about on tip of toes,
> And meets a frozen face where'er he goes."

The explanation of the lethargy of Poona was said to be because the G.O.C. made it a strict rule that on no account whatever was he to be disturbed after mid-day, and that no matter what messages might come to his office after noon, they were to be kept for him until the following morning. Owing to this rule, the official telegram announcing the signing of the Armistice lay on an office desk and Poona was the last place in the Empire to be officially informed of the victory.

Possibly the General was the same Staff officer whom C. E. Montague quotes in his " Disenchantment " as having said " At the War office we never used to open the afternoon letters till the next day."

Perhaps owing to the correspondence in the *Times of India* backed up by the growing indignation of the populace, the powers at Poona at length decided to bow to popular opinion and give their official sanction to some form of public rejoicing.

On November 27th, only sixteen days after the signing of the Armistice, a monster procession took place. Children in their hundreds, of both sexes, and of every colour, from flaxen-haired, blue-eyed Europeans, through all the various shades of the Eurasiatic, to the pure-blooded Parsee, Hindu and Mohammedan, marched in columns of four, waving little flags. Roused at last to a proper sense of their duties, the powers brought the day's rejoicings to a close by a not-too-costly display of fireworks, and the stain on the fair name of Poona was washed away.

CHAPTER X

THE JOURNEY HOME

NO sooner had the glorious news of peace oozed out than Poona became a hive of every sort of rumour; one being that we "temporary gents" were to be sent back at once to England to be demobilized; another, though less positive, maintained that a number of the R.A.M.C. were to be dispatched to serve with the army of occupation in Bulgaria. This last appeared to me most attractive, for although I was pretty well informed about the birds of Bulgaria I knew nothing whatever of its smaller mammals and saw an opportunity to make an interesting collection for the British Museum.

Losing no time I applied to be transferred to Bulgaria, but learnt to my disappointment that nothing was known at headquarters about any such design. Everyone now began to discuss and devise schemes for getting back to England to be demobilized. Most of us R.A.M.C. officers had left private practices at home which had by then fallen into other hands, and those who got back the soonest would have the best chance to retrieve what was left and to begin to build them up afresh. Many of these doctors had little beyond their army pay as captains to support their families.

Then all of a sudden there was issued from Simla one

of those subtle army-forms which appeared on the face of it to settle all our difficulties, and to promise early release.

It was one of the class which invited the credulous to state which of several alternatives they preferred, and insinuated that whichever they fancied most was to be had for the asking.

We were given three alternatives to choose from:

- *A* Those who had urgent family or business reasons for being sent home forthwith.
- *B* Those who wished to be sent home but were in no particular hurry.
- *C* Those who were willing to continue to serve in India, on a temporary commission basis, as long as their services were required.

No one applied under the heading *C*, and everyone except myself desired to be sent home at once under Schedule *A*.

As I had no great desire to return to a practice which I knew no longer existed, and as I had hopes of seeing other parts of India or even of Persia or Mesopotamia, I signed on for *B*.

Having handed back our forms, duly filled in, all the *A*'s packed up their belongings and prepared to leave Poona at a moment's notice. After waiting impatiently for eight or nine days, one morning while we were all congregated in the hospital common room discussing the burning question of demobilization, an orderly arrived with an envelope addressed to me. Amidst breathless silence I opened it to find it contained the following order:

THE JOURNEY HOME

Headquarters, Poona Division.
Poona.   28th November, 1918.
No: 54/83/Medl/2.

Copy of a telegram No: 6754/1 dated 25th November, 1918, from Medl India Simla to Genl: Divn: Poona.

In communication Embn Bombay arrange despatch England Captain P. H. G. Gosse, R.A.M.C. earliest possible opportunity to report on arrival to Director of Air Organization Adastral House, London. A.A.A. Addsd Genl: Divn: Poona. Reptd Embn Bombay who should wire usual information.

This incomprehensible but exciting piece of news from the far off Himalaya mountains was indeed a bombshell. I had not asked to be transferred to the Air Force, nor had I ever given the subject a moment's thought. However it was not for me to question why; in any case this settled the matter once and for all, and solved the looming difficulty of my personal luggage, which when packed up for travelling filled twenty-four bulky boxes and packages mostly filled with stuffed specimens of birds and mammals.

As my orders had been repeated in sextuple, in distinction to the usual triplicate, I felt justified in packing up and saying good-bye to Poona and my friends there, and setting off for Bombay accompanied by my ever faithful Kerudin, who saw me and my twenty-four packages safely aboard R.I.M.S. *Northbrook*.

I almost missed the boat anyhow for as we were approaching Bombay I was seized by a severe attack of malaria. Exactly how I got from the railway station to the ship I do not remember; in fact it was all a blank until I recovered consciousness and found myself lying in a bunk and the vessel out of sight of land.

As soon as the fever left me I staggered up, and crept out to search for my precious luggage and was relieved to find that all twenty-four packages were safely on board.

We called at only one port on our voyage to Suez, Karachi, where we shipped a crowd of officers going home to be demobilized. They were an amazing collection of stout-hearted, undaunted adventurers. Many of them had been members of the famous Dunster force, and most of them had been in strange places and done strange things for a long while. All of them were in high spirits at being on their way home at last.

The *Northbrook* was packed with officers by the time we left Karachi, but we had on board a disturbing influence, two unchaperoned Red Cross nurses. These two ladies had, I think, the time of their lives on this all too short voyage to Suez. For them it was love all the way, nothing but love from morning till night, and even then Cupid did not lay aside his bow and arrow, for after the sun had sunk beneath the dark horizon their resolute adorers never flagged in their ardent wooing and the good ship *Northbrook* became a floating temple of the goddess Venus.

One must be very circumspect when making statements of this kind about events which took place years ago. Time plays tricks on memory.

I said just now the two ladies travelled unchaperoned; but on consideration I have an impression that one of them, the elder, was probably travelling in the capacity of guardian or duenna to the younger.

In those far-off days, although no doubt sex-appeal did exist, it certainly was never mentioned.

There can be no doubt that these two ladies, though of course quite innocently and all unconsciously, did send out an appeal of this nature, and not in vain. The call was answered by a hundred brave and willing hearts.

At first the elder, a plump fair lady of perhaps five and forty summers, and her pretty ward were inseparable. Timidly they seemed to cling to each other as though for mutual protection amongst so many bold adorers. But by the end of the second day they were seldom seen together, except at meals in the saloon, when scarcely a word passed between them. The rest of the day Venus took up her quarters in the bows of the ship, while Aphrodite held her court on the poop, each enchantress being concealed from view by a press of ardent worshippers, who swarmed about them as bees swarm round the queen bee in summer time.

It was very close and hot for all of us as we steamed through the placid Red Sea.

Owing to recurring attacks of malaria I was unable to take any active part in this mass homage to our two lovely Circes, for a man needed to be in fine fettle to stand a chance in such a swarm of suitors, where the prize went to the strongest.

When, all too soon for some, our ship arrived at Suez, we disembarked and travelled by train alongside the canal to Port Said, a journey spoiled for me by the trouble I had in persuading the railway officials to allow my voluminous baggage to go with me. It completely blocked up the corridor, and I had to be on guard the whole time to prevent infuriated fellow passengers, who wanted to pass to the lavatory at the other end of the corridor, from throwing my boxes out of the window.

The long journey over, we marched to a dusty camp just outside the town of Port Said. Nothing occurred there worth mention except that some Australian officers set fire to and burnt down the mess hut. This they did as a just protest against the deplorable food provided by the caterers, which consisted of nothing else but bad mutton, thinly disguised by curry powder. I did not remain long enough at Port Said to learn whether these energetic measures brought about a much needed improvement in the messing arrangements for all of a sudden I was ordered to embark immediately, not as I expected for England, but for Salonika.

At any other time or under any other circumstances I should have been overjoyed to be sent to Salonika, but my one aim in life just then was to get home with my collections as quickly as I could, for I was far from well and very tired.

I knew this Salonika order must be a mistake, so I went at once to see the responsible officer and shewed him my orders from Simla, which stated in sextuple, that I was to proceed to England by the first available steamer; and I pointed out to him that the Director of Air Organisation at Adastral House was eagerly awaiting my arrival. Expostulations, and the orders from Simla were of no avail, and with my twenty-four boxes and a flea in my ear I went off to the quay where

I was to embark on board the good ship *Hunslet*. When I arrived there and had unloaded my baggage from the mule-cart I had hired, I was surprised to find the wharf deserted, without a vessel large or small alongside. While I was sitting on one of my boxes wondering what I ought to do next, a sergeant came up and asked me if I was the medical officer for whom they were waiting. When he heard I was the man, he pointed towards a disreputable-looking tramp steamer lying at anchor about a mile out at sea, from which came frequent impatient hoots of its siren. The sergeant said the ship was only waiting for me, but when he saw my luggage his face fell. However, he managed to procure a barge, manned by six swarthy cut-throats, and at last after a lot of bargaining, they pulled me alongside the steamer. From over her sides hundreds of interested soldier spectators were looking down to watch the arrival of their medical officer. Then a loud, gruff voice bellowed down from above to know what in hell all that cargo was in the barge. I called back that it was medical comforts for the troops. The angry one then roared out that the medical officer was to come aboard but bring only two pieces of baggage with him and no more. I replied that I would not go on board until all my baggage was there and I sat back comfortably in the barge and waited. After a good deal of wrangling and some blasphemous dialogue between the sergeant and the roaring quartermaster above, all my twenty-four packages were safely carried up the ladder and I followed.

I had never been anywhere, in a ship or out of one, so full of flies as was the *Hunslet*; the vessel swarmed with them, and our food was black with flies the moment the stewards uncovered a dish on the dining-table. I never knew there could be so many flies together in one place. Afterwards when I read Mr. A. P. Herbert's book *The Secret Battle*, the memory of the *Hunslet* helped me to visualise the awful scenes he describes so vividly in the fly-infested trenches of Gallipoli.

About Salonika there is little to say.

Having handed over my troops I was sent to a base hospital to await further orders, where as usual my luggage came in for a good deal of hostile comment.

After India and the Red Sea, Salonika was cold and cheerless. I arrived just in time for Christmas dinner, and kind as everybody was to the stranger, I felt myself to be an intruder at the Christmas festivities. I sold two of my guns at considerable profit, for guns were in great request just then at Salonika.

Also I nearly got killed.

During one of the Christmas parties a nurse took me for a little stroll to admire Mount Olympus by moonlight. Outside the building we discovered there was no moon, but the heavens were aglow with twinkling stars which we agreed did just as well, if not better. Whilst we stood close together, much moved by the marvellous spectacle, the shrill blast of a steam whistle made us leap aside and a railway engine rushed past, missing us both by inches. We must have been so engrossed studying the heavens that we had not noticed we were standing on a railway line nor heard the approaching engine.

I had not spent many days at this hospital before I got orders to proceed by motor omnibus over the

Albanian mountains to embark for Italy at a port on the Adriatic. I made some enquiries and learned that the road was apt to be blocked with snow in the winter and that absolutely no baggage could be taken except what could be carried in the hand. This was really serious, for by no means whatever could I have carried all mine, even in both hands. So I interviewed the transport officer to whom I put my case, and spun the usual story I was so weary of reciting.

I told him with perfect frankness about the twenty-four boxes; explaining that they were not my private property but belonged to the British Museum, and hinted there would be the devil and all to pay with the British Government if any of them were lost or damaged.

The transport officer was surprisingly sympathetic over my dilemma, countermanded the order for the bus, and the next day sent me instead as medical officer on a troop-ship going to Taranto, at the extreme south of Italy.

Once again I met with trouble on the wharf over my luggage, but five shillings in the palm of a sergeant smoothed all difficulties, and it was stowed away on board in the large cabin which as M.O. I had all to myself.

Once safely on board I took to my bed with another bout of fever, but happy to feel that I was one stage further towards the end of all my cares and anxieties. After a few idle days spent at Taranto I met with another stroke of good fortune, for I was chosen out of all the R.A.M.C. officers to go as medical officer in charge of a train leaving for Havre.

This train had attached to it a brand-new hospital

carriage painted white inside and out. Besides the ward with cots for the sick, it had a kitchen, sleeping quarters for the staff, a very comfortable cabin for the doctor in charge, and there was no one to say a word about all my goods and chattels, which were safely installed where I could keep an eye on them.

When the train pulled out from the railway siding in the camp, no one knew if we were to travel by the Riviera or over the Alps. The first part of the journey was delightful. The railway ran northwards close beside the shores of the Adriatic; the sea was blue and calm, the sky cloudless, and the countryside basked in the January sunshine. We passed by many picturesque old Italian towns such as Vasto d'Ammone, Ortona, Pescara, and Ancona.

Leaving the sea-coast at Rimini the train carried us to our first stopping place, Faenza, where all the passengers left the train to spend half a day in the noted rest camp there.

It was wonderfully laid out with gravel paths, neat grass plots and flower beds and frequent notices to keep off the grass and not to do this and that, and everything was very spick and span. From the soldiers' point of view it was a little too spick and span; they would have preferred something rather less of a show place. As one of my orderlies afterwards confided to me, the camp at Faenza made him feel he was trespassing all the time.

We re-embarked on our train the same evening and by the next morning found a great change in the temperature. All our passengers had served for months, in most cases for years, in tropical and sub-tropical countries, such as India, Persia, Mesopotamia and East Africa, and a large percentage suffered on and off from malaria. They soon began to feel the cold, and having no clothes but light drill uniforms, often with shorts instead of trousers, many were in a wretched state.

In addition to this, scarcely one carriage other than the hospital carriage, boasted of a whole glass window. This train had been used to carry British troops during the hot weather, and with the Englishman's notorious love of fresh air, the soldiers had smashed and knocked out most of the windows. The further north we went the more bitter the cold became and I soon had my hospital and my hands full with sick men. Some of these developed pneumonia and were seriously ill, and had to be left on the way whenever we went through a town which had an army hospital.

I had an interesting companion in the officer who acted as quartermaster on the train. He was very uncomfortable in his windowless carriage so I made him share my luxurious cabin. In civil life he had been in the Metropolitan police and was a detective in the branch which deals with the white slave traffic. He was full of surprising anecdotes and hair-raising stories of his experiences.

Very early one winter's morning, we stopped at Modane on the frontier between Italy and France. The platform was a foot deep in snow. I was fast asleep in my warm bunk when one of my orderlies woke me to say that a soldier had asked to be allowed to board our train as he had got left behind by the one before. I told the orderly to bring the man into the cabin, and in walked a middle-aged soldier wearing nothing but his trousers and boots with a towel thrown over his shoulders. For an instant we gazed at one another, and then both burst out laughing. By an extraordinary coincidence he was one of the last men I had seen in France when I left for India seventeen months before. He was the bandmaster of our famous Field Ambulance silver band, and used to march at the head of the column and beat time with his " bâton " while his musicians played " Colonel Bogey." In private life he was a tram-driver at Glasgow.

Almost directly after I left it, the 23rd Division had been sent post-haste to Italy at the time the Austrians so nearly broke through at Caporetto. Sergeant McGill was travelling back to England in a troop train just ahead of ours, and at Modane, in spite of the snow and ice, had taken off his tunic and shirt and gone on to the platform to have a wash. While he was thus engaged his train went off, leaving him without money, clothes, or his precious army pay-book. It was great good luck for him that a friend was on the next train as M.O., for I found him a cot in the sick-bay, supplied him with a shirt, tunic and cap, and lent him some money.

Naturally he had a lot to tell me about the exploits and adventures of the Division in Italy and news of all my friends, officers and others in the ambulance, particularly of Bob Church and Jim the terrier.

The long journey seemed nearly over when the train pulled up in a siding just outside Lyons. After a while we began to ask each other why we had stopped; then some got out to make enquiries. There were no officials so I went forward to the engine to ask the driver how long we should be there. Both the driver and his fireman had gone on strike and decamped. For twenty-four hours we remained beleaguered in that siding and no one dared walk back to the city to get a meal for fear the train might suddenly start off. Next day another engine driver was procured and without even a warning whistle the train set off, and there was a wild rush to jump on board.

After several more delays on the way we at last reached Havre and went on board a Clyde river paddle-steamer. I have never seen so many human beings packed into so small a space.

There was one large saloon, into which I was one of the first to enter, after having got my luggage safely stowed away on deck. Then I got into a panic about it, and tried to return to the deck to sit and guard it during the voyage. But it was impossible to get out, for hundreds of officers were struggling slowly down the companionway. On and on they came, pushed forwards by those behind. The press was overpowering and the atmosphere suffocating. Several fainted and had to be lifted up and passed from hand to hand over the heads of the crowd, up to the fresh air on deck. The sweat poured down our faces and bodies and no one could move a step from where he stood, and had he managed to sit down on the floor he would never have been able to get up again. But no one grumbled, or appeared to care. The war was nearly over for us now, and civilian life was going to be so wonderful.

After a trying passage we steamed at last into Southampton Water and tied up alongside the wharf. It took a long while for those of us at the further end of the saloon to reach the deck, where we gratefully inhaled deep draughts of cool, clean air.

By a happy miracle the malaria had not attacked me during the voyage. I waited until everybody had left the ship and then hurried to look after my precious boxes; I counted them, they totalled only twenty-two; two alas, were missing, after all the vicissitudes of travel from Poona to Southampton. There was nothing to do but inform the railway officials on the dock, and with my twenty-two remaining boxes, catch the train for London.

A few days afterwards the two missing ones followed me to London; Providence was kind to me throughout the Great War.

Printed at the BURLEIGH PRESS, *Lewin's Mead*, BRISTOL

www.ingramcontent.com/pod-product-compliance
Lightning Source LLC
Chambersburg PA
CBHW032124160426
43197CB00008B/511